BROADWAY DECODED

BROADWAY DECODED

Musical Theatre's Forgotten References

THOMAS S. HISCHAK

APPLAUSE
THEATRE & CINEMA BOOKS
Essex, Connecticut

APPLAUSE
THEATRE & CINEMA BOOKS

An imprint of Globe Pequot, the trade division of
The Rowman & Littlefield Publishing Group, Inc.
4501 Forbes Blvd., Ste. 200
Lanham, MD 20706
www.rowman.com

Distributed by NATIONAL BOOK NETWORK

Library of Congress Cataloging-in-Publication Data

Names: Hischak, Thomas S., author.
Title: Broadway decoded : musical theatre's forgotten references / Thomas
S. Hischak.
Description: Essex, Connecticut : Applause, 2023. | Includes
bibliographical references and index.
Identifiers: LCCN 2023001237 | ISBN 9781493074327 (paperback) | ISBN
9781493074334 (epub)
Subjects: LCSH: Musicals--Miscellanea. | Musicals--Encyclopedias. |
Musicals--Dictionaries. | LCGFT: Trivia and miscellanea. |
Encyclopedias. | Dictionaries.
Classification: LCC ML2054 .H47 2023 | DDC 782.1/402--dc23/eng/20230224
LC record available at https://lccn.loc.gov/2023001237

♾️™ The paper used in this publication meets the minimum requirements of American
National Standard for Information Sciences—Permanence of Paper for Printed Library
Materials, ANSI/NISO Z39.48-1992.

For Mark A. Robinson,
whose idea it was

CONTENTS

PREFACE
You Say Pinch-beck, I Say Pinch-back; Let's Call Professor Harold Hill

An' the next thing ya know
Your son is playin' for money
In a pinch-back suit . . .

If you are like me, you've enjoyed certain lyrics or lines of dialogue from favorite Broadway musicals for years, but when you stop and consider some of them, you realize you don't know to what they are referring. In *The Music Man*, for example, I get the reference to Hester and her scarlet letter *A*, but I certainly don't know what a demijohn is, or what is meant by a pinch-back suit. Not knowing doesn't subtract from the enjoyment. I'm sure 1957 Broadway audience members watching *The Music Man* didn't know what a pinch-back suit was, either—unless one was very old and grew up in a rural community. A pinch-back suit must not be a good thing, because Professor Harold Hill paints a picture of a young man wearing one while gambling in a pool hall. And the citizens of River City, Iowa, must not wear pinch-back suits, or else Hill wouldn't use the term in such a derogatory manner.

I was curious, so I looked into it. There was an eighteenth-century watchmaker named Christopher Pinchbeck who must have made flashy but cheap watches in London, because soon the phrase "pinch-beck" meant something that was not as good as it looks. Over time the association with timepieces was lost, and "pinch-beck" referred to clothes—specifically, poorly made garments that tried to look expensive. In America, the term was altered to "pinch-back," and that is how Hill uses it in the song "Ya Got Trouble." Did Meredith Willson go looking through an antiquated dictionary to find the expression "pinch-back suit" when he was writing *The Music Man*? My guess is he grew up hearing it in Mason City, Iowa. When a dandified traveling salesman came to town dressed in fancy duds, Aunt So-and-So might have said, "He isn't foolin' anyone with that pinch-back suit." Young Meredith may have heard her and never forgotten it, in future scrutinizing the suits worn by all traveling salesmen.

Broadway musicals, particularly those set in the past and in faraway places, are filled with pinch-beck suits, so to speak. This book is a guide to hundreds of those references—names, products, slang, and other forgotten phrases that we have heard in musicals, perhaps many times, just accepting them as part of the atmosphere without really knowing what they meant. Yet as I "decoded" these many references, I found that they make the lyric or the libretto richer and sometimes more clever than I imagined.

I have chosen fifty oft-produced American musicals that have a significant number of these long-lost expressions and names. You will find few contemporary musicals in this book, as we tend to recognize all of their modern references. Of course, in time, musicals such as *Legally Blonde* and *Dear Evan Hansen* will have to be explained for new audiences.

Consider the 1960 musical *Bye Bye Birdie*. It was an up-to-the-minute story taken from the headlines; everyone knew who Ed Sullivan was, and the news of Elvis Presley being drafted into the army was recent newspaper fodder. While that kind of knowledge cannot be assumed today, *Bye Bye Birdie* still holds the stage and entertains new audiences. So does *Oklahoma!*—and how many people today know what a "surrey" is? If they do, it's probably because of the Rodgers and Hammerstein song, "The Surrey with the Fringe on Top."

Some musicals have a marvelously vivid way of re-creating past and distant worlds onstage, be it a Russian village with Jewish citizens in 1905, as in *Fiddler on the Roof*, or a Scottish town lost in time, as in *Brigadoon*. Whether you are a director or a performer preparing a production of one of these fifty musicals, or just someone who wants to know more about the atmospheric details in your favorites, it is hoped you will find this book entertaining and informative.

I have limited myself to American musicals and, for the most part, shows that are frequently revived. Yet I had to include some beloved musicals that are not often produced, as they have such rich scores filled with many long-lost references. I have tried to keep the explanations lively throughout; we are dealing with the wonderful world of musical theatre, after all. And, unlike a pinch-back suit, this world is made with quality material.

ACKNOWLEDGMENTS

Many thanks to Mark A. Robinson, Robbie Roselle, Robert Spitzer, Jessie Rutland, and the staff of the Proctor Library at Flagler College. I would also like to thank Todd Ifft and the staff at Photofest, Inc.; Barbara Claire; John Cerullo; Jessica Thwaite, Melissa Hayes, and the staff at Applause Theatre & Cinema Books; and Cathy Hischak.

CHRONOLOGICAL LIST OF MUSICALS

Show Boat (1927)
Anything Goes (1934)
Pal Joey (1940)
Oklahoma! (1943)
On the Town (1944)
Carousel (1945)
Brigadoon (1947)
Kiss Me, Kate (1948)
Finian's Rainbow (1949)
South Pacific (1949)
Guys and Dolls (1950)
The King and I (1951)
Wonderful Town (1953)
The Pajama Game (1954)
Damn Yankees (1955)
My Fair Lady (1956)
West Side Story (1957)
The Music Man (1957)
Flower Drum Song (1958)
Gypsy (1959)
The Sound of Music (1959)
Bye Bye Birdie (1960)
Camelot (1960)
How to Succeed in Business without Really Trying (1961)
Hello, Dolly! (1964)
Fiddler on the Roof (1964)

Man of La Mancha (1965)
Cabaret (1966)
Mame (1966)
Sweet Charity (1966)
Hair (1967)
1776 (1969)
Company (1970)
Follies (1971)
Grease (1972)
Pippin (1972)
Chicago (1975)
Annie (1977)
Sweeney Todd: The Demon Barber of Fleet Street (1979)
Dreamgirls (1981)
Little Shop of Horrors (1982)
Big River (1985)
The Secret Garden (1991)
Assassins (1991)
Rent (1996)
Ragtime (1998)
Hairspray (2002)
In the Heights (2008)
Shrek the Musical (2010)

ANNIE

Libretto by Thomas Meehan, based on the comic strip *Little Orphan Annie* by Harold Gray. Lyrics by Martin Charnin. Music by Charles Strouse. Original Broadway production: January 2, 1977. Alvin Theatre. 2,377 performances. Broadway revivals in 1997 and 2012.

The setting for *Annie* is very specific: December 11 to 25, 1933, in New York City. The year 1933 is considered the low point of the Great Depression. Franklin D. Roosevelt was inaugurated as the thirty-second president of the United States in March of that year, so the impact of his New Deal programs would not be seen for a few years. Harold Gray's comic strip ran in hundreds of newspapers from 1924 to 2010. (Gray died in 1968, but other cartoonists continued the strip for Tribune Media Services.) Librettist Thomas Meehan chose to place *Annie* during the Depression, specifically the holiday season of 1933, in order to set Annie's optimism against the bleak situation in America. Both Meehan and lyricist Martin Charnin

ANNIE *When the orphans sing "You're Never Fully Dressed Without a Smile," they include such snappy dressers from the past as Dapper Dan and Beau Brummell.*
Photofest

filled the libretto and songs with many references to the 1930s, some of which are now forgotten.

Expressions, references, names:

Al Smith: The American Democrat politician Alfred Smith (1873–1944) served four terms as governor of New York, but when he ran for president of the United States in 1928, he was defeated by Republican Herbert Hoover. In the song "We Want to Thank You, Herbert Hoover," the homeless of New York City sing, "They offered us Al Smith and Hoover . . . [and] we paid through the nose."

Andrew Mellon . . . Madame Chiang Kai-shek: The American banker, industrialist, and philanthropist Andrew Mellon (1855–1937) oversaw a huge business empire. His private art collection became the National Gallery of Art in Washington, DC. Madame Chiang Kai-shek (1898–2003), or Madame Chiang, was a Chinese political figure who was First Lady of the Republic of China. Planning the adoption party in the musical, Daddy Warbucks tells Annie, "And you can have anyone in the world you want to come to it. Who would you like? Andrew Mellon? Madame Chiang Kai-shek?"

Astor Place: Named for the multimillionaire John Jacob Astor, Astor Place is a street in East Greenwich Village in Lower Manhattan. In *Annie*, the Dog Catcher tells his assistant, "There's s'posed to be a whole bunch of [dogs] runnin' wild over to Astor Place."

Baby Face Nelson . . . Dillinger: The American bank robber George Nelson (1908–1934) was known as Baby Face Nelson. He was the criminal partner of John Dillinger, and he helped Dillinger escape from prison. The violent Nelson had killed more FBI agents than any other criminal. The American bank robber and murderer John Dillinger (1902–1934) was Public Enemy #1 for a time. Dillinger was eventually gunned down in 1934. At the Cabinet meeting in *Annie*, Louis Howe tells President Roosevelt, "The FBI caught Baby Face Nelson, didn't they? They're bound to catch Dillinger."

Beau Brummelly: In Regency England, the arbiter of men's fashion was George Bryan "Beau" Brummell (1778–1840), a close friend of the future king, George IV. Ever since then, the expression "Beau Brummell" means a person of high fashion. When Bert Healy performs "You're Never Fully Dressed without a Smile" on the radio, he sings, "Your clothes may be / Beau Brummelly . . ." The orphans then reprise the song and the name.

Bentley . . . Duesenberg: Two of the most desirable (and expensive) automobiles in the 1920s and 1930s were cars made by the British manufacturer Bentley Motors Limited and those by the American company, Duesenberg. The butler Drake asks Warbucks, "Will you be wanting the Bentley, sir, or the Duesenberg?"

Bernard Baruch: The American financier and statesman Bernard Baruch (1870–1965) was one of the country's richest and most powerful men for over fifty years. Grace answers the telephone and tells Warbucks, "Excuse me, sir. Bernard Baruch calling."

Best's: Now long gone, Best's was a favorite store in New York City for clothing. Grace tells Annie, "We'll go to Best's and get you a warm winter coat."

"chicken in every pot": This phrase promising citizens that everyone will be able to have chicken for dinner goes all the way back to sixteenth-century France. "Chicken in every pot" was the Republican campaign slogan of the late 1920s, although candidate Herbert Hoover did not use it. All the same, the phrase is often associated with him. In the song "We Want to Thank You, Herbert Hoover," the residents of the Hooverville sing, "In ev'ry pot he said 'a chicken' / But Herbert Hoover, he forgot / Not only don't we have the chicken / We ain't got the pot."

Chrysler Building: In the first scene in *Annie*, Miss Hannigan orders the orphans to "clean this dump until it shines like the top of the Chrysler Building!" Still one of New York's most distinctive and beloved skyscrapers is the gleaming Art Deco–style Chrysler Building on the East Side of Manhattan. Using bright stainless steel extensively in its design, the steeple section of the Chrysler Building actually glows in the sun- or moonlight.

Collier's: The illustrated magazine known simply as *Collier's* was an American general interest publication founded by Peter Fenelon Collier in 1888. Until its demise in 1957, *Collier's* was known for its commentary, fiction, and photographs. The Hooverville resident Fred holds a copy of the magazine and says to the other homeless, "Hey, look at this. We made *Collier's* again."

Dapper Dan: Not a real person, but an old expression for the well-dressed man, Dapper Dan symbolized the very swanky and neatly groomed male. When the orphans perform "You're Never Fully Dressed without a Smile" along with the radio, they sing, "Hey, hobo man, hey, Dapper Dan."

Don Budge: The renowned American tennis player Don Budge (1915–2000) was the first to win the Australian, French, British, and United States singles championship, all in the year 1938. Making arrangements for Annie's tennis lessons, Grace tells the servants, "Oh, and get that Don Budge fellow if he's available."

fireside chats: Between 1933 and 1944, President Franklin D. Roosevelt delivered a series of "fireside chats" on the radio, broadcast from his office in the White House. These were not fiery speeches but more informal talks, helping Americans get through the Depression and World War II. In *Annie*, the newscaster on the radio says, "Mr. President, if you are listening, we've had enough of your fireside chats."

Franklin Roosevelt: Often referred to by his initials, FDR, Franklin Delano Roosevelt (1882–1945) served as the thirty-second president of the United States, from 1933 until his death in 1945, the longest term of office on record. He was a Democrat who introduced bills and programs to help ease the plight of Americans during the Depression. Daddy Warbucks in *Annie* is a Republican, but he respects FDR. When Warbucks has to break the news about Annie's real parents being dead, he says to her, "I've got something very difficult to tell you, and President [Roosevelt] is going to help me tell it to you."

Fred and Adele: A very popular dance team on the stage on Broadway and in London was the pairing of Adele Astaire (1896–1981) and her brother, Fred Astaire (1899–1987). They were American actors and singers but were most beloved for their dancing. Adele retired from the stage to become the British Lady Charles Cavendish, and Fred went on to have a renowned career in the movies. In the song "I Don't Need Anything But You," the servants sing about Warbucks and Annie: "They're two of a kind / The happiest pair now / Like Fred and Adele, / They're floating on air now."

Gershwins . . . Kaufman and Hart: In the song "NYC," Warbucks sings, "Go ask the Gershwins or Kaufman and Hart / The place they love the best / Though California pays big for their art / Their fan mail comes addressed to / NYC." One of Broadway's most distinguished songwriting teams was composer George Gershwin (1898–1937) and his lyricist brother, Ira Gershwin (1896–1983). Broadway's most popular playwriting team in the 1930s was George Kaufman (1889–1961) and Moss Hart (1904–1961). As famous and as successful as all four men were, in the Depression they had to go to Hollywood to find work.

Helen Trent: From 1933 to 1960, one of the most loved "soap operas" was *The Romance of Helen Trent* on CBS-Radio. The series followed the triumphs and heartbreaks of fictional Hollywood dress designer Helen Trent. In *Annie*, Miss Hannigan listens to the radio announcer say, "Once again we bring you the romance of Helen Trent . . ."

Hell's Kitchen: Originally called Hale's Kitchen after a restaurant there, Hell's Kitchen was a section of Midtown Manhattan, west of Times Square, formerly notorious for its slums and high crime rate. Today it is a gentrified and desirable neighborhood. Warbucks tells Annie, "I was born into a very poor family in what they call Hell's Kitchen, right here in New York."

Herbert Hoover: Often blamed for the Great Depression, Herbert Hoover (1874–1964) was an American politician and engineer who served as the thirty-first president of the United States, from 1929 to 1933. The Republican president was in office when the stock market crashed in 1929 and the Great Depression began. The residents of the Hooverville sing, "We'd like to thank you, Herbert Hoover . . . You made us what we are today."

Hoovervilles: During the Great Depression of the early 1930s, so many Americans either lost their homes or were evicted from apartments that ramshackle shantytowns sprang up across the nation. They were called Hoovervilles, mocking the president at the time, Herbert Hoover. Reading from a magazine, Fred says, "Thousands of once-affluent Americans are today living in makeshift towns called Hoovervilles . . . And in New York City alone, there are more than a dozen Hoovervilles."

Jack Dempsey: The world heavyweight boxing champion from 1919 to 1926 was William Harrison "Jack" Dempsey (1895–1983), nicknamed "the Manassa Mauler." When the orphan Pepper tries to start a fight, a fellow orphan mockingly calls her "the Jack Dempsey of the orphanage."

J. Edgar Hoover: The first and long-enduring director of the Federal Bureau of Investigation (FBI) was J. Edgar Hoover (1895–1972). From 1924 until his death, the sometimes ruthless Hoover built the FBI into a highly effective government organization. Warbucks calls Hoover on the phone and tells him to find Annie's parents. In the song "You Won't Be an Orphan for Long," Grace sings to Annie about Warbucks, "With all the favors that he's done / J. Edgar Hoover owes him one."

John D. Rockefeller . . . Mahatma Gandhi . . . Harpo Marx: Warbucks asks Grace if there have been any other phone calls while he was away, and she answers, "John D. Rockefeller, Mahatma Gandhi, and Harpo Marx." John D. Rockefeller (1839–1937), founder of the Standard Oil Company, became one of the world's wealthiest men. The lawyer-turned-statesman Mahatma Gandhi (1869–1948) used nonviolent resistance to lead the successful campaign for India's independence from British rule. The Marx brother who never spoke, Arthur "Harpo" Marx (1888–1964), was an American comedian, actor, mime artist, and musician.

Justice Brandeis: The American lawyer Louis Brandeis (1856–1941) was a justice on the Supreme Court from 1916 to 1939. Brandeis University is named for him. Warbucks tells his butler Drake, "Call Justice Brandeis and ask him to come over to sign the adoption papers [for Annie]."

Leavenworth: When Rooster first arrives at the orphanage, Miss Hannigan asks her brother, "They finally let you outta Leavenworth?" The largest maximum-security federal prison in the United States from 1903 until 2005 was Leavenworth Penitentiary in Leavenworth, Kansas.

Lou Gehrig: Renowned for his prowess as a hitter and for his durability, Henry "Lou" Gehrig (1903–1941) was an American professional first baseman who played seventeen seasons in Major League Baseball for the New York Yankees (1923–1939). He died of the rare disease amyotrophic lateral sclerosis (ALS), which is now known to the layman as Lou Gehrig's disease. When Warbucks first meets Annie, he asks her, "I don't suppose you'd like to meet Lou Gehrig?"

mayor five-foot-two: One of New York City's most popular mayors was Fiorello La Guardia (1882–1947), who served from 1934 to 1945. La Guardia was a short Italian politician who was only five feet, two inches tall. In the song "NYC," Warbucks sings, "What other town has the / Empire State [Building] / And a mayor five-foot-two?"

Mickey Finn: A drugged or doctored drink that is surreptitiously given to someone to make them drunk or insensible is called a Mickey Finn. In the song "It's a Hard-Knock Life," the orphans sing about Miss Hannigan: "Jab her with a safety pin / Make her drink a Mickey Finn."

mush: A thick porridge made with cornmeal boiled in water or milk was known as mush. The word applies to any substance that is reduced to a soft, wet, pulpy mass. Miss Hannigan tells the orphans, "You don't get hot mush this morning . . . You get cold mush."

Perkins . . . Hull . . . Morgenthau . . . Ickes . . . Howe: When Roosevelt introduces his cabinet to Annie, he names FDR's actual members: "Secretary of Labor [Frances] Perkins, Secretary of State [Cordell] Hull, Acting Secretary of the Treasury [Henry] Morgenthau, Secretary of the Interior [Harold L.] Ickes, and my friend and aide, Mr. Louis Howe."

Roxy . . . Rumpelmayer's: With its lush decor and 5,920 seats, the Roxy was one of the largest and most dazzling movie palaces ever built in North America. The New York City landmark was just off Times Square and opened to the public in 1927; sadly, it was demolished in 1960. Rumpelmayer's was a restaurant that specialized in ice cream and other desserts. It was once described as "the haunt of New York's most pampered children." Making plans for her first day seeing the city, Warbucks tells Annie, "You'll go to the Roxy. Then an ice-cream soda at Rumpelmayer's."

Saville Row: When the Boylan Sisters perform "You're Never Fully Dressed without a Smile" on the radio, they sing, "Who cares what they're wearing / On Main Street or Saville Row . . ." In Central London, a shopping street called Saville Row specialized in high-quality tailoring for men. The term "Saville Row" came to mean the best in men's clothing.

Waldorf . . . Automat: The Waldorf Astoria is a luxury hotel in Midtown Manhattan. The Art Deco landmark opened in 1931 and, until 1963, was the world's tallest hotel. The Waldorf was known for its plush rooms and fine dining. An automat is a cafeteria in which food and drink were purchased from glass boxes, much like a vending machine. Grace asks Miss Hannigan to guess where Annie and Warbucks had lunch, and Hannigan says, "The Waldorf?" but Grace tells her "The Automat."

William Howard Taft: The twenty-seventh president of the United States was William Howard Taft (1857–1930). He also served as chief justice of the Supreme Court after his presidency. Taft was inaugurated in 1909. Warbucks tells Annie, "I haven't waltzed since the inauguration of William Howard Taft."

Winchell . . . Tommy Manville: One of the most powerful journalists in the history of reporting was Walter Winchell (1897–1972), a syndicated American newspaper gossip columnist and radio news commentator. Tommy Manville Jr. (1894–1967) was a colorful socialite and heir to the Johns-Manville asbestos fortune. He was one of the richest men in America during the Depression. His record-breaking thirteen marriages to eleven women put him in the *Guinness Book of World Records*. Miss Hannigan says to Grace, "I read in Winchell's column that Oliver Warbucks has more do-re-mi than Tommy Manville." A slang term for money is "do-re-mi."

ANYTHING GOES

Libretto by Howard Lindsay, Russel Crouse, Guy Bolton, and P. G. Wodehouse. Revised by Timothy Crouse and John Weidman. Music and lyrics by Cole Porter. Original Broadway production: November 21, 1934. Alvin Theatre. 420 performances. Broadway revivals in 1987, 2002, and 2011.

Revived more often than any other 1930s musical, *Anything Goes* was a very modern work when it opened in 1934. It not only used the slang and referred to the topical items of the day, but it gloried in being an up-to-the-minute show. The libretto and Cole Porter's lyrics are filled with 1930s names in the news, products long gone, and literary references. Almost all of the action takes place on the fictitious ocean liner SS *American* in 1934. Revivals tend to keep the same time period of the original because of these references, and the exuberant nature of the silly plot feels most comfortable there. There is no one script used for reviving *Anything Goes*. Over the decades, songs have been dropped or added and the libretto (and even some characters' names) have changed. Included here are references in the songs and dialogue that have shown up in different revivals.

ANYTHING GOES   *Stowaway Billy Crocker (William Gaxton, left) disguised as a sailor, nightclub singer Reno Sweeney (Ethel Merman), and gangster Moonface Martin (Victor Moore) disguised as a minister, all speak with a 1930s slang in both the libretto and the song lyrics.* Photofest

Expressions, references, names:

Arrow collar: Ads for Arrow collars and shirts in the first half of the twentieth century depicted the ideal "Arrow collar man": handsome, dapper, and sophisticated. In the song "You're the Top," Reno sings to Billy, "You're an Arrow collar."

Bedlam: The Bedlam (or Bethlehem, or Bethlem) Royal Hospital in London was the first asylum for the mentally ill in England. Over the years, "bedlam" has come to mean chaos or madness. Billy insults British lord Evelyn Oakleigh when he tells Hope Harcourt: "He escaped from the family suite at Bedlam."

Bendel bonnet: A hat designed by renowned milliner Henri Bendel was a sign of high fashion in the 1930s. Reno compares Billy to "a Bendel bonnet" in the song "You're the Top."

Berlin ballad: When Reno sings to Billy, "You're a Berlin ballad" in the song "You're the Top," she is referring to renowned songwriter Irving Berlin (1888–1989), who had already been famous for two decades when *Anything Goes* premiered. Berlin's ballads were particularly popular.

Bojingles: Bill Robinson, nicknamed Bojangles (1878–1949), was a celebrated Black tap dancer, actor, and singer. Sir Evelyn gets the name wrong when he tells Reno that her nightclub act "had me dancing about like Bojingles!"

Brewster body . . . Nathan panning . . . Bishop Manning . . . Irene Bordoni: Several people in the news in 1934, but now long forgotten, are referred to in "You're the Top." Reno and Billy sing to each other, "You're a Brewster body . . . You're a Nathan panning, / You're Bishop Manning . . . You're the eyes / Of Irene Bordoni." A "Brewster body" may sound like a voluptuous model or actress named Brewster, but in fact it refers to the first effective body armor developed for the United States Army in World War I, designed by Dr. Guy Otis Brewster. Perhaps the most severe drama critic of the 1930s and 1940s was George Jean Nathan (1882–1958), who wrote for such magazines as *The Smart Set*, *The American Mercury*, and *The American Spectator*. A "Nathan panning" means a bad review (or "pan") by the controversial critic. William Thomas Manning (1866–1949) was the Episcopal bishop of New York City from 1921 to 1946. He is most remembered for raising the money to begin construction on the Cathedral of St. John the Divine. Irene Bordoni (1895–1953) was an Italian-born beauty who starred on Broadway in Cole Porter's first musical, *Paris*, in 1928. She was known for her alluring, seductive eyes.

brimstone . . . fire: In the song "Blow, Gabriel, Blow," Reno sings, "I've gone through brimstone and I've been through the fire." The expression "fire and brimstone" goes back to the fourteenth century, and referred to the tortures that sinners in hell suffered. The phrase later came to mean any difficult ordeal.

Bromo: An early form of Alka-Seltzer, a Bromo was a fizzy mixture used as a headache remedy, sedative, and antacid. When Sir Evelyn gets seasick, Hope Harcourt says to him, "I'll get you a Bromo."

Brooks Brothers suit: Founded in 1818, Brooks Brothers is still making superior clothing for men. During the Depression, the price was high, and wearing Brooks Brothers clothing was a status symbol. When he's in the brig, Billy says, "A week ago I was getting fitted for my first Brooks Brothers suit, now look where I am."

Camembert: Named after the French region in which it is made, Camembert is a rich, soft, creamy cheese with a whitish rind. It is considered highly desirable, so when Reno sings to Billy, "You're Camembert" in the song "You're the Top," it is meant as a compliment.

Camille: The beautiful but tragic Camille is a fictional character in novels, plays, operas, and movies, remembered for her coughing fits as she dies from consumption (or tuberculosis). The screen star Greta Garbo played Camille in a popular 1936 film of that name. Erma refers to the heartbroken Hope Harcourt when she says, "All she does is whine and cry and stand around looking like Garbo in *Camille*."

Cartier's: The French luxury goods conglomerate, which designs, manufactures, distributes, and sells jewelry, leather goods, and watches, was founded by Louis-François Cartier in Paris in 1847 and is still going strong. In the song "Buddy, Beware," Erma sings about "Pretty things Santy / Brings from Cartier's."

Charles Chaplin . . . *Mauritania*: The Purser informs the Captain that "Charlie Chaplin just wired. He's canceling his berth and sailing on the *Mauritania*." "Charlie" Chaplin (1889–1977) was the internationally famous English comic actor, filmmaker, and composer who rose to fame in the era of silent films but was still very popular in the 1930s. The *Mauritania*, a transatlantic passenger liner of the Cunard Line, was known as the "Grand Old Lady of the Atlantic."

Cicero: The suburb of Chicago named Cicero was known for its gangsters, corrupt police, and Al Capone, who ran the town in the 1920s. When Billy and Moon are thrown in the brig, Moonface says, "This place ain't so bad. Were you ever in jail in Cicero?"

cognac . . . Cointreau: Cognac is high-quality brandy, the best distilled in the town of Cognac in western France. Cointreau is a colorless orange-flavored liqueur. Billy says to Mrs. Harcourt: "Cognac . . . Cointreau—whatever makes you happy, Mom."

Coolidge dollar: When Calvin Coolidge (1872–1933) was president of the United States from 1923 to 1929, the economy was booming. Reno tells Billy he is a "Coolidge dollar" in the song "You're the Top," meaning he is like money when the dollar was most valuable.

Dillinger: The infamous gangster John Dillinger (1903–1934) and the Dillinger Gang were known for robbing banks during the Depression. Moonface claims to have known the notorious outlaw when he says, "It's like Dillinger once told me . . ."

Drumstick lipstick . . . Irish Svipstick: In the last of seven refrains for "You're the Top," Billy sings to Reno, "You're a Drumstick lipstick, / You're da foist / In da Irish Svipstick." In the 1930s, the company Drumstick not only made lipstick but also face powder and makeup compacts. Billy mangles the word "sweepstakes" when he tells Reno that she has come in first in the Irish "Svipstick." Founded in 1930 to raise money for Irish hospitals, the Irish Sweepstakes was a lottery with a huge payoff that flourished until a state lottery replaced it, in 1987.

Eli: Elihu Yale (1649–1721) was a British-American colonial administrator and philanthropist who was one of the founders of Yale University. The character of Elisha Whitney and other graduates of Yale call themselves "Eli's" and often burst into the school song. Whitney even goes by the familiar Eli.

five-year plan: The song "Kate the Great" was in the original production of *Anything Goes* but is usually cut now. There is a delightful reference made to 1930s Russia in the lyric. "Empress Catherine of Russia" is called "Kate the Great," and "she knew where women should stay . . . She never laid a five-year plan" but laid "a plan for a man." In the 1920s and 1930s, Soviet Russia had various "plans" that had a number of years in the name. The first "five-year plan" was instigated by Josef Stalin in 1928; another was announced in 1933.

Flying Dutchman: There is a seventeenth-century Dutch legend about a ghost ship that was said to be doomed to sail the seas forever. Noticing the lack of celebrities on board, one of the newspaper reporters comments, "This tub is deader than the *Flying Dutchman*."

Gabriel: The angel Gabriel is known as the messenger of good news, supposedly blowing his trumpet to make big announcements. The angel is summoned several times in the gospel song "Blow, Gabriel, Blow" sung by Reno and her Angels.

Gold and White Ball . . . Newport Cotillion: Two high-class formal balls in which young debutantes were presented to society in the 1930s were the Gold and White Ball in New York and the Newport Cotillion in Rhode Island. A reporter asks Hope Harcourt if she is "presiding at the Gold and White Ball this year? How about the Newport Cotillion?"

GOP: Since 1880, the Republican political party has been called the Grand Old Party, or the GOP. Billy sings, "I'm the nominee of the GOP" in the song "You're the Top."

Great Durante: Jimmy Durante (1893–1980) was an American actor, comedian, singer, vaudevillian, and pianist, most distinguished by his "schnozzola," or large nose. Reno tells Billy, "You're the nose / On the Great Durante" in the song "You're the Top."

hawsers: Thick ropes or cables used for mooring or towing a ship are called hawsers. Erma uses the double-entendre form when she says the sailors are "gonna show me how to grease the hawsers."

Henley Regatta: Ever since 1839, the rowing event called the Henley Royal Regatta is held annually on the River Thames by the town of Henley-on-Thames in England. It was—and still is—one of the major social events of the year. At the beginning of *Anything Goes*, Elisha Whitney tells the bartender Fred that he is sailing to England to attend the Henley Regatta.

Indoor China: Indochina is the Southeast Asian peninsula that was known as French Indochina until 1950. In the musical, the Minister asks Moonface if he was stationed in Indochina, to which Moonface responds, "That's it, I was in Indoor China."

Keats . . . Shelley . . . Botticelli: In the duet "You're the Top," Billy sings to Reno, "You're Keats," and she replies, "You're Shelley." John Keats (1795–1821) and Percy Bysshe Shelley (1792–1822) were both English poets of the Romantic school. The Italian painter Sandro Botticelli (1445–1510) portrayed beautiful women in such works as *Primavera* and *The Birth of Venus*. When Billy sings to Reno, "You're a Botticelli," he can be comparing her to one of those women, or simply saying she is like a valuable painting.

Lady Astor: When Billy sings to Reno, "You're Lady Astor" in the song "You're the Top," he is referring to Lady Astor of that time period, Nancy Witcher Langhorne Astor, an American-born British politician who was the first woman seated as a Member of Parliament, from 1919 to 1945.

L. B. Mayer . . . Elaine Barrie: Louis B. Mayer (1885?–1957) ran Metro-Goldwyn-Mayer studio for many years. In the song "It's De-Lovely," the couple sings about their future son growing up so handsome that Mayer "makes a night flight to New York and tells him he should / Go Hollywood." The son then makes so much money that "Elaine Barrie's his fiancée." Elaine Barrie (1915–2003) was an actress who schemed to become the fourth, and last, wife of actor John Barrymore (1882–1942).

Leavenworth: The city of Leavenworth in northeastern Kansas was most known in the 1930s for its large prison. Moonface has evidently spent some time there, for he says to Erma, "Sounds like meatloaf night at Leavenworth."

Life: During its golden age from 1936 to 1972, *Life* magazine was a weekly publication particularly known for the quality of its photography. To be on the cover of *Life* was quite an accomplishment. Reno refers to Hope Harcourt when she asks Billy, "The one who chases foxes on the cover of *Life*?"

Mae West: The movie star Mae West (1893–1980) was *the* sex symbol of Hollywood for several decades. Reno sings, "If Mae West you like" in the song "Anything Goes." Also, in the song "You're the Top," Billy sings to Reno, "You're the moon over Mae West's shoulder."

Melba: Nellie Melba (1861–1931) was a world-famous Australian operatic soprano, so popular that products were named after her. Moonface sings about "an old Australian bush song / That Melba used to sing" in the song "Be Like the Blue Bird."

Missus Ned McLean: The multimillionaire Edward McLean (1885–1941) became the owner and publisher of the *Washington Post* in 1916, and often promoted seemingly radical ideas. His wife, Evalyn Walsh McLean (1886–1947), insisted he buy her the Hope Diamond, even though it was said to be cursed. Years later, Ned went insane and Evalyn died in poverty. In 1933, the year *Anything Goes* opened, Ned lost the *Washington Post*, and Evalyn's plan to stop revolutions by inviting the common folk to her lavish parties ceased. In the title song, Reno sings, "When Missus Ned McLean (God bless her) / Can get Russian reds to 'yes' her, / Then I suppose / Anything goes."

National Gall'ry . . . Garbo's sal'ry . . . cellophane . . . Derby winner: Billy compliments Reno in "You're the Top" when he sings, "You're the National Gall'ry, / You're Garbo's sal'ry, / You're cellophane . . . You're the time of the Derby winner." Two world-class art museums are the National Gallery in London and the National Gallery in Washington, DC. Which one Billy is referring to is unknown. The stunning Swedish-American movie star Greta Garbo (1905–1990) was one of the highest-paid actresses in Hollywood. Her salary was considerable. The invention of clear, thin cellophane in 1912 changed the way food was packaged. It was still considered a marvelous homemaking improvement in the 1930s. The Derby Stakes, also known as the Epsom Derby or the Derby, is Britain's most popular horse race, an annual event that goes back to 1780. In England it is pronounced "dar-bee."

Noel Coward: The acclaimed British playwright, composer, director, and actor Noel Coward (1899–1973) was considered the height of sophistication in the 1930s. When Sir Evelyn does a clichéd impersonation of movie star James Cagney as a gangster, saying "You dirty rat!," Moonface sarcastically says, "Noel Coward?"

Normandie . . . **Jimmy Walker . . . Machine Gun Kelly:** The Captain is upset to learn that celebrities are on their rival ship after the Purser tells him, "The *Normandie* has Jimmy Walker and Machine Gun Kelly." The SS *Normandie* was a French ocean liner and, in its day, was the largest and fastest passenger ship afloat. James John Walker (1881–1946), known colloquially as Beau James and "Jimmy," was mayor of New York City from 1926 to 1932. He was a flamboyant politician who was very popular. Machine Gun Kelly (1895–1954) was an American bootlegger, bank robber, and kidnapper, often in the headlines in the 1930s.

O'Neill drama: Eugene O'Neill (1888–1953) is generally considered America's greatest playwright. He was at the peak of his popularity in the 1930s. In the song "You're the Top," Reno sings to Billy, "You're an O'Neill drama."

Ovaltine: Ovaltine is a brand of milk-flavoring product made with malt extract, sugar, and whey. The product is still available today, but it was much more popular in the twentieth century. In the song "You're the Top," Billy sings to Reno, "You're Ovaltine."

Purser: An officer on a ship who keeps the accounts is called the purser. The term is sometimes applied to the head steward on a passenger vessel. The Purser in *Anything Goes* seems to have several jobs, looking for Public Enemy #1 being the most important.

Rockefeller . . . Max Gordon: In the title song, Reno sings, "When Rockefeller still can hoard enough money to let Max Gordon / Produce his shows, / Anything goes." John D. Rockefeller (1839–1937), possibly the richest man in America during the Depression, because of Standard Oil, sometimes invested in Broadway shows. Max Gordon (1892–1978) was an American theatre and film producer who used wealthy friends to finance his Broadway productions.

Roxy usher: The Roxy Theatre was a plush movie palace in New York City. The ushers wore colorful and elaborate uniforms. Reno sings to Billy, "You're the pants on a Roxy usher" in the duet "You're the Top."

Sam Goldwyn . . . Anna Sten: Movie producer Samuel Goldwyn (1882–1974) discovered the Ukrainian-born actress Anna Sten (1908–1993) in German movies and tried to turn her into a Hollywood screen star, but her accent was too thick and audiences didn't warm up to her. In the title song, Reno sings, "If Sam Goldwyn can with great conviction / Instruct Anna Sten in diction, / Then Anna shows / Anything goes."

Saville Row: In London, Saville Row is a street in Mayfair known for its traditional and high-class tailoring for men. Moonface says about Sir Evelyn, "I was taking him down to Saville Row for a new straitjacket when he gave me the slip."

Sing Sing: When things go wrong in the second act of *Anything Goes*, Moonface says to Erma: "With your big mouth you can land us in Sing Sing!" The infamous prison on the Hudson River at Ossining, New York, is called Sing Sing.

Stork Club: One of the most prestigious nightclubs in the world was the Stork Club in Manhattan. From 1929 to 1965, it was a symbol of café society and catered to movie stars, celebrities, showgirls, aristocrats, etc.

Because there are no celebrities on board and it is time to shove off, the Captain tells the Purser: "Run down to the Stork Club and see if anyone's left over from last night."

Straddlevarious: Violins made by the Stradivarius family during the seventeenth and eighteenth centuries are considered the finest and the most valuable in the world. When Moonface's cheap violin case opens and his Tommy gun falls out, he mangles the Italian name with, "Whoops, my Straddlevarious!"

Strauss: Reno sings to Billy, "You're a melody from a symphony by Strauss" in the duet "You're the Top." There is more than one Strauss in music history, but she is most likely referring to Johann Strauss II (1825–1899), also known as Johann Strauss Jr. or Johann Strauss the Younger. Known to music lovers as "The Waltz King," he was a master of melody in such works as "The Blue Danube" and "Tales from the Vienna Woods."

Tin Pan–tithesis: In the song "It's De-Lovely," Hope Harcourt sings to Billy: "This verse I've started seems to me / The Tin Pan–tithesis of melody." This is a portmanteau word that Cole Porter made up, combining "Tin Pan" with "antithesis." The latter part of the word comes from the expression Tin Pan Alley, a name for the music business.

Tower of Babel . . . Whitney Stable: Billy sings to Reno in "You're the Top" that she is "the Tower of Babel . . . the Whitney Stable / By the River Rhine." A Bible story in Genesis tells of the construction of a tower by the Babylonians that hoped to reach the heavens, but God thwarted their plans by giving the different workers different languages, so they could not communicate with each other. John Hay Whitney (1904–1982) came from the wealthy Whitney family and was active in politics, moviemaking, art museums, and publishing. "Jock" Whitney also raised and raced Thoroughbred racehorses and had extensive stables in Europe and the States.

Vincent Youmans: A renowned composer for Broadway and Hollywood was Vincent Youmans (1898–1946), who was a friend of Cole Porter. Billy sings of "gifted humans like Vincent Youmans" in the song "You're the Top."

Waldorf salad: Consisting of apples, walnuts, celery, and mayonnaise, the Waldorf salad was named after the Waldorf Astoria Hotel in New York, where it was first served. In the duet "You're the Top," Reno sings to Billy, "You're a Waldorf salad!"

Whistler's mama: The most famous painting by American-British artist James Abbott McNeill Whistler (1834–1903) is commonly called *Whistler's Mother*. Billy sings to Reno, "You're Whistler's mama" in the song "You're the Top."

Yellow Pages: Now rather scarce, a telephone directory with a section printed on yellow paper was called the "Yellow Pages" and could be found in every city and town phone book, before the Internet took over. The pages listed businesses and other organizations according to the goods or services they offered. Erma gets Billy a fake passport that has "Murray Hill Flowers" for the name. When Billy asks her, "Where'd he get a name like that?," Erma answers, "The Yellow Pages."

Zuider Zee: A shallow bay of the North Sea in the northwest part of the Netherlands is known by the Dutch name Zuider Zee. In the song "You're the Top," Reno sings to Billy: "You're the boats that glide on the sleepy Zuider Zee."

ASSASSINS

Libretto by John Weidman. Music and lyrics by Stephen Sondheim. Original Off-Off-Broadway production: December 18, 1990. Playwrights Horizons. 73 performances. Broadway revivals in 2004 and 2012.

Among the many distinctive features of this fascinating musical is the cast of characters, just about all of whom are real people. Librettist John Weidman and lyricist Stephen Sondheim have brought these characters to life in a humorous, chilling, even devastating way. The range of *Assassins* is also unique. Events are not depicted in chronological order, but include assassinations and assassination attempts of various US presidents from 1865 to 1981. The locations for the action are also all over the map of the United States. *Assassins* is a concept musical that explores a dark side of the American Dream without being limited by chronological history.

Expressions, references, names:

Abraham Lincoln: The musical begins its look at specific assassinations with Abraham Lincoln (1809–1865), the first US president to be killed by an assassin's bullet. The Civil War had just concluded when John Wilkes Booth, a furious Confederate, shot Lincoln in Ford's Theatre in Washington while the president was watching the comedy *Our American Cousin*. In the musical, the wounded and defeated Booth dictates to his co-conspirator, Herold: "An indictment. Of the former President of the United States, Abraham Lincoln, who is herein charged with the following High Crimes and Misdemeanors . . ."

Anton Cermak: The mayor of Chicago in 1933 was Czech-born Anton Cermak (1873–1933), who was in Miami Beach's Bayfront Park with president-elect Franklin D. Roosevelt when Italian immigrant Giuseppe Zangara attempted to assassinate the future president. When Zangara drew his pistol, a bystander hit him with her purse, and the bullet hit and killed Cermak. In *Assassins*, the Announcer reports, "There's been a shot! I can't see—wait! Mr. Roosevelt is waving! He's all right! But Mayor Cermak has been hit!"

brother made you jealous: In the song "The Ballad of Booth," the Balladeer sings to Booth, "Your brother made you jealous, John, / You couldn't fill his shoes." The brother being referred to is Edwin Booth (1833–1893), arguably the finest American actor of his time. While John was a dashing matinee idol, Edwin was roundly applauded as the better actor. Edwin's acting career was nearly destroyed by his brother's crime, but he eventually won over the public once more.

Brutus: Marcus Junius Brutus (c. 85–42 BCE) was a Roman politician, orator, and the most famous of the assassins of Julius Caesar. Booth says to Oswald, "Ah! You know his name. Brutus assassinated Caesar, what? Two thousand years ago? And here's a high school dropout with a dollar-twenty-five-an-hour job in Dallas, Texas, who knows who he was. And they say fame is fleeting."

Charles Guiteau: The writer, preacher, and lawyer Charles Guiteau (1841–1882) believed he had played a major role in James Garfield's election victory and felt he deserved the reward of a consulship or ambassador post. He assassinated Garfield in a Washington, DC, train station in 1881 and subsequently was executed at the gallows. In the song "The Ballad of Guiteau," Guiteau quotes from his actual writings when he sings, "I'm Charles J. Guiteau, / Charlie Guiteau / Never said 'never'/ Or heard the word 'no.' "

Charlie Manson: An infamous cult based in California called the Manson Family was led by Charles Manson (1934–2017) in the late 1960s. The "family" committed nine murders at four locations in July and August of 1969. Although Mason was not among those to do the killing, he was convicted of first-degree murder in 1971, the court declaring that his ideology constituted an overt act of conspiracy. "Squeaky" Fromme was a member of the cult. In the musical, she tells Sara Jane Moore, "Charlie says that in America the chickens are finally coming home to roost, rotting and reeking with the oozing pus of a society devouring its own anus."

Dick Nixon: President of the United States from 1969 to 1974, Richard Nixon (1913–1994) was faced with almost certain impeachment for his role in the Watergate scandal, so he became the first American president to resign from office. In *Assassins*, Samuel Byck is obsessed with Nixon and asks the Bartender, "Has Dick Nixon been in today?"

Emma Goldman: The anarchist and political activist Emma Goldman (1869–1940) was an active force in the development of anarchist political philosophy in North America and Europe during the first half of the twentieth century. Goldman says to the confused immigrant Czolgosz, "Come, Leon. Come. You are a beautiful young man . . . Your life has made you beautiful. Your suffering has made you fine."

Gerald Ford: The only US president never to have been elected to the office of president or vice president, Gerald Ford (1913–2006) became president when Richard Nixon resigned in 1974. Two unsuccessful attempts were made on his life in 1975; by Sara Jane Moore and by Lynette "Squeaky" Fromme. The Moore attempt is portrayed farcically in *Assassins*. Picking up loose bullets from the ground, Ford tells Sara Jane, "Say, you should be more careful with these things. They're bullets."

Giuseppe Zangara: Italian immigrant Giuseppe Zangara (1900–1933) attempted to assassinate president-elect Franklin D. Roosevelt in 1933, seventeen days before Roosevelt's inauguration. Zangara was executed by electric chair. In the song "How I Saved Roosevelt," Zangara sings, "You think I am Left? / No Left, no Right, / No anything! / Only American!"

Hoover: Herbert Hoover (1874–1964) had the ill luck to be president of the United States in 1929, when the Great Depression struck. Many blamed the hard times on Hoover, and the shantytowns of homeless and unemployed that sprang up across the nation were mockingly called Hoovervilles. In the song "How I Saved Roosevelt," Zangara sings, "First I . . . figure I kill Hoover, / I get even for the stomach. / Only Hoover up in Washington . . . Roosevelt, Hoover—No make no difference."

James Garfield: The Civil War general James Garfield (1831–1881) was elected US president but only served six months because he was assassinated by civil servant Charles Guiteau in 1881. In *Assassins*, Guiteau says to Garfield at the train station, "President Garfield! . . . I want to be Ambassador to France!"

Jodie Foster: American film actress Jodie Foster (born 1962) has received numerous accolades, including two Academy Awards, in a career that began when she was a child. Foster's breakout role was the child prostitute Iris in *Taxi Driver* (1976). This role was one of the reasons John Hinckley becomes obsessed with the actress. In the song "Unworthy of Your Love," Hinckley sings, "You are wind and water and sky, / Jodie. / Tell me, Jodie, how I / Can earn your love."

John Hinckley: Inspired by his obsession for the actress Jodie Foster and hoping to impress her, John Hinckley (born 1955) attempted to assassinate President Ronald Reagan in Washington, DC, in 1981. In 2016, a federal judge ruled that Hinckley was no longer considered a threat to himself or others and could be released from institutional psychiatric care, with restrictions. In *Assassins*, Hinckley says to his photo of Jodie Foster, "My dearest Jodie, I am humiliated, by my weakness and my impotence. But, Jodie, I can change . . . With one brave, historic act I will win your love."

John Wilkes Booth: A well-known stage actor from an illustrious acting family, John Wilkes Booth (1838–1865) is remembered today as the man who assassinated Abraham Lincoln at Ford's Theatre in Washington, DC, in 1865. Booth was a zealous Confederate and organized a group of Southerners to kill several political figures on the same night as he shot Lincoln. Booth died in a barn fire when he was hiding from the law. The Balladeer introduces Booth in the song "The Ballad of Booth" with, "Johnny Booth was a handsome devil . . . Had him a temper, but kept it level. / Everybody called him Wilkes."

Lee Harvey Oswald: A US Marine veteran with an unhappy past and a broken marriage, Lee Harvey Oswald (1939–1963) is believed to have assassinated President John F. Kennedy on November 22, 1963, in Dallas. While in police custody, Oswald was murdered by Jack Ruby two days later, leaving many unanswered questions about the assassination. In the musical, a desperate and confused Oswald says to Booth, "I'm going to kill myself! Don't you think I've given it up!" Booth suggests an alternative: Kill President Kennedy.

Leonard Bernstein: The first American conductor to receive international acclaim was Leonard Bernstein (1918–1990), who was also a composer, musician, music educator, author, and humanitarian. Samuel Byck says into his tape recorder, "Hello, Mr. Bernstein? Lenny? How you doin'? My name is Sam Byck. We've never met. You're a world-renowned composer and conductor who travels the world over, enjoying one success after another, and I'm an out-of-work tire salesman, so I guess that's not surprising."

Leon Czolgosz: The steelworker and anarchist Leon Czolgosz (1873–1901) assassinated President William McKinley at the 1901 Pan-American Exposition in Buffalo. Although the bullet wound itself was not fatal, McKinley died a week later after his wound became infected. Czolgosz says to Emma Goldman, "Miss Goldman, I am alone, with no one and with nothing! I am a grown man, twenty-seven, but I have no life! What do I know? Nothing! What have I learned? Nothing!"

Pan-American Exposition: The 1901 Pan-American Exposition was a World's Fair held in Buffalo, New York, with exhibits and buildings covering 350 acres. It is remembered today primarily for being the location of the assassination of US president William McKinley at the Temple of Music on September 6, 1901. The Balladeer sings, "Czolgosz, / Working man, / Born in the middle of Michigan, / Woke with a thought / And away he ran / To the Pan-American Exposition / in Buffalo."

Roosevelt: Franklin D. Roosevelt (1882–1945) was the US president with the longest term of office, from 1933 to 1945. He was in office for most of the Great Depression and World War II. After listening to Giuseppe Zangara complain about his stomach ills, Booth asks him, "Have you considered shooting Franklin Roosevelt?"

Samuel Byck: Obsessed with President Richard Nixon, in 1974 Samuel Byck (1930–1974) planned to kill him by hijacking a plane and crashing it into the White House. Instead, Byck killed a policeman and a pilot, but was shot and wounded by another policeman before committing suicide. Making a tape to send to Leonard Bernstein, Byck says into his tape recorder, "I'm gonna change things, Lenny. I'm gonna drop a 747 on the White House and incinerate Dick Nixon. It's gonna make the news. You're gonna hear about it."

Sara Jane Moore: Divorced five times and unable to keep a job, Sara Jane Moore (born 1930) turned to revolutionary politics in the 1970s. In 1975 she attempted to assassinate US president Gerald Ford in San Francisco. Moore was given a life sentence for the attempted assassination and was released from prison in 2007, after serving thirty-two years. In the musical *Assassins*, Sara Jane tells Squeaky Fromme, "I love your beads . . . I must have spent an hour on Haight Street trying to find a string of beads like that, but all I found were these. The salesman told me they were groovy."

"Squeaky" Fromme: One of the two women to have attempted to assassinate a president, Lynette "Squeaky" Fromme (born 1948) was a member of the Manson Family, a cult led by Charles Manson. Though not involved in the Tate–LaBianca murders for which the Manson Family is best known, she attempted to assassinate President Gerald Ford in 1975. It was within three weeks of Sara Jane Moore's attempt to kill Ford. For that crime, she was sentenced to life, but was paroled after thirty-four years in prison. In the song "Unworthy of My Love," Squeaky sings, "Charlie, / Take my blood and my body / For your love."

William Howard Taft: The only person to have served as a president and chief justice of the United States, William Howard Taft (1857–1930) was president from 1909 to 1913. Taft was the heaviest of all the presidents, weighing 340 pounds. Sara Jane Moore says to Charles Guiteau about her poor marksmanship, "I couldn't hit William Howard Taft if he were sitting on my lap."

William McKinley: President during the Spanish-American War, William McKinley (1843–1901) was the twenty-fifth president of the United States, serving from 1897 until his assassination in 1901. He was killed by Leon Czolgosz at the Pan-American Exposition in Buffalo. In *Assassins*, the Attendant at the Pan-American Exposition says, "Single line, ladies and gentlemen. Line forms here to meet the President of the United States. Single line to shake hands with President William McKinley."

Willy Loman: In Arthur Miller's acclaimed play *Death of a Salesman* (1949), the main character, Willy Loman, tragically learns that all his values for success are lies. Booth explains the plot of *Death of a Salesman* to Lee Harvey Oswald, then says, "I'll tell you something—I'm an actor, Lee. And I'm a good one. But Willy Loman is a part I could never play."

BIG RIVER

Libretto by William Hauptman, based on Mark Twain's *The Adventures of Huckleberry Finn.* Music and lyrics by Roger Miller. Original Broadway production: April 25, 1985. Eugene O'Neill Theatre. 1,005 performances. Broadway revival in 2003.

Mark Twain's classic American tale *The Adventures of Huckleberry Finn* is narrated by Huck on the page, so the novel is filled with regionalisms, some of them still heard today, but many lost to time. The musical *Big River* retains some narration by Huck, and such slang is found throughout the dialogue and lyrics for many of the characters. The time period is the 1840s, some two dozen years before the Civil War and the emancipation of enslaved people. The story takes place in several towns and places along the Mississippi River, as well as on the river itself.

Expressions, references, names:

britches: In the song "Guv'ment," Pap complains about the government, singing, "You got your damn hands in every pocket of my britches." Rural slang for trousers, breeches, knee pants, knickerbockers, or any form of men's pants is britches.

Cairo: The city of Cairo, Illinois, is located at the confluence of the Ohio and Mississippi Rivers. In the nineteenth century, it was a booming community with a population of over fifteen thousand people, and a place where steamboats and later trains converged. Today it is something of a ghost town, with fewer than two thousand residents. The runaway slave Jim tells Huck, "I'm going down that river, Huck. To Cairo, where the Mississippi joins the Ohio. Then I'm following the Ohio north to the Free States."

calico gown . . . seegars: Cotton fabric printed with colorful patterns is known as calico and was very popular for women's wear in the past, particularly in the rural South. The regional pronunciation of "cigar" is *see*-gar, with the accent on the first syllable. Jim has collected various treasures that came floating down the river at high water. Huck looks through them and says, "Here's a calico gown . . . and some seegars."

cottonmouth: The large, deadly, semi-aquatic pit viper that inhabits lowland swamps and waterways of the southeastern United States is the cottonmouth. It gets its name from the white interior of its mouth. In his drunken delirium, Pap sees a stick on the floor of the cabin and thinks it's a snake, shouting, "It's a cottonmouth! Don't go near it!"

dad gum: This is an expression of annoyance, mostly associated with redneck speech; a fractured alternative for "God damn." In the song "Guv'ment," Pap frequently says, "you dad gum guv'ment."

d'bloon: An old gold coin from Spain or Spanish America is called a doubloon. The term is often heard when describing pirate loot in the eighteenth and nineteenth centuries. When Huck finds a coin inside of a fish he caught, he tells Jim, "Spanish . . . I think. This is a Spanish d'bloon, Jim, it's pirate gold!"

Dolphin: The eldest son of a king of France, and thereby the future king, is called the Dauphin. Huck tells Jim, "Some say King Louis the Fourteen of France had a little boy, the Dolphin, who came over here to America when his pa got his head chopped off." Later in the musical, the con man King announces, "I am the late Dolphin."

Fido: Coming from the Latin word for "faithful," the word *Fido* was once the most popular name given to a pet dog. Canines have been affectionately called Fido since Roman times. In the song "Hand for the Hog," Tom Sawyer sings, "You might get bit by the old Fido."

forty-rod whiskey: Huck says to drunken Pap, "You been bit by that forty-rod whiskey." Huck is referring to a homemade brew of whiskey that was said to be so powerful it supposedly has the power of killing at the distance of forty rods. It was also known as Taos Lightning, or by other local names. The contents might include grain alcohol, a twist of tobacco, red chilies, a bar of soap, a rattlesnake's head, and a little Pecos River water.

hayseeds: A derogatory term for rural members of the American working class; the stereotypical hayseed is someone who is naive, easily fooled, and ripe for a swindle. In the song "When the Sun Goes Down in the South," the Duke and King sing, "And the hayseeds stand in line."

Injun Joe's cave: In the novel *The Adventures of Tom Sawyer*, the caves outside of town where Injun Joe hid after the murder was later called Injun Joe's cave. At the beginning of *Big River*, Huck tells the audience, "Tom and me found the gold the robbers had hidden in Injun Joe's cave, and it made us rich." A bit later in the musical, Huck, Tom Sawyer, and the boys hold their secret meeting in Injun Joe's cave.

Iron Mask: The unidentified "Man in the Iron Mask" was a French prisoner who spent thirty-four years in prison in the seventeenth century. No one is known to have seen his face, as it was hidden by a mask of black velvet cloth. This was later changed to an iron mask when Voltaire wrote about the mystery man. The prisoner is the subject of books and movies, and it's likely Tom Sawyer ran across the story in his quest for adventure. Tom makes plans to rescue Jim in a contrived but dramatic way, telling Huck, "He's got to have a rope ladder—we'll send it in a pie—and he can write notes, using rust and tears for ink . . . That's what the Iron Mask done."

medicine show: Very popular in the nineteenth century, a medicine show was a traveling entertainment using one or more performers to attract a crowd with the intention of selling them some kind of miracle cure. The local man Lafe says to his friend Hank about the Duke's theatricals, "It's another one of them medicine shows."

Nonesuch: A nonesuch is person or thing unrivaled or unequaled. The Old English word was derived from "there is none such thing elsewhere." In 1538, Henry VIII built a palace in London that he titled Nonesuch. The Duke uses the word to create attention, announcing his show by saying, "A freak of nature, brought to you from the jungles of Borneo at great expense, the Royal Nonesuch!"

"Out, out damned spot": The Duke quotes from Lady Macbeth's famous "Out, out damned spot" speech in *Macbeth*, but then goes on to mix in phrases from other Shakespeare plays, ending with Marc Antony's speech, "Friends, Romans, countrymen!" from *Julius Caesar*.

phrenology: In the past, the science of phrenology studied the shape and contours of the skull with the belief that they would explain a person's mental faculties and character. Huck tells the audience that "the Duke lectured on the science of phrenology."

rakafratchits: A regional slang term for a rascal or dishonest person, all but forgotten today. In the song "Guv'ment," Pap calls the government "You sorry rakafratchits."

St. Petersburg: Mark Twain grew up in the Missouri river town of Hannibal, but he calls it St. Petersburg in both *The Adventures of Tom Sawyer* and *The Adventures of Huckleberry Finn.*

shoe fittin' fire starters: An old expression for an arsonist or firebug is "fire starter." In the song "Guv'ment," Pap calls the US government "Dead pan shoe fittin' fire starters."

sugar hogshead: An old-fashioned word for a cask or a barrel is hogshead. These large containers were usually filled with molasses, tobacco, or sugar. Huck says he misses the ramshackle cabin he used to live in. Forced to live with the Widow Douglas in a proper house, Huck tells the audience, "I'd rather live in a sugar hogshead again, like in the old days, and be free and satisfied."

Thunderation!: When someone was surprised or agitated or just annoyed, the exclamation "Thunderation!" might be used. It was a colorful rural expression, probably derived from thunder and lightning. When Huck suggests to Tom Sawyer that they run off to the Western territories, Tom says, "Thunderation!"

unities . . . boards: When Huck asks the Duke why they keep Jim chained up, he replies, "Chains are the correct things at all times. We must preserve the unities, as they say on the boards." The unities are the "unities of time, place, and action," a method of storytelling going back to the ancient Greeks. The "boards" is a familiar expression for the theatre, coming from the phrase "to trod the boards."

BRIGADOON

Libretto and lyrics by Alan Jay Lerner. Music by Frederick Loewe. Original Broadway production: March 13, 1947. Ziegfeld Theatre. 581 performances. Broadway revivals in 1950, 1957, 1963, 1980, and 2010.

The romantic fantasy *Brigadoon* is the most famous musical set in Scotland. Because the village of Brigadoon is awash in the mists of time, it often has a fairy-tale quality. The village is located in one of the glens in the Scottish Highlands. In fact, it is so hidden that when it disappears for a hundred years, it is not missed. Angus MacLaren says at one point, "This is the second day of our blessing." Tommy and Jeff, two Americans touring Scotland, are contemporary (that is, from the year 1946), but during the previous night, Brigadoon slept for one hundred years. If the "miracle" first appeared two nights ago, the date would be 1746. And, according to the wedding date written in the MacLaren family Bible, the day is May 24. But this is a fantasy, and time seems to be irrelevant in *Brigadoon*.

Expressions, references, names:

bairn: The Scottish word for a child; the villagers sing, "Come ye, bairn / Come ye men" in the song "Down on MacConnachy Square."

bonnie: Something attractive or beautiful is called "bonnie" in Scottish jargon. It's usually used in referring to a pretty girl, most commonly as "a bonnie lass." Archie Beaton says to Angus, "An' good morning to your two bonnie daughters."

brae: The Scottish word for a hillside or a place on high ground; when the villagers are searching for Harry Beaton, Angus sings, "Ye, there, head to the brae!"

braw: Something that is fine or good is said to be "braw" in Scotland. Meg tells Jeff, "Ye're a braw an' handsome lad."

Brigadoon: The fictitious word "Brigadoon" was created by Lerner for the name of the village where the musical takes place. In Scottish, a "brig" is a bridge. "Doon" might have been inspired from *Lorna Doone*, an 1869 British romance novel by Richard Doddridge Blackmore.

canna: "Can't" or "cannot" is expressed with "canna" in Scottish dialect. When Tommy asks Fiona to explain the "miracle," she replies, "I canna say."

claret: Originally a red wine from the Bordeaux region in France, claret now means a wine with a deep purplish-red color. Angus offers a bottle of claret to toast Charlie's wedding.

daft: An Old English expression for silly or foolish or even crazy; Mr. Lundie tells Tommy and Jeff that if the story of the "miracle" was told to them by "someone in the town, they'd think the lass or lad was daft."

dinna: In the Scottish dialect, "did not" or "didn't" comes out as "dinna." Angus MacGuffie says, "Just as well you dinna talk too much."

dram: Angus asks Charlie to "have a dram o' good luck with me." A small amount of liquid, usually strong whiskey, served in a little glass is known in Scotland as a dram. Because of its small size, folks usually say "a wee dram."

glen: A glen is a narrow valley. Because of the mountainous terrain of the Scottish Highlands, there are many famous glens. The townspeople sing, "Come ye in the glen" in the song "Down on MacConnachy Square."

gloamin': A poetic expression for twilight or dusk is "the gloaming." In "The Heather on the Hill," Tommy sings, "The mist of May is in the gloamin'."

Haig and Haig: A brand of Scotch whiskey that was first manufactured in Scotland is known as John Haig & Co., or "Haig and Haig." Jeff tells Tommy that Meg "never heard of Haig and Haig," which strikes both men as odd.

heather: The purple wildflower that grows abundantly on the moorland and hillsides of Scotland and northern England is called heather. Fiona and Tommy sing about leaving the town to go out and gather "The Heather on the Hill."

Highlands: The mountainous part of Scotland north of Glasgow is called the Highlands. Often associated with Gaelic culture, this region has its own dialect, dress, and traditions. *Brigadoon* takes place in the Highlands, as introduced by the song "Once in the Highlands."

high road: When Jeff and Tommy are lost in the Highlands, Jeff says, "Maybe we took the high road instead of the low road." He is referring to the song "Loch Lomond," which begins "O ye'll take the high road, and I'll take the low road / And I'll be in Scotland afore ye."

ken: An old expression for one's range of knowledge or sight is "in my ken," or the opposite, as with "outside my ken." *Ken* is also used for "know" in Scottish, as with the lyric, "Don't ye ken / There's a fair / Down on MacConnachy Square."

kirk: A church in Scotland is called a kirk. Mr. Lundie refers to Mr. Forsythe as "an old minister of the kirk."

laddie: In Scotland and some other cultures, a boy or young man is called a lad, or, more informally, a laddie. The villagers sing, "Come ye to the fair, laddie" in "Down on MacConnachy Square."

lassie: The feminine equivalent to a lad or laddie is a lass or lassie. Now that Charlie is getting married, Angus asks him if he's "through with the lasses for good?"

lea: A lea is any area of grassy or open land. Fiona sings that waiting for a true love is "sweeter to me / Than wooin' any laddie on the lea."

loch: A lake or an arm of the sea that stretches inland is called a loch in Scotland. Loch Lomond and Loch Ness are two famous lochs.

Loch Lomond: A famous lake in west-central Scotland, Loch Lomond is known around the world because of the nineteenth-century ballad, "Loch Lomond." Tommy sings, "I could swim Loch Lomond / And be home in / Half an hour" in "Almost Like Being in Love."

Lowlands: To most of the world, the Lowlands refers to Belgium and the Netherlands, but in Scotland the Lowlands is the area that lies south of the Highlands. In "The Love of My Life," Meg sings of a fellow she knew from the Lowlands, and "of all the Lowland laddies there was never one so low!"

Rand McNally: The publishing company Rand McNally & Co. has been printing maps since 1868. Named after co-founders William H. Rand and Andrew McNally, the Chicago firm still produces printed and digital maps. Jeff and Tommy are using a Rand McNally map in Scotland. When they see a village that is not on the map, Jeff says, "Wait till Rand McNally hears about this!"

rill: A small stream, usually one that cuts a shallow channel in the surface of soil or rocks, is called a rill. Tommy sings of the "lazy music in the rill" in the song "The Heather on the Hill."

sable: Something that is black or very dark is said to be sable. In the song "Brigadoon," the chorus sings, "Brigadoon, Brigadoon, blooming under sable skies."

shilling: A shilling is a former British coin and monetary unit equal to one-twentieth of a pound, or twelve pence. When Tommy tries to pay for the milk with a contemporary shilling, the villagers are astounded to see the twentieth-century date on the coin.

thistle: Growing abundantly in the Highlands, the thistle is the Scottish national emblem, a plant with a prickly stem and leaves and rounded heads of purple flowers. Archie teases Jeff that he might rip his trousers on a thistle.

waistcoat: A vest, especially one worn by men over a shirt and under a jacket, is still called a waistcoat in the British Isles, and is pronounced *wescut*. Fiona tells Archie that she needs to buy "a waistcoat for my father for the weddin'."

wee: Anything little is wee in Scottish jargon. It could be a person, such as a "wee child," or a thing, such as a "wee dram."

winna: Scottish for "will not," *winna* is used throughout *Brigadoon*, as with "The cow winna take it back" and "Ye winna forget to come over this afternoon?"

ye: An Old English (and Scottish) word that means "you" in both the singular and the plural. Harry tells his father, "Ye know it well." The villagers sing, "Come ye, to the fair" in the song "Down on MacConnachy

Square." Over the years, "ye" has also become a quaint form of "the," as in Ye Olde Gift Shoppe.

BYE BYE BIRDIE

Libretto by Michael Stewart. Lyrics by Lee Adams. Music by Charles Strouse. Original Broadway production: April 14, 1960. Martin Beck Theatre. 607 performances. Broadway revival in 2009.

While *Bye Bye Birdie* was the first Broadway musical about rock 'n' roll, its score is mostly in the conventional Broadway style. In fact, the new rock sound is mostly parodied in this contemporary musical that was filled with idioms, names, and references everyone knew in 1960. Recently in the news at the time was the coverage of Elvis Presley being drafted and inducted into the army. This provides the premise for *Bye Bye Birdie*. As the years pass, the time period for the musical grows more distant, yet the

BYE BYE BIRDIE   *There was no question in 1960 that heartthrob Conrad Birdie (Dick Gautier, center) was based on rock 'n' roll favorite Elvis Presley.*
Photofest

popularity of the show continues on. Knowing these references will only aid in the enjoyment.

Expressions, references, names:

Abbe Lane: The popular American actress and singer Abbe Lane (born in 1932) was known in the 1950s and 1960s for her sexy outfits and sultry style of performing. She was married to the Spanish-born bandleader Xavier Cugat and often sang Latin songs. In the song "Spanish Rose," Rosie sings, "I'll be more Espagnol than Abbe Lane!" which is a joke, because Lane was Jewish and born in Brooklyn.

Albert Schweitzer: The renowned humanitarian, philosopher, and physician Dr. Albert Schweitzer (1875–1965) was a symbol of goodwill around the world. When Rosie complains about how awful men are, Kim says, "All men can't be like that!" to which Rosie responds, "Every one of them! Except maybe Albert Schweitzer. And I'm not his type."

all-clear: An indication that danger or a threat is over, usually signaled by a loud siren. When Rosie hears a loud moan from Albert's mother, Mae Peterson, offstage, she comments, "It's either her or the all-clear."

Almaelou: Almaelou Music Corporation is a fictional record company named after Albert Peterson; his mother, Mae; and their deceased wire-haired terrier, Lou. When Albert wants to get out of the music business and dissolve Almaelou, his mother is shocked and insulted.

"Amapola": The Latin-flavored hit song "Amapola (Pretty Little Poppy)" was a number-one record for Jimmy Dorsey in 1941. Rosie refers to the Joseph M. Lacalle (music) and Albert Gamse (English lyrics) song when she declares, "From now on the sky's the limit . . . parties . . . balls . . . dances! Amapola, my pretty Ama!"

Arpège: First sold in 1927, the perfume Arpège is very expensive. Albert quotes the perfume's famous advertising slogan when he says, "Promise her anything, but give her Arpège."

Benedict Arnold . . . Mussolini: The famous traitor Benedict Arnold (1741–1801) and the infamous Italian dictator Benito Mussolini (1883–1945) are among the men Rosie refers to when she tells Kim, "They're all the same. From puberty to senility . . . from Benedict Arnold to Mussolini!"

bickerish: To bicker is to argue or complain. Albert creates the word "bickerish" to rhyme with "licorice" in the song "Put on a Happy Face" when he sings, "If you're feeling cross and bickerish, / Don't sit and whine!"

bolero: The bolero is a style of music as well as a famous Spanish dance, often associated with gypsies. In the song "Spanish Rose," Rosie sings, "With Albert I will dance the bolero."

Chichi Costenango: There is a city in Guatemala called Santo Tomás Chichicastenango, also known as Chichi Costenango. Rosie sings in "Spanish Rose," "I'll be the toast of Chichi Costenango."

Conrad Birdie: The fictional rock star Conrad Birdie is an obvious spoof of superstar Elvis Presley (1935–1977). In 1958, Presley was drafted into the US Army, and his induction, training, and two-year duration were all widely covered by the press. Librettist Michael Stewart used Presley's being drafted as the premise for *Bye Bye Birdie*.

Daisy Air Rifle: An air gun or air rifle is a weapon that fires projectiles pneumatically with compressed air. Instead of bullets, the Daisy brand fired BBs at its target. When Mr. MacAfee hears that his daughter Kim has run off with Conrad Birdie, he tells his son Randolph to fetch his Daisy Air Rifle so he can shoot Conrad with BBs.

dentifrice: Another word for toothpaste or any tooth-cleaning substance; in the song "One Last Kiss," Albert sings, "Oh one last kiss; it gives so much bliss . . . what is your dentifrice!"

Dolores del Rio: The Mexican-born movie actress Dolores del Rio (1904–1983) is regarded as the first major female Latin American crossover star in Hollywood. Del Rio is mentioned when Albert recalls the 1933 movie *Flying Down to Rio*: "Gosh, I'll always remember that great cast. Dolores del Rio—"

Ed Sullivan: The famous newspaper columnist Ed Sullivan (1902–1974) is most remembered for his very popular TV variety program, *The Ed*

Sullivan Show, which ran live on Sunday nights from 1948 to 1971. Like many performers, Elvis Presley's popularity skyrocketed when he appeared on Sullivan's show in 1956. In the song "Hymn for a Sunday Evening," the MacAfee family sings sincerely about their beloved idol, Ed Sullivan.

Fidel Castro: Fidel Alejandro Castro Ruz (1926–2016) was a Cuban revolutionary and politician who was the leader of Cuba from 1959 to 2008. When a phone call comes for Rosie at the dive, Maude's Roadside Retreat, the bartender mockingly says to her, "Hey, Fidel Castro! I got a guy named Peterson wants to talk to you."

Flying Down to Rio . . . Greed: Albert mentions two classic films when he says, "Great double bill tonight . . . *Flying Down to Rio* and *Greed*!" It is an amusing pairing, for *Flying Down to Rio* is a 1933 movie musical and *Greed* is a 1924 silent drama.

Gene Raymond: The dashing film actor Gene Raymond (1908–1998) of the 1930s and 1940s is mentioned by Mr. MacAfee when he and Albert talk about the movie musical *Flying Down to Rio* (1933).

Geoffrey Chaucer . . . William Morris: In the song "An English Teacher," Rosie laments how Albert gave up a teaching career for show business with, "It was good-bye, Geoffrey Chaucer, / Hello, William Morris." Geoffrey Chaucer (c. 1340–1400) was the early English poet and author most known for writing *The Canterbury Tales*. America's most famous talent agency, the William Morris Agency, has handled the biggest names in movies, music, theatre, sports, and the literary market.

GI: Any member of the US armed forces is called a GI, a term that came from the initials for "General Issue" on uniforms. In the song "A Healthy Normal American Boy," Albert sings that Conrad Birdie is "proud to be a plain GI."

"Granada": The 1931 hit song "Granada" by Augustin Lara (music) and Dorothy Todd (English lyrics) was a Latin-flavored favorite for over thirty years. In the song "Spanish Rose," Rosie sings, "The only song I'll sing will be 'Granada.'"

Indo-China: The former French colonial empire in Southeast Asia, including much of the eastern part of the Indochinese peninsula, was known as Indo-China for a time. In the song "A Healthy Normal American Boy," Rosie sings that Conrad Birdie was "born in Indo-China, / Son of missionaries there."

IRT: The Interborough Rapid Transit Company (IRT) was New York City's original underground subway line that opened in 1904. The initials IRT were retained as one of the subway's lines beginning in 1940. When Mae Peterson refuses her son's help getting home, she says, "I'll take the IRT. That's the worst subway."

jerries: A derogatory term used by the Allies for the Germans in World War II. During the song "A Healthy Normal American Boy," Albert gets carried away and says that Conrad Birdie hopes to get assigned to the front lines so he'll "be sure to get [him] one of those dirty jerries."

Mr. Keen: The radio show *Mr. Keen, Tracer of Lost Persons* debuted in 1937 and entertained listeners through 1957. In the program, the "kindly old investigator" Mr. Keen tracked down individuals who had mysteriously vanished. When Kim runs off with Conrad Birdie, her father cries out, "Call Mr. Keen, Tracer of Lost Persons!"

Loop-the-Loop: A popular ride at amusement parks was the Loop-the-Loop, a roller coaster that made a complete circle and was considered very daring. Conrad sings, "Loop-the-loop and laugh at the view" in the song "A Lot of Livin' to Do." When Mr. MacAfee hears that Kim has gone out with Conrad Birdie, he says, "My daughter has run off to loop-the-loop with a fiend!"

Mr. Luce: Henry Luce (1898–1967) was one of the most successful and powerful publishers of the twentieth century and the founder of *Time* and *Life* magazines. When Luce calls Albert on the phone, Albert thinks the call is from a "Mr. Lewis," who prints pulp publications. Albert shouts, "You can print that in whatever cheap paper you happen to represent! (pause). It's not a paper, it's a magazine (another pause). And it's not Mr. Lewis . . . It's Mr. Luce!"

mantilla: A traditional item of dress in Spain is the mantilla, a lace or silk scarf worn over the hair and shoulders. Rosie sings in "Spanish Rose" that "Beneath my mantilla I'll pose, / The beauty that nobody knows."

Margo . . . Shangri-La: In the popular 1933 book and 1937 film *Lost Horizon*, Shangri-La was a magical place where one never ages. When one of the characters, played by the beautiful actress Margo in the movie, leaves Shangri-La, she immediately decays and is an old woman. Mae Peterson insults Rosie when she says, "This is Rose? I can't believe it. She looks like Margo when they took her out of Shangri-La."

"Mexicali Rose": A Latin-flavored song by Jack B. Tenney (music) and Helen Stone (lyrics), "Mexicali Rose" had a big hit recording by Bing Crosby. Mae Peterson slyly refers to Rosie as "Mexicali Rose."

Mounted Police: The Royal Canadian Mounted Police has been the national police force in Canada since 1920. When he finds out that his daughter Kim has gone off with Conrad Birdie, Mr. MacAfee says, "Call the Mounted Police!"

Murad: An exotic brand of cigarettes that uses Turkish tobacco. Kim has never smoked a Murad, or probably any other kind of cigarette, so when Conrad Birdie gives her one and she tries it, she says, "Mmm, that is refreshing. Of course, I do prefer a Murad, but these'll do."

NYU: New York University (NYU) is one of the oldest and largest universities in New York City. In the song "An English Teacher, "Rosie sings, "You were going to college . . . You were going to NYU and become / An English teacher."

Parliament . . . Magna Carta . . . Nero: When Mr. MacAfee puts his foot down and tries to maintain dominance in his own home, he says, "Parliament has been dissolved; the Magna Carta is revoked; and Nero is back in town!" Parliament is the governing body of Great Britain; the Magna Carta is the document King John was forced to sign in 1215 that outlined the liberties guaranteed to the English people; and Nero was the Roman emperor who supposedly played his fiddle while Rome burned in the year AD 64.

Peter Lawford: The movie star Peter Lawford (1923–1984) was a member of the "Rat Pack" and was in the news in 1960 because he married into the Kennedy family. When Mr. MacAfee gets angry, he says, "I intend calling the FBI! Who's the head of it now, dear? Is it Peter Lawford yet?"

Phi Beta Kappa: In the song "An English Teacher," Rosie sings, "I could have been . . . Missus Albert Peterson, / Missus Phi Beta Kappa Peterson, / The English teacher's wife." The honorary society of college and university students to which members are elected on the basis of high academic achievement, Phi Beta Kappa is one of the most prestigious of honor societies.

pinned: Once a very popular courting ritual, giving a girl your fraternity pin as a token of attachment was called "being pinned." It later referred to any two people dating on a steady basis. In "The Telephone Song," all the teenagers sing about the news that Hugo and Kim "got pinned."

Postum: Postum was the brand name for a coffee substitute invented by C. W. Post and made with chicory and roasted grains. When Albert gets upset, his mother, Mae, suggests that he have a "nice cup of Postum."

reform school: Two of the news reporters ask Albert and Rosie, "Is it true that you found Conrad in a reform school?" Not so much a school as a penal institution for reforming young offenders, reform school was associated with juvenile delinquents.

"A rose is a rose is a rose": This phrase was written by Gertrude Stein as part of the 1913 poem, "Sacred Emily," and has remained her most famous quotation. In the song "Rosie," Albert sings about her being "A rose is a rose is a rose."

Sammy Kaye: "Swing and Sway with Sammy Kaye" was the tagline for American bandleader Sammy Kaye (1910–1987), one of the most famous stars of the Big Band Era. Mr. MacAfee, singing the song "Kids," wonders, "What's wrong with Sammy Kaye?"

***The Shadow*:** A radio show that was long remembered after it stopped broadcasting in 1957, *The Shadow* was a mystery-suspense program narrated by Lamont Cranston. When Mr. MacAfee panics, thinking his daughter has been kidnapped, he cries out, "Call the Shadow! Look him up under Lamont Cranston!"

Shriners: A fraternal order that is an auxiliary of the Masonic order, the Shriners have local chapters that socialize and promote charitable causes. When Rosie goes to the dive, Maude's Roadside Retreat, the Shriners are having a meeting in the back room, and she decides to join them, resulting in the hilarious Shriners' Dance.

"Sibonny": The 1929 song "Sibonny" by Ernesto Lecuona (music), Alfredo Brito (Spanish lyrics), and Dolly Morse (English lyrics) was a Latin favorite. When Rosie arrives at Maude's Roadside Retreat, she orders a double bourbon and says "Bring on the dancing boys! . . . Sibonny!" and sings the popular song with, "Da da da da, da da da da da, da dum dum dum!"

Terramycin: An antibiotic used to treat skin conditions, such as acne. When Conrad Birdie is recovering from being slugged by Hugo, Mrs. Peterson makes the ridiculous offer, "Wait for me, Conrad! I'll make you a nice hot cup of Terramycin."

CABARET

Libretto by Joe Masteroff, based on the play *I Am a Camera* by John Van Druten and *Berlin Stories* by Christopher Isherwood. Lyrics by Fred Ebb.

CABARET   *The rise of the Nazi Party in Germany is personified by the character of Ernst (Edward Winter, foreground) in this sobering musical about the Holocaust.*
Photo by Thomas Hollyman / Photofest

Music by John Kander. Original Broadway production: November 20, 1966. Broadhurst Theatre. 1,165 performances. Broadway revivals in 1987, 1998, and 2014.

A musical about the coming of the Holocaust seems bold and sobering today; imagine what audiences in 1966 thought. *Cabaret* took the "musical play" to places never before explored. The setting is a crucial time in the history of the Nazi Party. The musical begins on New Year's Eve of 1929, when the Nazis and Adolf Hitler were far from powerful. But over the months that follow, the Third Reich and its leader are getting stronger. Cliff sees this and leaves Germany. Sally, like too many others, refuses to see it and, consequently, allows it to happen. Here are some of the expressions used in the musical, most of them coming from the German language.

Expressions, references, names:

bloomers: Introduced by Amelia Bloomer in Upstate New York in the mid-nineteenth century, bloomers were loose trousers gathered at the knee, formerly worn by women as part of a gymnasium, riding, or other sports outfit. By the early decades of the twentieth century, bloomers referred to women's undergarments, particularly in Great Britain. Sally tells Cliff about her school friend Sybil: "We were utterly wild—smoking cigarettes and not wearing bloomers!"

Chelsea: In the song "Cabaret," Sally sings, "I used to have a friend known as Elsie / With whom I shared four sordid rooms in Chelsea." The district of western London called Chelsea sits on the north bank of the Thames River. It has been popular with writers and artists since the late eighteenth century.

Frau . . . *Damen* . . . Herr . . . *Herren*: The German equivalent to "Mrs." is "Frau," used to address a married woman. The plural *Damen* also refers to women, but not to their marital status. It is best translated as "ladies." The courtesy title for a married or single male is "Herr" in German-speaking regions. In *Cabaret*, Cliff and Schultz are addressed as Herr Bradshaw and Herr Schultz. The plural, meaning "men," is *Herren*, as when the Emcee addresses the audience at the Kit Kat Klub with, "*Meine Damen und Herren—*"

Fraulein: The German language honorific for unmarried women, comparable to "Miss" in English and "Mademoiselle" in French. Since the 1960s, "Fraulein" has been used less and less in Germany and Austria, many considering it sexist. Sally is introduced at the Kit Kat Klub as "Fraulein Sally Bowles," and Schultz respectfully addresses the landlady as "Fraulein Schneider."

groschen: An Austrian coin worth only one-one-thousandth of a schilling is the *groschen*. It was discontinued in 2002. To explain why she is outside Herr Schultz's door, Fraulein Schneider tells Fraulein Kost, "I am looking for—I think I dropped—a small coin—a *groschen*. It rolled this way."

ja: The German word *ja* means "yes," but can be used for any affirmative response. "*Ja*" is also frequently used as a filler word in random German speech. When Cliff asks Ernst if the train is slowing down for the German border, he replies, "*Ja*."

marks: Fraulein Schneider shows Cliff a room to rent and says, "You see! All comforts! And with breakfast only one hundred marks!" The basic unit of money in the former Germany currency is the mark, available in both coin and paper. To distinguish from other currencies, it was often called a Deutsche Mark, or a German mark. Today marks have been replaced by Euros.

mazel: A Jewish phrase expressing congratulations or good luck; the expression is not as old as many Hebrew words, *mazel* being introduced in print in 1862. Herr Schultz says to Cliff, "I want to wish you *mazel* in the New Year."

Meeskite: Yiddish for an ugly person; in the song "Meeskite," Herr Schultz sings, "Meeskite, meeskite, / No one ever saw a bigger Messkite, meeskite." In an alternate ending to the song "If You Could See Her," the Emcee looks at the gorilla and sings, "If you could see her through my eyes . . . She isn't a Meeskite at all!"

Mein Kampf: Adolf Hitler's 1925 autobiographical manifesto was titled *Mein Kampf*, which can be translated as *My Struggle* or *My Battle*. In the book, Hitler describes the process by which he became anti-Semitic, and outlines his political ideology and future plans for Germany. Sally looks at the book Cliff is reading and says, "It's in German! *Mein Kampf?*"

***Prosit!*:** When toasting one's health and happiness, one says *Prosit* in German-speaking regions. Cliff says to Sally and Ernst, "We're going to be rich! Here—drink up! I mean, *Prosit!*"

Rhine: The Rhine River, which flows from the Swiss Alps to the North Sea, handles more traffic than any other river in the world. Much of the river is in Germany, where there is a province also called the Rhine. In the song "Tomorrow Belongs to Me," the Waiters sing, "The Rhine gives its gold to the sea."

ruble . . . yen . . . franc . . . buck: During "The Money Song," the Emcee introduces the Kit Kat Klub chorus girls, each one dressed with coins and paper money from different nations: "Meet Olga, my Russian ruble . . . Sushi, my Japanese yen . . . My French franc, Viola! . . . And now, ladies and gentlemen, my American buck!"

CAMELOT

Libretto by Alan Jay Lerner, based on T. H. White's novel *The Once and Future King*. Lyrics by Alan Jay Lerner. Music by Frederick Loewe. Original Broadway production: December 3, 1960. Majestic Theatre. 873 performances. Broadway revivals in 1980, 1981, 1993, 2011, and 2023.

Running over six hundred pages and filled with dozens of characters, T. H. White's 1958 epic novel *The Once and Future King* was not going to be easily adapted into a musical. Less obvious but even more difficult, the book is a fanciful mix of fantasy and realism, lighthearted exuberance and tragic consequences. Alan Jay Lerner's libretto for *Camelot* opts for modern dialogue with a few medieval words here and there. Also, several names from Arthurian legend are brought up. Lerner sets the time period of the play with the simple "A long time ago." The legend of King Arthur has been told frequently over the centuries, and most versions place the setting as the fifth century in a rather primitive Britain. Most productions of *Camelot* tend to romanticize the legend, which is how audiences prefer it.

Expressions, references, names:

Arthur: Also called Arthur Pendragon, King Arthur is the legendary British king who appears in a cycle of medieval romances. It is not certain how these legends originated or whether the figure of Arthur was based on a historical person. Yet there is some evidence that Arthur was real, a great leader named Arturus, who championed the Celtic Britons' cause against the Anglo-Saxons in the fifth century. How he became king—by pulling the sword Excalibur from a stone—was also part of the legend. Arthur explains to Guenevere, "That's how I became king. I never knew I would be. I never wanted to be. And since I am, I have been ill at ease in my crown."

Camelot: The castle and court of King Arthur is known as Camelot, though that place name was not mentioned until twelfth-century French romances. It is believed that Camelot was situated near Exeter in southwest England. In the song "Camelot," Arthur sings to Guenevere, "In short, there's simply not / A more congenial spot / For happy-ever-aftering than here / In Camelot."

"C'est moi": The French for "It is I" is "C'est moi." In the song "C'est Moi," Frenchman Lancelot sings, "C'est moi! C'est moi, / I'm forced to admit! / Tis I, I humbly reply."

Chamberlain: The word *chamberlain* has been used to denote a variety of government positions over the centuries. In the time of *Camelot*, a chamberlain was an officer who manages the household of a king. Arthur says to Pellinore, "Pelly, please tell the Chamberlain the order of jousts tomorrow will be Dinadan, Sagramore, and Lionel."

Channel: The English Channel is so well known that it is usually just called "the Channel" in news reporting and literature. The Channel is an arm of the Atlantic Ocean that separates southern England from northern France, and links to the southern part of the North Sea by the Strait of Dover at its northeastern end. It remains the busiest shipping area in the world. For centuries, anyone traveling from France to England had to "cross the Channel" by boat, as Lancelot did. Sir Dinadan says of the overly pious Lancelot, "He probably walked across the Channel."

chivalry: A combination of qualities and behavior can be used to describe chivalry. In the Middle Ages, an ideal knight was expected to display courage, honor, justice, and a readiness to help the weak, in particular, women in distress. Arthur says to Guenevere, "Jenny, suppose we create a new order of chivalry? . . . A new order where might is only used for right, to improve instead of destroy."

derry down dell: In the song "Fie on Goodness," Mordred and the knights sing, "Derry down dell / Damn, but it's hell!" "Derry down dell" is an alliterative but meaningless refrain or chorus heard in very old English songs. *Derry* is Celtic for a grove, and a dell is a secluded hollow or small valley usually covered with trees or turf.

en brochette: In French cooking, *en brochette* means meat or any other food that is roasted or grilled on a skewer. In the song "Then You May Take Me to the Fair," Sir Sagramore sings to Guenevere, "I'll serve him [Lancelot] to your highness *en brochette!*"

Excalibur: The legendary sword of King Arthur; the name of the magical weapon was first used in fifteenth-century romances in France and England. When they first meet, Arthur says to Guenevere, "I swear by it! By the Sword of Excalibur! I swear I won't touch you!"

fie: A very old expression of mild disgust or annoyance; the first use of the word in writing goes back to the fourteenth century. Mordred and the knights sing, "Oh, fie on goodness, fie / Fie, fie, fie!"

"Gaul will be divided": When Julius Caesar wrote the chronicle of his conquest of Gaul (today's France), he began the account with "Gallia est omnis divisa in partes tres," meaning "All of Gaul is divided into three parts." In the song "Then You May Take Me to the Fair," Sir Lionel sings to Guenevere, "Oh, give me the opportunity to fight him [Lancelot] / And Gaul will be divided once more!"

Guenevere: Often spelled "Guinevere," Guenevere was the queen of Britain, wife of King Arthur, and lover of Sir Lancelot in the Arthurian legends. She is best known from Sir Thomas Malory's *Le Morte d'Arthur* (1485). In *Camelot*, she is betrothed to Arthur and is not happy about the prospect of marrying him. Guenevere says to Arthur before she knows he is the king, "But if you mean [Merlyn] is some sort of fortune-teller, I'd give a year in Paradise to know mine."

Joyous Gard: The castle from which Sir Lancelot hails is called Joyous Gard (*Joyeuse Garde* in French). According to French legend, Lancelot succeeded in his conquest to remove the formidable fortress from the forces of evil. Arthur recalls Merlyn's words, "He said to me one day: 'Arthur, keep your eye out for Lancelot du Lac from the castle of Joyous Gard.'"

kith and kin: Any familiar friends, neighbors, or relatives can be referred to as kith. *Kin* (or *kinfolk*) is a word for a group of persons of common ancestry, such as those belonging to the same family or clan. In the song "The Simple Joys of Maidenhood," Guenevere sings, "Shall kith not kill their kin for me?"

Lancelot: Also spelled Launcelot, and known as Lancelot of the Lake, the French knight Lancelot was the lover of King Arthur's queen Guenevere, one of the greatest knights in Arthurian romance, and was the father of the pure knight Sir Galahad. In *Camelot*, Arthur introduces Lancelot to the court, saying, "This is the Lancelot [that] Merlyn spoke of. He's come all the way from France to become a Knight of the Round Table."

mail: Part of a medieval knight's armor was mail, or chain mail. It was made of small metal rings fashioned together to form a mesh, which was then tailored to cover various parts of the body. In the song "C'est Moi," Lancelot sings that he can "swim a moat in a coat of heavy iron mail."

Malory . . . Tennyson: Of the many printed versions of the Arthurian legend, two old ones stand out. The English author Sir Thomas Malory (c. 1415–1471) either wrote or compiled the chronicle titled *Le Morte d'Arthur* (*The Death of Arthur*), first published in 1485. Malory's identity has never been confirmed. Four centuries later, the Victorian poet Alfred Tennyson (1809–1892) wrote a cycle of twelve narrative poems titled *Idylls of the King*. The poems were written over a period of twenty-five years, and were first published together in 1885. When Arthur is hiding in a tree, Merlyn tells him, "And where is the King? Swinging in the trees. Thank heaven History never knew. Thank heaven Malory and Tennyson never found out."

marzipan: A sweet confection consisting primarily of sugar, honey, and ground almonds; this dessert is sometimes augmented with almond oil or extract. In the song "The Persuasion," Mordred tempts Morgan Le Fey with "Fudge by the van! / Fresh marzipan!"

Merlyn: An alternate spelling of Merlin, a wizard in the Arthurian legend who first appeared in print in the twelfth century. Mostly known as an enchanter, he is usually portrayed as a good wizard, as in the tales concerning King Arthur. Arthur explains to Guenevere, "Merlyn. My teacher . . .

He lives backwards. He doesn't age. He youthens. He can remember the future so he can tell you what you'll be doing in it."

Mordred: The illegitimate son of King Arthur and his half-sister Morgause, Mordred is best remembered for his betrayal of Arthur, and for launching the battle that led to his father's demise. In *Camelot*, he reveals his identity to Arthur with "That's not a very kind way to treat the son of Queen Morgause . . . Yes, Your Majesty, I am Mordred."

Morgan Le Fey: The enchantress Morgan Le Fey is sometimes depicted as an evil wizard, other times as a helpful spirit. In the Arthurian legend, she is usually described as Arthur's sibling. Arthur explains to Guenevere, "We have an enchanted forest where the Fairy Queen, Morgan Le Fey, lives in an invisible castle. Most unusual."

Nimue: One of the most powerful of all legendary British witches, Nimue—also known as "the Queen of Blood" or "the Lady of the Lake"—lived during the reign of King Arthur and was beloved by Merlyn, who told her all of his secrets. She later used this knowledge to imprison him in a grave for eternity. In the musical *Camelot*, Merlyn says to the unseen spirit, "Oh, Nimue! So it's you! Must you steal my magic now? Couldn't you have waited a bit longer?"

noblessely obliged: The French expression *noblesse oblige* means, literally, "nobility obligates," and refers to the responsibility that people from a noble ancestry have, to act honorably and generously to others. Alan Jay Lerner twists the words a bit in the song "What Do the Simple Folk Do?" in which Guenevere refers to "The folk not noblessely obliged."

Pellinore: First mentioned in old French romances, King Pellinore is the king of Listenoise, or "of the Isles." In the Arthurian legend, Pellinore is fated to spend his life chasing after the Questing Beast. In the musical, King Pellinore explains to Guenevere, "You say you haven't seen a beast with the head of a serpent, the body of a boar . . . Called the Questing Beast, what? The Curse of the Pellinores. Only a Pellinore can catch her."

Prometheus: In Greek mythology, Prometheus was a Titan who defied Zeus and gave fire to mankind. For this transgression, Prometheus was bound to a rock and an eagle was sent every day to eat his liver. His liver would then grow back overnight, only to be eaten again the next day.

This myth was turned into a Greek tragedy by Aeschylus, titled *Prometheus Bound*. In the song "C'est Moi," Lancelot sings, "C'est moi! C'est moi, / So admir'bly fit; / A French Prometheus unbound."

rigor mort: The Latin expression *rigor mortis* literally means "stiffness of death." It is today a medical term for the stiffness that sets in quickly on a dead body. In the song "The Seven Deadly Virtues," Mordred sings, "Take Courage! now there's a sport / An invitation to the state of rigor mort!"

Round Table: First appearing in literature in the mid-twelfth century, the Round Table and the knights who were dedicated to it are an essential part of Arthurian legend. To ensure peace in Arthur's kingdom following an early warring period, he founded the Round Table. These same knights would later go on the mystical quest for the Holy Grail. Guenevere asks Arthur, "Won't there be jealousy? All your knights will be claiming superiority and wanting to sit at the head [of the table]," to which Arthur replies, "Then we shall make it a round table so there is no head."

St. Geneviève: The fifth-century French saint Geneviève is the patron saint of Paris because she allegedly saved that city from the Huns. In the song "The Simple Joys of Maidenhood," Guenevere prays to her patron saint: "Dear Genevieve, Sweet Genevieve, / Shan't I be young before I die?"

Sermon on the Mount: In the New Testament, Jesus' longest and most detailed sermon is recorded in St. Matthew's Gospel, and is known as the Sermon on the Mount. The sermon contains some of the most essential principles for living a genuine Christian life. Sir Dinadan irreverently says to the pious Lancelot right before the joust, "Do you know what I shall be thinking, Lancelot, when I see you on your horse? There he is, the Sermon on the Mount."

Unstatusing . . . Beelzebubble: Several times in *Camelot*, Alan Jay Lerner creates a new word from old ones or changes a noun into a verb for comic effect. In the song "The Seven Deadly Virtues," Mordred sings, "You'll never find a virtue / Unstatusing my quo, / Or making my Beelzebubble burst." *Status quo* is a Latin phrase meaning the existing state of affairs, or the way things are now. Beelzebub is a name for the devil, derived from a Philistine god, and later adopted as a major demon in certain religions.

CAROUSEL

Libretto by Oscar Hammerstein, based on the play *Liliom* by Ferenc Molnár. Lyrics by Oscar Hammerstein. Music by Richard Rodgers. Original Broadway production: April 19, 1945. Majestic Theatre. 566 performances. Broadway revivals in 1949, 1954, 1957, 1994, and 2018.

The darkest of all the Rodgers and Hammerstein musicals, *Carousel* is set in the past—from 1873 to 1888—but it is far from a nostalgic look back. There is a hard reality in the musical, and the unpleasant issues it brings up are not easily resolved. All the action takes place in or near an unnamed New England coastal town. Several of the characters have a strong dialect, but it is usually made clear what is being said. There are some weaving and whaling terms heard in the musical, but they are not too difficult to follow. Here are some that are not as clear or familiar.

Expressions, references, names:

barker: Any person who is employed to draw customers onto a ride or into an attraction can be called a barker. Such jobs were mostly found in carnivals or circus side shows. Billy Bigelow is barker for Mrs. Mullen's carousel, and his job is not only to attract customers, but also to flirt with the young women as he rides with them, encouraging them to ride over and over again. Mrs. Mullen says to Billy, "Can y'imagine how the girls'd love that? A barker who runs home to his wife every night! Why, people'd laugh theirselves sick."

blackguard: An old expression rarely used anymore, a blackguard is a man who behaves in a contemptible manner. Referring to Billy, Mr. Bascombe tells Julie, "You heard what kind of blackguard this man is."

capuluptic fit: An angry Carrie says to Mrs. Mullen, "Suppose he did [put his arm around her]. Is that a reason to hev a capuluptic fit?" Carrie probably means a "cataleptic fit," a sudden attack of catalepsy in which a person loses consciousness and goes into a seizure or trance.

carousel: Whether it's called a merry-go-round, a roundabout, a horse-about, a jumper, or flying horses, a carousel is perhaps the oldest amusement park ride, variations of it going back to the seventeenth century. The first such attraction in North America was the "wooden horse circus ride" in Salem, Massachusetts, in 1799. At the time of *Carousel*, the ride usually featured horses that moved up and down, powered by a steam engine.

chippies: An antiquated word for a prostitute or any female with loose morals. Mrs. Mullen purposely insults Julie and Carrie when she says, "I don't run my business for a lot o' chippies!"

clambake: A traditional clambake is a picnic or social gathering at the seashore at which clams and other seafood are baked, sometimes with corn and other items, traditionally on hot stones under a covering of seaweed. The chorus sings, "This was a real nice clambake / And we all had a real good time!"

dickey: An article of clothing that has changed meaning over the years. Today it refers to a fragment of a garment worn under another garment, such as a turtleneck dickey. In the late 1800s, a dickey was a fake shirt front, possibly with a tie and vest, to look like one had a full shirt on under a jacket. During the bench scene, Billy imagines himself married and sings to himself, "I'd throw away my sweater and dress up like a dude / In a dickey and a collar and a tie."

doubtin' Thomases: In the Gospel of St. John, the apostle Thomas refused to believe that Jesus had risen from the dead until he could see and feel Jesus' crucifixion wounds. Ever since then, an incredulous or habitually doubtful person has been called a "doubting Thomas." In the song "June Is Bustin' Out All Over," Nettie sings, "And a crowd of doubtin' Thomases / Was predictin' that the summer'd never come!"

lallygaggin': To waste time by puttering aimlessly, loafing around, or goofing off; Enoch says to Carrie, "I can't abide women who are free, loose, and lallygaggin'!"

lorgnette: An old-fashioned pair of spectacles or opera glasses held in front of a person's eyes by a long handle at one side; in the song "Soliloquy," Billy sings about a snobby woman who looks "through a lorgnette!"

Penobscot . . . Augusty: Penobscot is a coastal village in Maine. Augusta is the state capital of Maine. In the song "June Is Bustin' Out All Over," Nettie twists the name of Augusta to sing, "From Penobscot to Augusty / All the boys are feelin' lusty."

roustabouts: Any unskilled or semi-skilled laborer can be called a roustabout. They were very common in the past with traveling circuses and carnivals, erecting and dismantling tents and handling animals and equipment. Today the term is mostly used with workers in an oil field or refinery. Nellie says, "Hey, you roustabouts! Time to get goin'! Come and help us carry everythin' on the boats!"

shuttle . . . warp . . . woof: In the song "You're a Queer One, Julie Jordan," Carrie sings to Julie, "And half the time yer shuttle gets twisted in the threads / Till y'can't tell the warp from the woof!" Both women work at the looms, and these are weaving terms. A shuttle is a tool designed to neatly and compactly store a holder that carries the thread of the yarn. At the time of *Carousel,* simple "stick shuttles" were made from a flat, narrow piece of wood with notches on the ends to hold the weft yarn. The woof are the threads that cross over and under the other threads (called the warp) in weaving the fabric.

Virginia creepers . . . bejeepers: The Virginia creeper is a climbing vine of the grape family with bluish-black berries. A variant of "bejesus," bejeepers is a mild euphemistic oath. In the song "June Is Bustin' Out All Over," Nettie sings, "That the young Virginia creepers / Hev been huggin' the bejeepers / Outa all the mornin'-glories on the fence."

vittles: A very rural and rustic word for any food substance; in the song "This Was a Real Nice Clambake," the chorus sings, "The vittles we et / Were good, you bet!"

wharf yarns . . . spoondrift: A yarn is a long or rambling story, especially one that is difficult to believe. *Spoondrift* is slang for the spray blown up from the surface of the sea. Carrie tells Jigger, "Now look here, Mr. Craigin, I ain't got no time fer no wharf yarns or spoondrift."

CHICAGO

Libretto by Fred Ebb and Bob Fosse, based on the play *Chicago* by Maurine Dallas Watkins. Lyrics by Fred Ebb. Music by John Kander. Original Broadway production: June 3, 1975. 46th Street Theatre. 898 performances. Broadway revival in 1996.

This musical satire is not only set in the Jazz Age, but all the songs are pastiches of popular songs of the 1920s. Both the lyrics and the dialogue are filled with the slang and names in the news that were popular during that era. Few are known to modern audiences, but that doesn't stop *Chicago* from being one of the most often-produced musicals. Here are some terms that are uniquely Roaring Twenties.

Expressions, references, names:

bunny hug: An American ballroom dance in the 1920s with a ragtime rhythm was called the bunny hug. The couple holds each other closely while they dance to a rapid beat. In the opening number, "All That Jazz," Velma sings, "Hold on, hon, we're gonna bunny-hug."

cellophane: Cellophane goes back to 1912, when Swiss chemist Jacques E. Brandenberger invented the thin, transparent sheet made of regenerated cellulose. Combining the words cellulose and diaphane ("transparent"), cellophane changed the way food was packaged. Amos sings that he is like the product, "'cause you can look right through me."

deuce: A two-dollar bill is sometimes referred to as a "deuce" or a "Tom." In the song "Class," Velma and Mama Morton sing, "Any girl'd touch your privates for a deuce."

Father Dip: In "All That Jazz," Velma sings, "I hear that Father Dip is gonna blow the blues." The renowned American trumpeter and vocalist Louis Armstrong (1901–1971) had several nicknames, including "Satchmo," "Satch," "Pops," and "Father Dip." As a young boy he was called Dippermouth because of his large mouth and lips. Later, fellow musicians gave him the affectionate nickname Father Dip.

finagle: To obtain something by devious or dishonest means is to finagle; Billy sings, "Throw 'em a fake and a finagle" in the song "Razzle Dazzle."

CHICAGO *The murderesses Velma Kelly (Chita Rivera, left) and Roxie Hart (Gwen Verdon) end up as stars of vaudeville more because they are notorious than for their talent.*
Photofest

flasks: These small containers of alcohol were popular during the Prohibition, as they were narrow enough to be concealed in one's pocket or under a garter belt. Velma sings, "Find a flask, we're playing fast and loose" in the opening song, "All That Jazz."

flim flam flummox: Billy puts together two slang expressions when he sings, "Give 'em the old flim flam flummox" in the song "Razzle Dazzle." To "flummox" someone is to confuse or bewilder them, while "flim flam" refers to a swindle or a way to cheat someone.

garters break . . . shimmy shake: An elastic band worn to hold up a stocking or sock, a garter became a sensual item of clothing in the Roaring Twenties, and was rarely hidden. The jazz dance known as the shimmy shake was characterized by a shaking of the body from the shoulders down. In the opening number, "All That Jazz," the chorus sings about Velma, "She's gonna shimmy till her garters break."

jazzing: A euphemism for sexual intercourse during the 1920s was "jazzing." Amos says to Roxie, "You told me he was a burglar and all the while you're up here jazzing him."

lavaliere: The French term for a pendant on a fine chain that is worn as a necklace. Roxie sings about wearing one in her own vaudeville act in the song "Roxie."

Leopold and Loeb: One of the most notorious crimes in 1920s Chicago was the murder of fourteen-year-old Bobby Franks by Nathan Leopold Jr. and Richard Loeb, two wealthy, intelligent students at the University of Chicago. In 1924 they pulled off what they considered the perfect crime, later admitting they killed Franks just for fun. Velma compares Roxie becoming a mother to "making Leopold and Loeb Scout Masters."

Lucky Lindy: An oft-used nickname for American aviator Charles Lindbergh (1902–1974). After he made the first nonstop flight from New York City to Paris in 1927, Lindbergh was so famous that several songs were written about him. One was called "Lucky Lindy." Velma sings, "I betcha Lucky Lindy never flew so high" in "All That Jazz."

Marshall Field: The most famous department store in Chicago, Marshall Field's opened in 1852 and was considered the best retail establishment outside of New York City. When Roxie learns that she may get a life sentence, she asks Mama Morton, "In jail?" to which Morton answers sarcastically, "Where else? Marshall Field?"

matron: The term *matron* has many meanings, from a middle-aged married woman to the lady in charge of a hospital ward. The matron Mama Morton in *Chicago* is the woman in charge of the female inmates in the Cook County jail.

Methuselah: In the Bible, Noah's grandfather Methuselah was said to have lived for 969 years. In the song "Razzle Dazzle," Billy sings how people have enjoyed being bamboozled "Back since the days of old Methuselah."

Packard cars: The Packard brothers started manufacturing a line of automobiles in 1899, and the Packard remained a luxury car for several years. Billy sings, "I don't care for drivin' Packard cars" in the song "All I Care About Is Love."

Palace: Mama Morton tells Velma that the baseball star Babe Ruth is "playing the Palace and earning five thousand a week." She is referring to the Palace Theatre in New York City, considered the finest venue in American vaudeville.

Princeton crew: In the song "When You're Good to Mama," Matron Mama Morton sings, "Let's all stroke together like a Princeton crew," referring to the rowing team at Princeton University.

ragout: A hearty, seasoned Italian sauce of meat and tomatoes that is used chiefly in pasta dishes is called a ragout. Mama Morton sings, "pepper my ragout," and Velma sings, "fezzle my ragout"—both meaning to "spice up my sauce."

silk cravats . . . ruby studs . . . satin spats: High style for men in the Roaring Twenties was a band or scarf worn around the neck called a cravat. A stud is a solid button with a shank or eye on the back, inserted (as through an eyelet in a garment) as a fastener or ornament. A man's cufflinks are an example. Up until the 1930s, many men and women wore spats, a cloth or leather covering for the instep and ankle of a shoe. In "All I Care About Is Love," Billy sings, "I don't care for wearin' silk cravats / Ruby studs, satin spats."

sob sister: A slang term for a journalist who specializes in writing or editing sob stories or other sentimental material is a sob sister. In *Chicago*, Mary Sunshine is the sob sister who takes an interest in Roxie.

Sophie Tucker: The American singer, comedian, actress, and radio personality Sophie Tucker (1886–1966) was one of vaudeville's biggest stars. Roxie imagines how jealous the celebrity will be when she sings, "And Sophie Tucker'll shit, I know, to see her name get billed below" her. Tucker was known by the nickname "The Last of the Red-Hot Mamas," and the character of Mama Morton in *Chicago* is clearly inspired by her.

United Drug: A drugstore chain in the first half of the twentieth century, the United Drug Company had hundreds of stores across the country. Velma sings about buying "some aspirin down at United Drug" in the opening song, "All That Jazz."

Vanderbilt: The Vanderbilts were once the wealthiest family in America, a dynasty founded by industrialist Cornelius Vanderbilt (1794–1877) that flourished during the Gilded Age. Billy sings, "I don't care for any attire Vanderbilt might admire" in the song "All I Care About Is Love."

vaudeville: The 1920s was the peak of vaudeville, a stage entertainment consisting of various acts, from singers and dancers to comics and animal acts. Sometimes celebrities, such as Babe Ruth, appeared in vaudeville for top dollar. At the end of *Chicago*, Velma and Roxie go into vaudeville together and perform "Nowadays."

William Morris: The William Morris talent agency handles actors, singers, and any famous person whom people will pay to see onstage or on the screen. Founded in 1898 by William Morris, the agency is still active today. Mama Morton tells Velma that she's "been talkin' to the boys at William Morris" to get her vaudeville bookings after she is acquitted.

COMPANY

Libretto by George Furth. Music and lyrics by Stephen Sondheim. Original Broadway production: April 26, 1970. Alvin Theatre. 705 performances. Broadway revivals in 1993, 1995, 2006, and 2021.

When *Company* opened on Broadway in 1970, it was not only revolution-ary in its development of the concept musical, but it was also thoroughly contemporary in words and music. Instead of faraway places in past times, George Furth's libretto was set in New York City "today," and the char-acters onstage were not all that different from the New Yorkers in the audience. They are smart, educated, neurotic, funny urban dwellers who might be a bit jaded but still approach life with ferocity. And they speak the Manhattan lingo.

Expressions, references, names:

Ann Miller: One of Hollywood's premiere tap dancers, Ann Miller (1923–2004) appeared in several classic movie musicals. She was known for her rapid-fire tapping and exuberant personality on the screen. At the nightclub, Joanne tells her husband, Larry, "I find it unbelievably humiliat-ing watching my own husband flouncing around the dance floor, jerking and sashaying all over the place like Ann Miller."

Bellevue: Bellevue Hospital Center in New York City is the oldest public hospital in the United States, as well as one of the largest. Histori-cally, Bellevue has often been associated with its treatment of mentally ill patients, meaning that the term "Bellevue" became a local pejorative slang term for a psychiatric hospital. On her wedding morning, Amy says to her husband, Paul, "If you say 'thank you' I will go running right out of this apartment and move into the Hopeless Cases Section at Bellevue, where they'll understand me."

Boeing: The Boeing Company is a multinational American corporation that designs, manufactures, and sells airplanes, rockets, satellites, and mis-siles worldwide. Many of the commercial aircraft active in the United States were made by Boeing, including the plane April will be working on. Asked by Robert where she is going, April sings, "Barcelona . . . And Madrid . . . On a Boeing."

Eliza on the ice: One of the most famous passages in Harriet Beecher Stowe's 1852 novel, *Uncle Tom's Cabin*, is a scene where the runaway slave Eliza tries to cross the icy Ohio River to get to freedom. In the song "Not Getting Married," Amy sings, "But why watch me die / Like Eliza on the ice?"

Fourteenth Street: A major crosstown street in Manhattan, considered the border between Lower Manhattan and Midtown Manhattan. The street is also a busy crossroads where buses, the subway, and taxis converge. Marta tells Robert, "And Fourteenth Street. Well, nobody knows it, but *that* is the center of the universe."

Goliath: In the Bible, the Philistine warrior giant, Goliath, was slain by the youth David. Since then, any huge person or thing can be described as Goliath. In the song "Poor Baby," Joanne sings, "Tall? She's tall enough to be your mother . . . Goliath!"

Harold Teen: A long-running American comic strip about a naive but eager adolescent, seen in newspapers from 1919 to 1959. At the nightclub, Joanne says to Robert, "Don't talk. Don't do your folksy Harold Teen with me."

"hog butcher for the world": One of the most famous poems by the American writer Carl Sandburg (1878–1967) was "Chicago" (1916), which sang of the glories of the city. The opening line is, "Hog butcher for the world," and later in the poem Sandburg writes, "proud to be Hog Butcher." At the nightclub, Joanne recalls how she left her first husband when he wanted them to move to Chicago, saying, "And least of all would I ever want to go to a place where they actually feel honored being called 'hog butcher for the world'!"

Kamasutra: The ancient Sanskrit text *Kamasutra* (or *Kama Sutra*) is a guide to finding love and desire, but is most known today as a work of eroticism, giving instructions on physical lovemaking. In the song "Have I Got a Girl for You," Peter sings of a girl who is "Into all those exotic mystiques: The Kamasutra and Chinese techniques."

Krafft-Ebing case history: Baron Richard von Krafft-Ebing (1840–1902) was a German psychiatrist noted for his writings on case studies of sexual deviance. Joanne mocks Robert's way of being "always outside, looking in the window," and says to him, "You are lifted right out of a Krafft-Ebing case history."

Librium: A very popular tranquilizer of the benzodiazepine group is Librium, used mainly to treat anxiety and alcoholism. Joanne takes a deep drag on her cigarette and tells Robert, "That's the best. Better than Librium."

Life: Known mostly for its outstanding photography, *Life* was an American magazine published weekly from 1883 to 1972. It was a general-interest magazine with a wide range of topics, none of them explored too deeply. In the song "The Ladies Who Lunch," Joanne mocks the wives who are, "Keeping house but clutching a copy of *Life* / Just to keep in touch."

Mahler: The Austro-Bohemian romantic composer and conductor Gustav Mahler (1860–1911) was an innovative artist who bridged the nineteenth-century Austro-German tradition and the modernism of the early twentieth century with his work. In the song "The Ladies Who Lunch," Joanne sings, "Perhaps a piece of Mahler's—I'll drink to that. / And one for Mahler."

Mary Baker Eddy: The American religious leader and author Mary Baker Eddy (1821–1910) founded the Church of Christ, Scientist, in New England in 1879. In *Company*, Sarah, who is on a diet and craves Sara Lee desserts, says to Robert, "Sara Lee is the most phenomenal woman since Mary Baker Eddy."

NSEW Airlines: A fictional airline company that George Furth created for *Company*, NSEW Airlines is mostly likely an acronym for North South East West Airlines. April is a stewardess for the company and at one point announces, "Final departure call for NSEW Airlines Flight One-Nineteen."

Pinter play: English playwright, actor, and director Harold Pinter (1930–2008) is known for his puzzling plays that are associated with the Theatre of the Absurd. Despite the difficulty of the plays, theatregoers who wanted to be sophisticated never missed a new Pinter work. In the song "The Ladies Who Lunch," Joanne sings, "Another thousand dollars, / A matinee, a Pinter play."

sampler: A piece of embroidery worked in various types of stitches to depict a scene with words and letters of the alphabet. In many cases, the sampler spelled out a motto or a wise saying. When Paul tells Amy, "Just because some of the people might be wrong doesn't matter . . . [marriage] is still right," Amy says, "Yes, well, I'll put that on a sampler, Paul."

Sazerac slings: A Sazerac is a cocktail originally from New Orleans using cognac or whiskey. A Sazerac sling usually has several base ingredients: a type of alcohol, fruit flavors, and sugar. It is served in a large glass and is a relatively fruity, light drink. In the song "Have I Got a Girl for You," Larry sings about a girl "with a weakness for Sazerac slings."

Seagram Building: The sleek Park Avenue skyscraper known as the Seagram Building is a stunning example of a rectilinear prism sheathed in glass and bronze. The high-rise was designed by Ludwig Mies van der Rohe and Philip Johnson in the International Style. During the song "Side by Side by Side," David says about Robert, "You know what comes to my mind when I see him? The Seagram Building. Isn't that funny?" Perhaps David means Bobby is sleek, modern, and somewhat aloof.

Shaker Heights . . . Radio City: Shaker Heights is an affluent suburb east of Cleveland, Ohio. "Radio City" is the familiar term for Radio City Music Hall, a large entertainment venue in Rockefeller Center in Midtown Manhattan. April, who is from Ohio, tells Robert, "I was getting ready to go back to Shaker Heights when I decided where I really wanted to live more than any other place was—Radio City. I thought it was a wonderful little city near New York."

vodka stinger: A stinger is a duo cocktail, using only two ingredients: a spirit and a liqueur. A vodka stinger is a cocktail made with vodka and white crème de cacao. At the nightclub, Joanne is drinking heavily, and in the song "The Ladies Who Lunch," she sings, "Another reason not to move, / Another vodka stinger . . . I'll drink to that!"

West End Avenue: A very desirable neighborhood on the Upper West Side of Manhattan is West End Avenue, filled with large historic buildings that make for roomy apartments and condos. April tells Robert that she has a male roommate, and that "We just share this great big apartment on West End Avenue."

DAMN YANKEES

Libretto by George Abbott and Douglas Wallop, based on Wallop's novel *The Year the Yankees Lost the Pennant.* Music and lyrics by Richard Adler and Jerry Ross. Original Broadway production: May 5, 1955. 46th Street Theatre. 1,019 performances. Broadway revival in 1994.

According to the authors, *Damn Yankees* is set in Washington, DC, "sometime in the future." Yet the musical is a fantasy rather than science fiction. The libretto is not futuristic, but rather very much a 1950s musical comedy. Broadway's only successful sports musical, *Damn Yankees* uses few baseball terms or slang, but the names of some famous ballplayers come up, most of them still widely recognized today. Most productions of *Damn Yankees* retain the 1950s setting and keep the action in the Washington, DC, area. As far as the real Washington Senators, they ceased to be after 1960, something the authors could not foresee.

Expressions, references, names:

Alibi Ike: In the 1915 short story "Alibi Ike" by Ring Lardner, a fictional baseball player constantly invents excuses for everything he does wrong. The expression lived on, and later meant anyone who constantly makes excuses, so as to shirk duty or responsibility. When Lola gives Applegate excuses for not being able to seduce Joe Hardy, he calls her "Alibi Ike."

Antoinette: The French queen Marie Antoinette (1755–1793), the wife of King Louis XVI, lived an extravagant lifestyle that led to widespread unpopularity, and, like her husband, she was executed during the French Revolution. In the song, "Those Were the Good Old Days," Applegate sings about "Antoinette, dainty queen, with her quaint guillotine."

Applegate: The devil has gone by many names in literature. Douglas Wallop calls him Applegate in the book and the musical—probably a nod to the tempting apple in the Garden of Eden, which the snake gave to Eve.

boffola: Something that is dazzling and surprising was once referred to as boffola. It often was used to describe a big success that was not expected. In the song "A Little Brains, A Little Talent," Lola brags to Applegate about "Just one more case she can erase with that old boffola."

Bonaparte: Napoleon Bonaparte (1769–1821) is the well-known French military leader and emperor who conquered much of Europe in the early nineteenth century. Because of Napoleon's ambitious and deadly pursuits, Applegate sings, "I see Bonaparte / A mean one if ever I've seen one" in the song, "Those Were the Good Old Days."

Channel: When she is asked if the Senators will win the pennant, reporter Gloria sarcastically replies, "When I swim the Channel." She is referring to the English Channel, which separates southern England from

DAMN YANKEES *The Washington Senators are no more, but they were a real major league baseball team when the musical opened in 1955.*
Photofest

northern France. A challenge for athletes has long been to swim across the Channel.

Chevy Chase: Joe and Meg Boyd live in Chevy Chase, a town in Maryland that straddles the northwest border of Washington, DC. It was built up as a convenient suburb, and today is a very expensive and desirable place to live. Joe Hardy has made arrangements to move into Meg's house, telling Lola, "I rented a room out in Chevy Chase this afternoon, and I promised to move in tonight."

Delilah: In the Bible, Delilah was the seductive beauty who betrayed Samson to the Philistines by revealing to them that the secret of his strength lay in his long hair. Ever since then, a Delilah means a dangerous female not to be trusted. In the song "A Little Brains, A Little Talent," Lola boasts, "I've done much more than that old bore, Delilah!"

diathermy: The surgical technique involving the production of heat in a part of the human body by high-frequency electric currents is called diathermy. It is done to stimulate the circulation, relieve pain, or cause bleeding vessels to clot. Sister has no idea what diathermy is when she lies to Mr. Welch, saying, "May I have your autograph, please? It's for my niece—she's sick—muscular diathermy."

Elks: The Benevolent and Protective Order of Elks, usually just called the Elks or the Elks Lodge, is an American fraternal order founded in 1868 as a social club, but is now also a major charitable organization. The Elks Lodge was often the site of community activities. Meg tells Joe Hardy, "Joe [Boyd] used to take me dancing at the Elks."

folderol: When Gloria keeps bringing up questions about Joe Hardy, Applegate tells her, "Folderol—what business is it of yours where Joe lives?" *Folderol* is an old-fashioned word for something trivial and not worth fussing over.

Gregory Peck: The tall, dashing American movie star Gregory Peck (1916–2003) was at the peak of his popularity in the 1950s and early 1960s. Sister is excited about possibly seeing the star when she tells Meg, "We're going down to the station to see Gregory Peck come in on the train from California."

Hank Bauer . . . Mickey Mantle: During the big game between the Washington Senators and the New York Yankees, the radio announcer in *Damn Yankees* mentions two real-life ballplayers when he says, "Coming up now for the Yankees is Hank Bauer. On deck, Mickey Mantle." Hank Bauer (1922–2007) was an American right fielder and manager and played with the Yankees from 1948 to 1959. Mickey Mantle (1931–1995), who was with the Yankees from 1951 to 1968, was a powerful switch-hitter (right- and left-handed) who hit 536 home runs during his career.

Hannibal: Famous as the boyhood home of Samuel Clemens (Mark Twain), Hannibal is a small city on the Mississippi River, about one hundred miles north of St. Louis, and the setting for some of Twain's books. Meg and Joe Boyd are from Hannibal, and she says to Joe Hardy, "Back home in Hannibal we had heat over 100 [degrees] lots of times." Also in *Damn Yankees*, Gloria leads the ballplayers in the song, "Shoeless Joe from Hannibal Mo."

Hercules . . . Mercury: In the song "Shoeless Joe from Hannibal Mo.," Gloria describes Joe Hardy using comparisons to mythological figures when she sings, "arms of steel like Hercules . . . Feet as fleet as Mercury's."

Hercules was the Greek hero of superhuman strength and courage, the son of Zeus, who became one of the gods. The Greek god Hermes was called Mercury by the Romans. He was the fleet-footed messenger of the gods, with a winged hat and staff.

Juicy Fruit: Juicy Fruit is a popular flavor of chewing gum made by the Wrigley Company. The gum was introduced in 1893 and is still a favorite today. Applegate says to Gloria about Joe Hardy, "He weighs 193 pounds, chews Juicy Fruit."

Listerine: First manufactured in 1895, Listerine was the first over-the-counter mouthwash sold in the United States. It remains the best-selling product of its kind. In the song "Shoeless Joe from Hannibal Mo.," Gloria and the ballplayers describe Joe Hardy as being "As fresh as Listerine."

Little America: Established by Admirable Richard E. Byrd of the US Navy in 1929, Little America is a maritime base in the Antarctic on the Bay of Whales. Many Antarctic expeditions set off from Little America. When real estate agent Joe Boyd worries about leaving his wife, Applegate says to him, "Tell her you're going to Little America, to interest the Eskimos in split-level houses."

mambo: The mambo is a Latin American dance, similar in rhythm to the rumba, which was derived from the ritual dance of voodoo. In the song and dance "Who's Got the Pain?," Lola and her dancing partner sing, "Who's got the pain when they do the mambo?"

Nero: Roman emperor Nero (AD 37–68) was infamous for his cruelty, executing leading Romans, including his own mother. During a great fire that destroyed half of Rome in AD 64, he supposedly played his fiddle. Although it is historically far from the truth, Nero's fiddling has become legend. In the song "Those Were the Good Old Days," Applegate sings about "Nero fiddlin' thru that lovely blaze."

pennant: If a baseball team wins their division title, they have won the "pennant" and will go on and play in the World Series. The name "pennant" goes back to the days when a physical pennant was raised on a flag-pole at the team's home when that ball team won their division. Lynch asks Mr. Welch, "Do you think Washington is going to win the pennant?"

Prince of Wales: The heir to the British throne is given the title Prince of Wales, an honor that goes back to the fourteenth century. In the song "A Little Brains, A Little Talent," Lola sings, "I took the starch out of the sails of the Prince of Wales."

rhubarb: An antique term for a heated dispute or controversy, this was often used in sportscasting when an argument broke out on the field. After a commotion in the game between the Washington Senators and the New York Yankees, the radio announcer says, "Well, the rhubarb's over."

Siam: Before 1939, the country of Thailand was known as Siam. The kings of Siam were symbols of Asian pomp and circumstance. In the song "A Little Brains, A Little Talent," Lola sings that she "took the zing out of the king of Siam."

Ty Cobb: The Baseball Hall-of-Famer Ty Cobb (1886–1961) has the highest lifetime batting average (.367) in major league history. The celebrated outfielder played for the Detroit Tigers from 1905 to 1926 and the Philadelphia Athletics in 1927 and 1928. Applegate says to Benny, "If Ty Cobb came here looking for a chance, you'd send him to Little Rock."

Washington Senators: The Washington Senators baseball team was founded in Washington, DC, in 1901, and was one of the American League's eight charter franchises. The team was bought in 1960 and is now known as the Minnesota Twins. When *Damn Yankees* opened on Broadway in 1955, the Washington Senators team was still firmly established in the nation's capital.

Willie Mays: The center fielder Willie Mays (born 1931) was a very popular baseball star in the 1950s. During his career, he played for the New York Giants, the San Francisco Giants, and the New York Mets. Mays was inducted into the Baseball Hall of Fame in 1979. In the song "Six Months Out of Every Year," the wives sing, "Instead of praising our goulash / They are appraising the plays of Willie Mays!"

Yale Regatta: The annual rowing race between Harvard University and Yale University began in 1859 and is still one of the premiere sporting events of the year. Known as the Harvard-Yale Regatta or the Yale-Harvard Boat Race, it is often referred to as simply "The Race." In the song "A Little Brains, A Little Talent," Lola boasts, "I can upset every male / In a Yale Regatta."

DREAMGIRLS

Libretto and lyrics by Tom Eyen. Music by Henry Krieger. Original Broadway production: December 20, 1981. Imperial Theatre. 1,521 performances. Broadway revivals in 1987 and 2001.

A fictional backstage musical with plenty of parallels to real singers, *Dreamgirls* is a thrilling musical drama that captures the world of Black people in show business in the 1960s. In addition to the Motown sound, the musical also has soul music, easy listening, and blockbuster Broadway numbers. Tom Eyen's libretto and lyrics include many references to 1960s artists, both Black and white. Few musicals capture an era like *Dreamgirls* does.

DREAMGIRLS   *There were more similarities between the Dreams and the Supremes than the rhyming names. Jennifer Holliday (left), Loretta Devine (right), and Sheryl Lee Ralph played fictional characters based on various girl groups.*
Photofest

Expressions, references, names:

Apollo Theater: At the beginning of *Dreamgirls*, the M.C. says, "Ladies and gentlemen, the Apollo Theater continues our legendary talent contest with the . . . Stepp Sisters!" The Apollo Theater in Harlem became a famous venue for Black performers in the 1930s, and many celebrated artists have played there since. It also offered talent nights for unknown performers, a practice it continues to this day. In 1983, both the interior and exterior of the building were designated as New York City Landmarks, and the building was added to the National Register of Historic Places.

Chiffons . . . Marvelettes . . . Supremes: Three actual Black girl groups are mentioned in *Dreamgirls*. Lorrell says to C.C., "We're going to be famous, just like the Chiffons, the Marvelettes, the Supremes!" The Chiffons were pioneers in the genre of all-girl groups. Originating in New York, by 1960 the sassy trio had a series of hit singles that are still enjoyed today. The Marvelettes went through five different combinations of singers but maintained a high standard of the up-tempo Motown sound on all of their recordings. The most successful of the girl-group acts was the Supremes. Coming from Detroit with the Motown style, the trio reached its peak in the 1960s, chalking up twelve number-one singles. The Supremes were so popular that they also became fashion icons for hair and clothing.

the Dreams: The announcer says, "Ladies and gentlemen, the Crystal Room is proud to present the club debut of America's new recording stars, the Dreams!" Because the name is so close to the Supremes, it is assumed that *Dreamgirls* is a pseudo-biography of the famous girl group. There are certainly many similarities, in particular the way Diana Ross eventually dominated the group, and how Florence Ballard was pushed aside and then fired. But librettist Tom Eyen insists that the Shirelles, the Chiffons, and Martha and the Vandellas were the real inspiration for the Dreams.

James "Thunder" Early: Several Black artists have been cited as the inspiration for the fictional Jimmy Early. The most likely candidates are James Brown (1933–2006) and Jackie Wilson (1934–1984). Often called the "Godfather of Soul," Brown was a singer, dancer, musician, record producer, and bandleader who promoted funk and soul. Wilson was a prominent figure in the transition of rhythm and blues into soul. He was a master showman and a dynamic performer in pop, R&B, and rock 'n' roll. Both Brown and Wilson come to mind in *Dreamgirls* when the M.C. announces, "The wildest man in show business, our headliner, James 'Thunder' Early!"

Johnny Mathis: Unlike most Black singers in the 1960s, Johnny Mathis (born 1935) established himself as a smooth crooner of song standards and easy listening recordings. The durable singer has seen several dozen of his recordings achieve gold or platinum status, and seventy-three of his albums made the Billboard charts. In the song "Rap," Jimmy Early sings, "I like Johnny Mathis / I can't do that stuff . . . 'Cause Jimmy got, Jimmy got, Jimmy got soul!"

kit and kaboodle: The American slang phrase "kit and kaboodle" or "kit and caboodle" means "all," or the entirety of something. The phrase goes back to the nineteenth century, and over the years, it has sometimes been misread as "kitten kaboodle." Perhaps Effie refers to this feline version when she sings "Take your cat, kit, and kaboodle" in the song "Move."

Pat Boone . . . "Fats" . . . Elvis . . . Big Mama Thornton: When the song "Cadillac Car" is turned into a hit for a white singing group, Marty explains to C.C., "Happens all the time, baby! Pat Boone had the big hit with Fats' 'Ain't That a Shame' and Elvis covered Big Mama Thornton's 'Hound Dog.' That's the way it happens in the world of R&B." Pat Boone (born 1934) is a squeaky-clean white singer, actor, and television personality who later became a motivational speaker and spokesman for various causes. Boone was a chart-selling pop singer of the 1950s and early 1960s. Fats Domino (1928–2017) was a Black pianist and singer-songwriter and a pioneer of rock-and-roll music. Elvis Presley (1935–1977), often dubbed the "King of Rock and Roll," was a significant cultural figure of the twentieth century, bringing rockabilly and then rock 'n' roll into fruition. Big Mama Thornton (1926–1984) was a Black R&B singer and songwriter who in 1952 was the first to record Leiber and Stoller's "Hound Dog," her version staying seven weeks at number one on the *Billboard* R&B chart.

payola: The practice of bribing someone to use their position to promote a particular product is known as payola. It has always been rampant in the music business, where undercover payments are made to a disc jockey for promoting a particular record. Marty tells Curtis, "We got limited distribution, we got limited bread for payola, and we got limited appeal."

Perry Como: The smooth-voiced, low-key white singer Perry Como (1912–2001) was the very definition of "easy listening." Como was a singer and television personality whose career stretched nearly fifty years. Effie tells Jimmy, "I saw you on TV last week. You sound like Perry Como now."

Ray Charles: Although he was blind and a poor Black man from the sticks, Ray Charles (1930–2004) became one of the most iconic and influential singers of the twentieth century. The singer, songwriter, pianist, and composer had a long and prodigious career in gospel, soul, and R&B music. Jimmy tells Curtis, "I been waiting so long, Ray Charles has had enough time to get himself another Grammy!"

Record World: The music industry trade magazine *Record World* started out in 1946 as *Music Vendor*, then changed its name in 1964. With articles and information about the music business, *Record World* lasted until 1982. Wayne says to Curtis, "Hey, Curtis, have you seen *Record World*? Effie has a song on the charts!"

Sammy Davis: Beginning his career in vaudeville at the age of three, versatile singer-dancer Sammy Davis Jr. (1925–1990) was a color barrier–breaking star of records, television, movies, and Broadway. When Curtis tries to get Jimmy and the Dreamettes booked into the Atlantic Hotel in Miami, Marty says, "You couldn't even get Sammy Davis in there. That place is so white, they don't even let our boys park the cars."

the Strip: A four-mile-long stretch of Las Vegas Boulevard, known for its concentration of resort hotels and casinos. Jimmy says, "I was driving down the Strip, just a-driving down the Strip, and I saw this electric sign twenty stories high—"

Tony Bennett: The durable Italian-American singer Tony Bennett (born 1926) has enjoyed one of the longest singing careers on record. His repertoire includes traditional pop standards, Big Band, Broadway songs, and jazz. Jimmy tells Lorrell, "Don't worry about a thing, baby . . . This Vegas crowd won't know the difference. Last time I played here, three women thought I was Tony Bennett! Tony Bennett!"

Vic Damone: The Italian-American pop and Big Band singer Vic Damone (1928–2018) sang traditional favorites on his many albums. He also had a substantial film career in Hollywood musicals. On the phone to the manager of the Atlantic Hotel, Curtis says, "You weren't sure of Vic Damone's availability and you said you'd tell me something today."

FIDDLER ON THE ROOF

Libretto by Joseph Stein, based on stories by Sholem Aleichem. Lyrics by Sheldon Harnick. Music by Jerry Bock. Original Broadway production: September 22, 1964. Imperial Theatre. 3,242 performances. Broadway revivals in 1976, 1981, 1990, 2004, and 2015.

Because of the popularity of *Fiddler on the Roof*, gentiles around the world now know a handful of Yiddish or Hebrew words and expressions. Such is the power of the American musical! *Fiddler on the Roof* is set in fictional Anatevka, a small village in Russia, in 1905. This was the time of Tsarist Russia, and Jews were a persecuted people. While this is presented in the musical, much of *Fiddler on the Roof* is about a way of life, a folk tale with iconic characters and classic situations.

Expressions, references, names:

dowry: In many cultures, a dowry is an important part of a marriage agreement. It is the goods or property that a wife brings to her husband in marriage. In Jewish culture, the amount of the dowry is not usually made public. Because Tevye is poor and has five daughters to marry off, he has nothing but a few goods to offer as a dowry for Tzeitel. Her mother, Golde, tells her, "A poor girl without a dowry can't be so particular."

Heinrich Heine: The German poet Heinrich Heine (1797–1856) is known today not only for his poems but for the songs (German *lieder*) made from his verses. Fyedka says to Chava, "Go ahead, take the book. It's by Heinrich Heine. Happens to be Jewish, I believe." Heine was not Jewish, but was educated in Catholic and Hebrew schools and was known for his radical ideas, which appealed to Jewish intellectuals.

kopeck: When Lazar gives the beggar Nahum one kopeck, he complains, "One kopeck? Last week you gave me two kopecks." In the Russian monetary system, a kopeck is a very small portion of the ruble (which today is worth 74 cents).

kosher: The Hebrew word *kosher* literally means "fit" or "fitting." Originally kosher laws defined the foods that are fit for consumption for Jews, but the word has come to refer more broadly to anything that is "above board" or "legitimate." In the opening number, Golde and the Mothers sing, "Who must know the way to make a proper home / A quiet home, a kosher home?"

L'Chaim: For more than two thousand years, Jews have used the expression *L'chaim*—literally "To life!"—as a toast. In the song "L'Chaim," Tevye and Lazar sing repeatedly, "Drink, *L'Chaim*, to Life!"

Mazeltov: Originally, the expression "Mazel tov"—literally translated as "Good luck"—was not a wish but a statement, suggesting "Good luck has occurred," or "Your fortune has been good." Over the years it has evolved to mean a wish, or "Congratulations!" During "Tevye's Dream," the chorus congratulates Tevye with "A blessing on your house, Mazeltov, Mazeltov, / Imagine such a spouse, Mazeltov, Mazeltov."

pogrom: In Russia and Eastern Europe in the late nineteenth and early twentieth centuries, an organized massacre of a particular ethnic group, particularly Jews, was called a pogrom. When the Constable tells Tevye, "Soon this district is to have a little unofficial demonstration," Tevye says, "A pogrom? Here?"

rabbi: The chief religious official of a synagogue who performs ritualistic, educational, and other functions as spiritual leader of the congregation is called a rabbi. But the word is also a term of respect for a Jewish scholar or teacher. Hodel says to her sisters, "We only have one rabbi and he only has one son. Why shouldn't I want the best?"

Reb: Roughly the equivalent of the English "mister," the Yiddish "Reb" is traditionally used for, and by, Orthodox Jewish men. Tevye says to the student Perchik, "And until your golden day comes, Reb Perchik, how will you live?"

Ruth . . . Esther: During the "Sabbath Prayer," Tevye and Golde sing, "May you be like Ruth and like Esther, / May you be deserving of praise." Both women were important figures in the Old Testament. Ruth was a woman of Moabite background who helped the Jews during the time of the Judges. The book of Esther is about the heroine who saved the

Jewish people. Both women are recognized for their strength, bravery, and dignity.

Sabbath: The seventh day of the Jewish week (Saturday) is the Sabbath, a day of rest and abstention from work, as commanded by God. The Sabbath meal is at sunset on Friday, and everything must be ready by then. Yente the matchmaker tells Golde: "Well, I must prepare my poor Sabbath table."

Shah! . . . the Evil Eye: "Shah!" is a Yiddish exclamation that can be translated as "Let there be quiet!," "Shut up, already!," or even "Silence!" The folk superstition known as the Evil Eye is not limited to Jewish culture. It is the belief that a person or supernatural being can bewitch or harm an individual merely by looking at them. Many wear the symbol of the Evil Eye in jewelry or other items to ward off the evil. When Tzeitel says she is "not yet twenty years old," her mother, Golde, says, "Shah! Do you have to boast about your age? Do you want to tempt the Evil Eye?"

Siberia: Siberia is an extensive geographical region, constituting all of north Asia, from the Ural Mountains in the west to the Pacific Ocean in the east. It has been a part of Russia since the tsar acquired the land in the latter half of the sixteenth century. Soon after, Siberia was used to house a system of penal labor camps known as the Katorga. Under Soviet rule, when Russia continued to send political prisoners to Siberia to perform forced labor under harsh conditions, the system was then known as the Gulag. Hodel tells Tevye that her beloved Perchik has asked her to join him. "It is far, Papa, terribly far. He is in a settlement in Siberia."

synagogue . . . a seat by the eastern wall: A synagogue is not only a house of worship in the Hebrew faith, but the word can also refer to the Jewish congregation. Inside the synagogue is the "mizrach" section, which faces east, where seats are reserved for the rabbi and other dignitaries. In the song "If I Were a Rich Man," Tevye imagines leisure time to "sit in the synagogue and pray" and "maybe have a seat by the eastern wall."

Tsar: The Romanov emperor on the Russian throne during the time of *Fiddler on the Roof* was Tsar Nicholas II (1868–1918). Ruling from 1894 until his abdication in 1917, Nicholas was the last emperor of Russia, murdered along with his family in 1918. In the song "Tradition," the Rabbi says, "A blessing for the Tsar? Of course. May the Lord bless and keep the Tsar—far away from us!"

Yente: The Yiddish word for a talkative, gossipy woman is *yente*. The matchmaker in *Fiddler on the Roof* is called Yente, and because of the popularity of the musical, many now think that *Yente* means "matchmaker." Hodel says to her sister Tzeitel, "I wonder if Yente found a husband for you?"

Yisroel: During the time in which *Fiddler on the Roof* takes place, the word *Yisroel* referred to the ancient biblical land that God promised to Abraham. Since 1946, the name also applies to the modern geographic region known as the State of Israel. In "Sabbath Prayer," Tevye and Golde sing, "May you come to be / In Yisroel a shining name."

FINIAN'S RAINBOW

Libretto by E. Y. Harburg and Fred Saidy. Lyrics by E. Y. Harburg. Music by Burton Lane. Original Broadway production: January 10, 1947. 46th Street Theatre. 725 performances. Broadway revivals in 1955, 1960, and 2009.

Finian's Rainbow is set in "Rainbow Valley" in "Missitucky." You won't find either place on any map. Yet this classic musical fantasy pointedly portrayed the world of sharecroppers in the tobacco states of Mississippi and Kentucky in the late 1940s. The Jim Crow laws were firmly in place at this time, and as delightful as much of the musical is, there is always the shadow of racial prejudice looming nearby. Throughout his career, E. Y. Harburg invented words in his lyrics, and *Finian's Rainbow* is no exception. But his and Fred Saidy's libretto is also filled with references and names from the late 1940s that actually existed. Even the leprechaun Og is very aware of the slang and celebrities of the day.

Expressions, references, names:

Abercrombie Fitch: David T. Abercrombie and Ezra Fitch founded Abercrombie & Fitch in Manhattan in 1892 as outfitters for the elite outdoorsman. Today the company focuses on casual wear. In the song "When the Idle Poor Become the Idle Rich," Sharon and the chorus sing, "We'll hide these incongruities / With cloaks from Abercrombie Fitch."

Astors: The wealthy American family whose fortune was rooted in the fur trade, the Astors were not only rich, but Mrs. Astor was the unrivaled head of society during the Gilded Age in New York City. In the song "When the Idle Poor Become the Idle Rich," the girls sing, "You won't know your Joneses from your Astors."

AWOL: The military acronym for "absent without leave." The little boy Henry tells Og the leprechaun that his rooster has run away and "[gone] AWOL."

Babbitts . . . bourgeoisie: A materialistic, complacent, and conformist businessman is known as a Babbitt. The name comes from the 1922 novel of the same name by Sinclair Lewis. In the song "The Begat," the Pilgrim Gospellers sing, "They Begat the Babbitts of the bourgeoisie." The French word *bourgeoisie* means the middle class or, more often, conventional middle-class values.

beat-beat-beat of the tom-tom: A tom-tom is a tribal drum used in several cultures, and today is favored by jazz musicians. Og quotes from the 1932 Cole Porter song standard, "Night and Day," when he asks Finian, "Does an optical illusion feel the beat-beat-beat of the tom-tom?"

begat: An antiquated expression for creating new offspring is to "beget" a son or a daughter. A long genealogical list in the Old Testament chronicles who begat whom; the list is known as "the begats." The Gospellers make their own merry list in the song "The Begat."

Benzedrine: Benzedrine (also called "bennies") is the brand name of amphetamine sulfate, which affects the central nervous system and treats attention-deficit hyperactivity, narcolepsy, and obesity. In the song "That Great Come-and-Get-It Day," one of the sharecroppers sings, "Come and get your beer and your Benzedrine."

Bogart . . . Baby Bacall: Humphrey Bogart (1899–1957), nicknamed Bogie, was one of Hollywood's most iconic stars. Lauren Bacall (1924–2014) was his wife and sometime co-star. The tobacco worker Lyn says her leaf of tobacco is going to Hollywood and asks, "Do you think Bogart will be smokin' it and puffin' it right into Baby Bacall's big blue eyes?"

bon vivant: Literally meaning "good living," the French expression "bon vivant" refers to a person who enjoys a sociable and luxurious lifestyle. In the song "When the Idle Poor Become the Idle Rich," Sharon sings, "When a rich man doesn't want to work, / He's a bon vivant."

Bromo-Seltzer: Once a formally registered symbol identifying the manufacturer or distributor of an antacid, Bromo-Seltzer, or just Bromo, refers to any such solution used to ease heartburn and acid reflux. When Senator Rawlins finds out he doesn't own the strip of land where gold is detected, he gets so upset he asks for a Bromo.

calico gown: A plain-woven cotton cloth printed with a figured pattern, usually on one side, is called "calico." Sharon tells Finian, "Father, how can you say that? We have calico gowns."

Carmen Miranda: The Brazilian samba singer, dancer, and film star Carmen Miranda (1909–1955) was nicknamed "The Brazilian Bombshell" for her funny, sexy persona. In the song "If This Isn't Love," the very Irish Sharon sings, "If this isn't love, I'm Carmen Miranda."

chemise: A woman's loose-fitting, one-piece undergarment was known as a "chemise." In the song "The Begat," the Gospellers sing about Adam and Eve living in the Garden of Eden "without pajamas and without chemise."

collateral: Something pledged as security for repayment of a loan, to be forfeited in the event of a default, is called collateral. One of the sharecroppers sings about how the dandelions "gonna smell without collateral" in the opening song, "This Time of the Year."

colleen: Since the early nineteenth century, the Irish have used this word to mean a young lady. Later, it became a proper first name in Ireland. Og tells Finian that living in Ireland is a poor situation, a place where "no colleens smile and no children sing."

crock of gold: According to Irish legend, if one captures a leprechaun's crock or pot of gold, one gets three (sometimes four) wishes, which the elf-like creature must grant. Because Sharon is standing near the buried gold when she says, "I wish to God he [Senator Rawlins] were [B]lack," the white senator magically becomes Black.

cyclotron: An apparatus in which charged atomic and subatomic particles are accelerated. When Finian asks Og if he used the crock of gold to wish Susan to have speech, Og replies, "It wasn't a cyclotron, Bub."

DAR: The Daughters of the American Revolution is a patriotic organization with a long history of conservatism. The Gospellers sing, "They Begat the Daughters of the DAR" in the song "The Begat."

Eisenhowzish: General Dwight D. Eisenhower (1890–1969) was an American military officer, statesman, and national hero, serving as the thirty-fourth president of the United States from 1953 to 1961. Og the leprechaun claims that Sharon makes him feel "Eisenhowzish" in the song "Something Sort of Grandish."

Eureka!: Legend says that Greek alchemist Archimedes shouted, "Eureka!" ("I have found it!") when he discovered a method of detecting the amount of alloy mixed with the gold in the crown of the king of Syracuse. Finian exclaims, "Eureka!" when he sees the perfect spot to bury his gold.

filibuster . . . filibusterers: A prolonged speech that obstructs progress in a legislative assembly is known as a filibuster. In the song "The Begat," the Gospellers sing, "Fat filibusterers Begat."

Fort Knox: Fort Knox is a US Army installation in Kentucky that is used to house a large portion of the United States' official gold reserves. Finian plans to bury his gold near Fort Knox, believing it will multiply by being near such a treasure trove.

Gabriel's horn: The biblical archangel Gabriel was known for bringing news from God. The expression "Gabriel's horn or trumpet" meant glorious good news. Woody sings, "[be]cause word has come from Gabriel's horn" in the song "That Great Come-and-Get-It Day."

Glocca Morra: The fictional place where Finian and his daughter Sharon come from in Ireland is called Glocca Morra. E. Y. Harburg invented the name for *Finian's Rainbow*. Because of the popularity of the song "How Are Things in Glocca Morra?," the name has come to mean a magical place out of one's reach.

GOP: The Republican Party has been known as the "Grand Old Party" (GOP) since 1874. In the song "The Begat," the Gospellers sing, "Who Begat the misbegotten GOP."

grandish: E. Y. Harburg invented the word *grandish* for *Finian's Rainbow*. It means a very grand feeling. Having created the word, Harburg then had to invent a handful of other new words that rhyme with *grandish* in the song "Something Sort of Grandish."

Guinevere: According to Arthurian legend, Guinevere (or Guenevere) was an early-medieval queen of Britain and the wife of King Arthur. The leprechaun Og mentions Guinevere in the song "Something Sort of Grandish."

habitués: A person who may be regularly found at a particular place or kind of place can be called a habitué. In the song "The Begat," the Gospellers sing, "Sons of habitués Begat."

heath: A tract of open uncultivated land that is harsh and not very fertile is called a heath or a moor in Ireland and northern Britain. When Og tells Finian that he's from Glocca Morra, Finian replies, "From Glocca Morra? That's my native heath!"

Honorary Aryans: The German expression *Ehrenarier* (Honorary Aryan) was used in Nazi Germany to describe the unofficial status of persons who were not recognized as belonging to the Aryan race but were approved of by the Party. The Gospellers sing in "The Begat" how "Strict vegetarians Begat, / Honorary Aryans Begat."

hungry yearning: Og quotes from Cole Porter's 1932 song standard, "Night and Day," when he asks Finian, "Does an optical illusion feel an, oh, such a hungry yearning burning inside of him, under the hide of him?"

Jezebel: The biblical Jezebel was a wicked, adulterous woman who fought against God. In the song "The Begat," the Gospellers sing, "It was pleasing to Jezebel."

Karl Marx: The German philosopher, economist, and socialist revolutionary Karl Marx (1818–1883) is best known for his Communist manifesto

Das Kapital. Finian names Marx as an economical giant who still cannot discover how gold multiplies at Fort Knox.

Killybegs, Kilkerry, and Kildaire: Killybegs is a fishing town in County Donegal, Ireland. Kilkenny (sometimes Kilkerry) is a historic city in east Ireland. Kildare is a town in County Kildare, Ireland. All three are mentioned in the song "How Are Things in Glocca Morra?"

kith and kin: With its roots in Old English, "kith and kin" is an antiquated expression for friends and family. Sharon tells Woody, "Your kith and kin here pinnin' their hopes on you—and you squanderin' your savin's on a music box!"

lass: In Scottish, Irish, and northern English jargon, a lass, or a lassie, is a young girl. Finian calls his daughter Sharon a lass on several occasions. At one point, he says, "Don't you see, lass, in six months we'll be rich!"

League of Women Shoppers: The League of Women Shoppers (LWS) was an American consumer advocacy group founded in 1935 that worked toward social justice for workers and fought against racial discrimination of all kinds. In the song "The Begat," the Gospellers sing, "It pleased the League of Women Shoppers in Duluth."

leprechaun: The mischievous elf of Irish folklore known as a leprechaun usually possesses a pot or crock of gold. It was believed that if one captured a leprechaun, it would reveal where the gold was hidden. Finian has stolen the crock of gold from Og, so the leprechaun has followed him to America to get it back.

***Life*, *Look*, *Click*, *Slick*, *Pic*, and the *Nicotine Digest*:** Two of the most popular magazines in the 1940s were the pictorial publications *Life* and *Look*. *Click* was an American magazine that debuted in 1938. *Slick* refers to any magazine printed on high-quality paper. *Pic* (or pix) is slang for "pictures." Today it usually refers to the photos sent through the Internet, but in the 1940s it was short for "picture magazines." There was no such publication called *Nicotine Digest*, which is making fun of the widely read magazine *Reader's Digest*. Woody tells the residents of Rainbow Valley that the Lucky Gold Tobacco Company is so happy about buying Rainbow Valley tobacco that they are "Shoutin' it out in *Life*, *Look*, *Click*, *Slick*, *Pic*, and the *Nicotine Digest*."

love-in-bloomish: "Love in Bloom" is a popular 1934 song with music by Ralph Rainger and lyrics by Leo Robin. Harburg uses the phrase "love-in-bloomish" in the song "Something Sort of Grandish."

Lucky Gold: The brand name of Lucky Gold cigarettes was inspired by the gold rushes of the nineteenth century. In *Finian's Rainbow*, when the retailers Shears and Robust try to make a deal with Finian, Woody informs everyone that "The Lucky Gold Company . . . just gave me an order for forty-thousand bales of . . . Rainbow Valley tobacco!"

Machiavellian: Derived from the name of the Italian statesman and political philosopher Niccolò di Bernardo dei Machiavelli (1469–1527), a person who is Machiavellian is cunning, scheming, and unscrupulous, particularly in politics. In his anger, Finian calls Og a "Machiavellian half-pint pirate, stealin' me property!"

Merchant Marine: The US Merchant Marine is an organization that oversees commercial and civilian vessels that enter American ports, rivers, and lakes. Woody Mahoney has worked for the Merchant Marine, where he earned enough money to pay off the taxes on his sister Susan's land.

mint julep: A popular Southern drink consisting of bourbon, crushed ice, sugar, and fresh mint. Buzz Collins tries to teach the new Black butler Howard how to slowly shuffle when he serves the senator his mint julep.

Mr. Ford and Mr. Cadillac and Mr. Serutan: When listing the millionaires he will be like once his gold matures, Finian mentions three names. Mr. Ford refers to auto manufacturer Henry Ford. But Finian thinks there is also such a person as Mr. Cadillac, which there isn't. Finian also mistakenly believes there is a Mr. Serutan, who is associated with the laxative Serutan.

Neutron . . . Proton . . . Nucleus: Finian uses the parts of an atom to name "the multitude of gnomes, elves, and fairy folk" that live inside the hunk of rock he holds, saying they are "ready to work for you and bring you all happiness." Not to be found in any physics book are Finian's "Neutron the Latent and Proton the Potent . . . and a friend of mine, named Nicholas the Nucleus."

Oak Ridge, Tennessee: Oak Ridge, Tennessee, was home to several massive Manhattan Project facilities employing thousands of workers during and after World War II. It was here that the atom bomb was first developed. At the end of *Finian's Rainbow*, Finian announces he is leaving Rainbow Valley and going "to Oak Ridge, Tennessee!" What is implied is that Finian is no longer interested in gold but has a new interest in uranium.

Ozymandias: In antiquity, Ozymandias was a Greek name for the Egyptian pharaoh Ramesses II. "Ozymandias" is also the title of an 1818 poem by Percy Bysshe Shelley. Og tells Finian that St. Ozymandias is "the patron saint of leprechauns in Glocca Morra," but Finian replies, "Never heard of him."

Park Avenue: Since the turn of the twentieth century, Park Avenue has been one of the most prestigious addresses in New York City. Sharon sings, "For when you're on Park Avenue, / Cornelius and Mike / Look alike" in the song "When the Idle Poor Become the Idle Rich." The name Cornelius refers to the wealthy industrialist Cornelius Vanderbilt.

pixie . . . pixified: If someone is behaving like the supernatural pixie, it is said that person is pixified. Sharon asks her father, "What pixified fancy of yours has brought us to America?" Later in the musical, Og relates how he got the Shears and Robust catalog: "The pixies left it for me in that tiny house yonder." The "tiny house" is an outhouse or privy; people often used pages from old catalogs as toilet paper.

poll tax: A poll tax, also known as a head tax or capitation, is a tax levied as a fixed sum on every liable individual. It is a very unpopular tax, especially for the poor. According to Woody, Senator Rawlins is using the poll tax to bleed the sharecroppers dry.

promised kiss of springtime: Asking about Og's new human feelings, Finian says, "Do you feel like the promised kiss of springtime that trembles on the brink of a lovely song?" This is a direct quote from the Jerome Kern (music) and Oscar Hammerstein (lyrics) song "All the Things You Are" (1939).

Rand and McNally: In 1856, William Rand and Irish immigrant Andrew McNally opened a printing shop in Chicago that became the most popular publisher and purveyor of maps, atlases, and globes. Finian consults his Rand McNally map, but Sharon says, "I don't know who Rand is, but I could never trust a McNally."

a river over Tennessee way: In 1933, the federal government dammed up some rivers in Tennessee and created the Tennessee Valley Authority (TVA), a federally owned electric utility corporation that still serves seven states. Woody Mahoney tells the sharecroppers what they did to "a river over Tennessee way," and how Senator Rawlins is afraid they'll do the same thing to Rainbow Valley, which would cut into his profits.

River Shannon: Winding over two hundred miles through Ireland, the River Shannon is the longest in the country. Sharon sings of "a River Shannon breeze" in the song "How Are Things in Glocca Morra?"

roaring traffic's boom: Og quotes from Cole Porter's 1932 song standard, "Night and Day," when he tells Finian he hears "the roaring traffic's boom in his lonely room."

Rockefellertive: An American industrial and banking family, the Rock-efellers made their vast fortune in the petroleum industry during the late nineteenth and early twentieth centuries. In the song "When the Idle Poor Become the Idle Rich," Sharon sings about "everyone's poor relative / Becomes a Rockefellertive."

round and round like an elevator: Finian asks Og about his new sense of human romantic feelings, "You go round and round like an elevator lost in the tide?" This is a mixed-up quotation from the song standard "That Old Black Magic" (1942), by Harold Arlen (music) and Johnny Mercer (lyrics), which goes: "The same old tingle that I feel inside / And then that elevator starts its ride / And down and down I go, round and round I go / Like a leaf that's caught in the tide."

Ruth: The biblical book of Ruth is named for a beloved Moabite woman who married an Israelite and fought for the Jews. In the song "The Begat," the Gospellers sing about the Begat being "pleasin' to Ruth."

Sambo: The derisive term "Sambo" refers to Black males. The term goes back to the 1700s, but was popularized by Helen Bannerman's 1899 children's book, *Little Black Sambo*. The Sheriff hands a guitar to Senator

Rawlins, who has been changed into a Black man, and says, "Here, Sambo—sing for the white folks."

sasperilla: A rural name for a root beer–like drink is sasperilla, or sarsaparilla. The tobacco worker Maude asks, "And what is it puts the fly in your sasperilla?"

sharecropper: In the Southern states, a tenant farmer who works the land and receives an agreed-upon share of the value of the crop, minus charges, was known as a "sharecropper," and their labors were known as "sharecropping." Many of the citizens, Black and white, in Rainbow Valley are sharecroppers and have little money.

sharper than a serpent's tooth: In Shakespeare's *King Lear*, the old king says, "How sharper than a serpent's tooth it is / To have a thankless child!" The quotation has been used ever since by parents with difficult offspring. When Sharon scolds Finian for stealing Og's gold, her father says, "You're sharper than a serpent's tooth."

Shears and Robust: American chain of department stores founded by Richard Warren Sears and Alvah Curtis Roebuck in 1892 began as a mail-order catalog company, eventually opening retail locations in 1925. Og pulls out a Sears, Roebuck catalog to show the kids and calls it "Shears-Robust . . . that's the two angels in charge of distribution." Later in the musical, Mr. Shears and Mr. Robust show up in Rainbow Valley to offer credit to the residents because the duo thinks there is gold in the ground.

smoke keeps coming out of me eyes: Og spoofs the popular song standard "Smoke Gets in Your Eyes" (1933), by Jerome Kern (music) and Otto Harbach (lyrics), when he tells Finian, "Yes, and what's worse, smoke keeps coming out of me eyes."

tetched in the head: The Irish pronunciation of "touched" is "tetched." If a person is tetched, it means the individual is not quite sane, or "tetched in the head." When Finian tells the Sheriff that Sharon is, indeed, a witch, Woody says, "He's tetched in the head."

Too-ra-lay: There is an ancient Irish folk song titled "Too-ra-lay," not to be confused with the 1913 Irish-American favorite

"Too-Ra-Loo-Ra-Loo-Ral" by James Royce Shannon. Sharon sings about a "lad that comes whistlin' 'Too-ra-lay'" in the song "How Are Things in Glocca Morra?"

tote that barge, lift that bale: "Ol' Man River," the folk song classic from *Show Boat* (1927), is spoofed when one of the Gospellers tells Senator Rawlins, who has been turned into a Black man, that he can make a living singing. "You can either tote that barge, lift that bale, shine that shoe—or sing," he says, quoting from the Jerome Kern (music) and Oscar Hammerstein (lyrics) song.

Tower of Babel: In the biblical city of Babel, the people began building a tower intended to reach heaven, but they were forced to abandon their work when God created confusion by giving everyone different languages. In the song "The Begat," the Gospellers sing, "So they Begat Cain, and they Begat Abel, / Who Begat the rabble at the Tower of Babel."

Tuskegee: Booker T. Washington founded the Tuskegee Institute in Tuskegee, Alabama, in the 1880s to educate Black people. In *Finian's Rainbow*, Howard is working during the summer as a butler to pay tuition for his last year at Tuskegee. When Buzz Collins asks what a Tuskegee is and Howard tells him it's a college, Buzz replies, "Don't mention the word college to Mr. Rawlins. It upsets him."

Tweedledum . . . Tweedledee: The fictional twins in Lewis Carroll's *Through the Looking-Glass, and What Alice Found There* (1871) were the rotund and silly Tweedledum and Tweedledee. In the song "When the Idle Poor Become the Idle Rich," Sharon and the chorus sing, "When poor Tweedledum is rich Tweedledee / This discrimination will no longer be."

William Tell: According to Swiss legend, the folk hero William Tell was an expert marksman with the crossbow and could pierce an apple sitting on someone's head. In the song "If This Isn't Love," Woody sings, "I'm feelin' like the apple / On top of William Tell."

Woody: Woody Guthrie (1912–1967) was an American folk singer, activist, and songwriter whose songs chronicled the plight of common people, especially during the Great Depression. The singing union organizer Woody Mahoney in *Finian's Rainbow* is most likely an homage to Guthrie.

FLOWER DRUM SONG

Libretto by Oscar Hammerstein and Joseph Fields, based on the novel by Chin Y. Lee. Lyrics by Oscar Hammerstein. Music by Richard Rodgers. Original Broadway production: December 1, 1958. St. James Theatre. 600 performances. Revised Broadway revival in 2002.

In its day, *Flower Drum Song* was a rare glimpse into the world of Asian Americans. Chin Y. Lee's novel and the libretto by Joseph Fields and Oscar Hammerstein are mostly comic. But the struggle to live in the New World and not discard the traditions of the Old World is a very serious theme. It can be found in the Asian American plays and novels of the 1970s and beyond. The setting is San Francisco's Chinatown, a world unto itself, and the time is 1958, when many were still trying to flee Communist China. All of the characters are Asian, which is why the musical is not frequently produced. There is no villain in the piece. Instead, both generations of characters are making mistakes, learning, and adjusting to the binary life of being both Asian and American.

Expressions, references, names:

Blue Cross: The medical insurance giant Blue Cross Blue Shield Association was formed in 1982, but since 1929 there was Blue Cross, which provided health care for millions of Americans. The young Wang San, who has been involved in fights at school, tells his aunt, "If I stay in that school, I better join Blue Cross."

Bollinger: Since 1829, Bollinger has produced champagne with a powerful and sophisticated taste. Sammy tells the waiter, "Bring a magnum of Bollinger to this table."

cukey: In the 1950s, a new word for something eccentric, strange, or just plain wild was "kooky." For the younger generation, saying something was kooky was not negative, but rather had a touch of admiration in it. Because the word evolved vocally, there are different ways of spelling it, such as "kookie" or "cukey," as used in *Flower Drum Song*. When young San asks Linda if she sings rock 'n' roll, she replies, "I like anything cukey. I dig that the most." Later, in the song "The Other Generation," Madame Liang sings to Wang, "Your younger son confuses me, the way he uses words, / He tells me I am 'cukey' and 'something for the birds!'"

FLOWER DRUM SONG *Getting out of Communist China in the 1950s was no easy task, but Mei-Li (Miyoshi Umeki, center) made it to San Francisco, where she is helped by Madame Liang (Juanita Hall) and Wang Chi-Yang (Keye Luke).*
Photofest

Drambuie: Made from Scotch whiskey, honey, herbs, and spices, Drambuie is a sweet, golden-colored liqueur with 40 percent alcohol content. In the song "Chop Suey," the chorus sings, "Milk and beer and Seven-Up and Drambuie—Chop Suey!"

Dr. Norman Vincent Peale: The American Protestant clergyman Norman Vincent Peale (1898–1993) wrote one of the most-read nonfiction books of the twentieth century, *The Power of Positive Thinking* (1952). In the song "Chop Suey," Madame Liang sings, "Dr. Norman Vincent Peale / Tells you how to feel," to which the younger generation sings, "Big deal!"

fan-tan game: Dating back at least two thousand years, fan-tan is a gambling game of Chinese origin. It was introduced in the western United States in the second half of the nineteenth century by Chinese immigrant workers. Speaking about Sammy, Wang Chi-Yang asks his sister, "How could you discuss our family problems with a man who runs a fan-tan game and a nightclub?"

flower drum: The *huagu*, or flower drum, is a type of double-skinned Chinese hand drum. It is normally painted with a red flower on the sides and is beaten with wooden sticks, like other Chinese drums. Wang Chi-Yang asks Mei Li, "Can you sing Flower Drum Songs?"

Formosa: The free and democratic Republic of Formosa declared its independence from mainland China in 1895. The nation consists of 168 islands at the junction of the East and South China Seas in the northwestern Pacific Ocean. Today the republic is called Taiwan, after its principal island. Dr. Li tells Wang Chi-Yang, "By the time we got to Formosa, our money was given away for bribes."

funny papers: An antiquated expression for the section of a newspaper containing comics and humorous matter is the "funnies," or the "funny papers." In the song "Sunday," Sammy sings, "While all the funny papers lie or fly around the place."

ginseng soup: A soup made from the root of the ginseng plant in Asian culture. Although ginseng has been used in traditional medicine for centuries, modern clinical research is inconclusive about its medical effectiveness. All the same, Ta says to Wang Chi-Yang, "Here, my father, take some ginseng soup. [Or] you'll get another coughing spell."

Harry Truman . . . Truman Capote . . . Dewey: In the song "Chop Suey," Madame Liang sings, "Harry Truman, Truman Capote, and Dewey—Chop Suey!" Harry S. Truman (1884–1972) was the thirty-third president of the United States, serving from 1945 to 1953. Truman Capote (1924–1984) was an American novelist, screenwriter, playwright, and actor. He was a very popular new talent in the 1950s, and today his books are considered modern classics. Thomas Edmund Dewey (1902–1971) was an American lawyer, prosecutor, and politician. He was governor of New York State from 1943 to 1954, and in 1944 he was the Republican Party's nominee for the presidency, but lost the election to Franklin D. Roosevelt. Dewey ran for president again in 1948 but lost to Truman.

hula hoops . . . Dr. Salk . . . Zsa Zsa Gabor: A hula hoop is a toy hoop that is twirled around the waist, limbs, or neck and has been used by children and adults since at least 500 BCE. The familiar plastic version of Hula Hoop was popularized in 1958 by the Wham-O toy company. Jonas Edward Salk (1914–1995) was an American scientist who developed one of the first successful polio vaccines. Zsa Zsa Gabor (1917–2016) was a Hungarian-American actress and socialite, frequently in the news because of her many marriages. In the song "Chop Suey," Madame Liang sings, "Hula Hoops and nuclear war, / Dr. Salk and Zsa Zsa Gabor!"

Hwang Ho Valley: Known in English as the Yellow River Valley, the Hwang Ho Valley was the birthplace of ancient Chinese civilization. The valley surrounds the Yellow River in northern China and is at the center of thousands of years of Chinese history. Ta recites lines from a poem that become the first lines of the song "You Are Beautiful": "Along the Hwang Ho Valley, / Where young men walk and dream."

Khan . . . Ali or the Aga: In the song "Don't Marry Me," Sammy sings to Mei Li, "Marry a dope, / Innocent and gaga. / Marry a Khan—Ali or the Aga . . ." Prince Aly Khan (1911–1960) was a Pakistani socialite, racehorse owner and jockey, military officer, and diplomat. The Aga Khan III at the time was Sir Sultan Mohammed Shah (1885–1957), who ruled Pakistan from 1877 to 1957. Both men were fabulously wealthy.

La Paloma . . . Perry Como: The Spanish lullaby-like song "La Paloma" ("The Dove") has been popular, in different versions, for more than a thousand years. A top-selling recording was made by Perry Como (1912–2001), an Italian-American singer, actor, and television personality. In the song "Chop Suey," Madame Liang sings, "Hear that lovely La Paloma / Lullaby by Perry Como."

Late Late Show . . . Clara Bow: In the 1950s, television stations started showing old Hollywood movies later at night, after "prime time." This programming was often titled *The Late Show*. Clara Bow (1905–1965), a vivacious flapper known as the "It Girl," was one of the most beloved stars and sex symbols of 1920s silent films. In the song "Chop Suey," Madame Liang sings, "Tonight on TV's late, late show, / You can look at Clara Bow."

litchi nuts: In the song "Don't Marry Me," Sammy sings to Mei Li, "I eat litchi nuts and cookies in bed, / And I fill the bed with nutshells and crumbs." Native to many Asian countries, the litchi (or lichee) nut is found inside the small, roundish fruit of the Chinese litchi tree. The whitish edible flesh that surrounds a single large seed tastes sweet or slightly acidic.

Maidenform bra: The manufacturer of women's underwear known as Maidenform was founded in 1922 by a group of seamstresses who rebelled against the flat-chested designs of the time for women. Among their most innovative products was the Maidenform bra, which accentuated the natural shape of a woman's figure. There was a famous advertising campaign in the 1950s and 1960s with illustrations of a woman wearing only underwear in a public place, appearing proud and cheerful. The tagline was: "I dreamed I . . . [was doing some ordinary activity] . . . in my Maidenform bra." In the song "Chop Suey," young San mockingly sings, "Dreaming in my Maidenform bra, / Dreamed I danced the cha-cha-cha!"

Nob Hill: For more than a hundred years, the Nob Hill neighborhood of San Francisco has been home to the city's upper class. Nob Hill is also known for its luxury hotels and historic mansions. It remains one of the most desirable and expensive real estate markets in the country. Referring to Mei Li, Sammy says, "Yeah, she's on her way up. She'll wind up in a mansion on Nob Hill."

Peking duck . . . Mulligan stew . . . Plymouth Rock and Little Rock: In the song "Chop Suey," everyone sings, "Peking duck and Mulligan stew, / Plymouth Rock and Little Rock, too." Peking Duck is a Chinese dish consisting of strips of roast duck served with shredded vegetables and a sweet sauce. On the other hand, Mulligan stew is an Irish dish made from whatever ingredients are available. The Pilgrims landed at Plymouth Rock in 1620, and Little Rock is the capital city of Arkansas.

picture bride: In the early twentieth century, immigrant workers from Asia working in Hawaii and the West Coast of America selected brides from their native countries via a matchmaker. A bride and groom were paired using only photographs and family recommendations. Such women were referred to as "picture brides." Sammy tells Wang, "I went to a progressive school. When I got out, my mother sent for a Hong Kong picture bride as a graduation present . . . The kid arrived in town today and I can't handle her!"

shark-fin soup . . . bean-cake fish: Shark-fin soup is a traditional soup or stewed dish served throughout Southeast Asia. The shark fins provide the texture while the taste comes from the other ingredients. In China, it is commonly served at special occasions, such as weddings and banquets. A common street food from Asia is bean-cake fish. The fish is shaped into a cake and is stuffed with red bean paste. In the song "Grant Avenue," Linda sings of the delicacies of Chinatown with, "Shark-fin soup, bean-cake fish!"

Thunderbird: In 1955, the Ford Thunderbird was introduced in order to compete with the Corvette. The Thunderbird was a sporty, tailor-made two-seater that was very popular with younger car buyers. Ford manufactured the model until 1997. Ta proudly announces that his date, Linda Low, is modern: "Miss Low has a Thunderbird."

Tiger Bone wine: As its name suggests, Tiger Bone wine is an alcoholic beverage originally produced in China using the bones of tigers as a necessary ingredient. The production process takes approximately eight years and results in a high alcohol concentration. When Ta asks Helen what she's been drinking, she replies, "Tiger Bone wine."

FOLLIES

Libretto by James Goldman. Music and lyrics by Stephen Sondheim. Original Broadway production: April 4, 1971. Winter Garden Theatre. 522 performances. Broadway revivals in 2001 and 2011.

Because of its casting, costume, and scenic demands, *Follies* is not frequently revived, but the musical is such an iconic piece that it belongs in this book. The "present" for the characters is 1971, but the flashbacks involving the four main characters are set in the late 1930s, when they were in their twenties. Several of the other characters are older, and their heyday was in the 1920s. Therefore, many of the references in the musical go back to the 1920s and 1930s. The setting is a theater in Manhattan about to be demolished, an ideal place for ghosts from the past to take the stage.

Expressions, references, names:

Abie's Irish Rose . . . **Dionne babies** . . . **Major Bowes:** In the song "I'm Still Here," Carlotta sings, "I got through Abie's Irish Rose / Five Dionne babies, / Major Bowes." Although the critics panned Anne Nichols's 1927 play *Abie's Irish Rose*, it was a hit with the public and ran a surprising five years, a record at the time. On May 28, 1934, a Canadian mother gave birth to five babies, the first quintuplets known to have survived infancy. The identical girls became world-famous and were featured in newspapers, magazines, and newsreels. Edward Bowes (1874–1946) was a popular American radio personality of the 1930s and 1940s whose program, *Major Bowes' Amateur Hour*, was the most famous amateur talent show on radio. The show ran from 1935 to 1952 and gave hundreds of contestants a shot at stardom.

Amos 'n' Andy: *Amos 'n' Andy* was an American radio sitcom with all Black characters, yet the show was voiced by two white actors whose broad depictions of the race perpetuated Black stereotypes. The comedy was very popular, running from 1928 to 1960, first on the radio, then briefly on television, where it featured Black actors. Carlotta sings, "I've been through *Amos 'n' Andy*" as she lists the fads of the past in the song, "I'm Still Here."

Arthur Murray franchise: When the American ballroom dancer Arthur Murray (1895–1991) retired, he founded a very popular chain of dance instruction studios across the country that still bear his name. Vaudeville and *Follies* dancer Vincent says, "We bought an Arthur Murray franchise" after he and his wife, Vanessa, retired from show business.

Battery Park . . . Washington Heights: While Battery Park is located at the southernmost tip of Manhattan, the section known as Washington Heights is at the northern part of the island. The old trouper Hattie sings in "Broadway Baby" about how the lights from her marquee are able "to pierce the dark / From Battery Park / To Washington Heights."

Braques and Chagalls: Georges Braque (1882–1963) was a major twentieth-century French painter who played an important role in the development of Cubism. Marc Chagall (1887–1985) was a Belarusian-French artist who was renowned for his work in several major artistic styles. Works by both artists are very expensive and highly sought after, so in the song "Could I Leave You?," Phyllis sings, "Leave me the Braques and Chagalls and all that."

Brenda Frazier: The American socialite Brenda Frazier (1921–1982) was so popular in the late 1930s that she appeared on the cover of *Life* magazine, even though she never did anything of importance. In the song "I'm Still Here," Carlotta sings, "I've lived through Brenda Frazier."

cablegrams: Before international phone service or e-mail, a fast but expensive way to contact someone overseas was with a cablegram, a telegram sent by underwater cable. Ben sings, "Some get a boot / From shooting off cablegrams" in the song "Live, Laugh, Love."

the first of May: One of the most celebrated holidays in the days of the Soviet Union was International Workers' Day, or May Day, celebrated on the first of the month. In the song "Ah, Paris!," Solange sings, "I've been to Moscow, / It's very gay— / Well, anyway, / On the first of May!"

Franz Lehár . . . Oscar Straus: Listening to the music from the four-piece combo, the aged operetta singer Heidi Schiller says, "It's my waltz they're playing. Franz Lehár wrote it for me in Vienna . . . or was it Oscar Straus?" Franz Lehár (1870–1948) was an Austro-Hungarian operetta composer best known for *The Merry Widow* (1905). Oscar Straus (1870–1954) was a Viennese composer of operettas and film scores, in particular *The Chocolate Soldier* (1908).

grand . . . spinet: Any piano with a horizontal frame and strings is called a grand, be it a concert grand or a baby grand. A spinet is a small and compactly built upright piano. Unless it is an antique, a spinet costs much less than any grand piano. That is why in the song "Could I Leave You?," Phyllis sings, "I'll take the grand, / Sugar, you keep the spinet."

hara-kiri: The ritual suicide by disembowelment, mostly practiced by the Japanese samurai, is known as hara-kiri. Young Phyllis naively sings, "Will it be birds in spring / Or hara-kiri . . . ?" in the sunny duet "You're Gonna Love Tomorrow."

heebie-jeebies . . . Beebe's Bathysphere: Used mostly in the 1920s, the expression *heebie-jeebies* refers to the jitters, the shakes, shivers, and other signs of nervousness. The American zoologist Charles William Beebe (1877–1962) invented the bathysphere, a spherical steel vessel with portholes for use in undersea observation. In the song "I'm Still Here," Carlotta does a play on similar sounds when she sings that she "Had heebie-jeebies / For Beebe's Bathysphere."

Herbert and J. Edgar Hoover: Carlotta sings of two very famous men named Hoover in the song "I'm Still Here." Herbert Hoover (1874–1964) was the thirty-first president of the United States, a Republican who had the misfortune to be in office when the stock market crashed in 1929. J. Edgar Hoover (1895–1972) was the director of the Federal Bureau of Investigation (FBI) for nearly forty-eight years. Having survived both men, Carlotta sings, "I've gotten through Herbert and J. Edgar Hoover . . . That was fun and a half."

Loreleis: There is a German legend of a beautiful maiden named Lorelei who threw herself into the Rhine River in despair over a faithless lover and was transformed into a siren, a mythical creature who lured fishermen to destruction. In the song "Beautiful Girls," the former *Follies* girls sing, "Faced with these Loreleis, / What man can moralize?"

Lothario: Lothario is a character in Miguel de Cervantes's 1605 novel, *Don Quixote*, who seduces several women without any remorse. Over the centuries, the word *Lothario* has come to mean any man whose chief interest is seducing females. In the song "Who's That Woman?," the ladies sing, "Whose Lothario let her down?"

modus operandi: A term originally used by law enforcement authorities to describe the particular manner in which a crime is committed. The phrase has come to mean any mode of operation that a person usually uses. In the song "Live, Laugh, Love," the chorus wants to know "the modus operandi / a dandy should use / When he is feeling low."

Neiman's: Neiman Marcus is an American chain of luxury department stores with its headquarters in Dallas, Texas. Buddy tells Sally that his lover, Margie, in Dallas "works at Neiman's."

pinko: Any person who holds radically liberal political or economic views can be termed a *pinko*. Communists, in particular, were often referred to as pinkos. In the song "I'm Still Here," Carlotta sings, "Been called a pinko / Commie tool."

Proust and Pound: The French novelist Marcel Proust (1871–1922) is known for his psychologically and allegorically dense writing, as with his seven-volume *Remembrance of Times Past*. The poet Ezra Pound (1885–1972) was an expatriate American who was a major figure in the early modernist poetry movement. Both men make for challenging reading, to say the least. In the song "Live, Love, Laugh," Ben sings, "Some like to be profound / By reading Proust and Pound."

"road you didn't take": One of poet Robert Frost's most beloved works is the 1915 poem "The Road Not Taken," which ponders the path one did not follow. Ben paraphrases the ideas in Frost's poem in the song "The Road You Didn't Take."

Samson . . . Delilah: In the song "Beautiful Girls," the former *Follies* girls sing, "This was how Samson was shorn: / Each in her style a Delilah reborn." The biblical Samson was a man of unmatched physical strength until he fell in love with the conniving Delilah, who cut off his hair while he slept, rendering him weak and seemingly helpless.

stock: Summer theatre and the circuit of semiprofessional theatres was known as "stock." In the song "I'm Still Here," Carlotta sings, "Top billing Monday, / Tuesday, you're touring in stock."

Toscanini broadcasts: The Italian conductor Arturo Toscanini (1867–1957) is considered one of the great virtuoso conductors of the first half of the twentieth century. Between 1937 and 1954, he conducted the NBC Symphony Orchestra on the radio, making him a household name. When Ben and Sally meet at the reunion, he asks her, "Did you fall asleep at Toscanini broadcasts?"

Weismann: The aging impresario Dmitri Weismann is a fictional character in *Follies* who is based on the great showman Florenz Ziegfeld (1867–1932). Like Ziegfeld, Weismann had his own Broadway theater, where he presented revues called *Follies*, featuring the Weismann Girls.

Wilson: When Buddy tells Ben, "I haven't read your book on Wilson yet," he is most likely referring to Woodrow Wilson (1856–1924), who served as the twenty-eighth president of the United States, from 1913 to 1921.

Windsor and Wally's affair: One of the most sensational news items of the 1930s was when Britain's King Edward VIII (1894–1972) abdicated the throne so he could marry the American socialite and divorced woman Wallis Simpson. In the song "I'm Still Here," Carlotta sings, "I've been through . . . Windsor and Wally's affair."

WPA: During the Great Depression, the Works Progress Administration (WPA) brought some relief for the unemployed by providing jobs. By 1938, over 3.3 million Americans were employed through the WPA. In the song "I'm Still Here," Carlotta sings, "I've slept in shanties, / Guest of the WPA."

GREASE

Libretto, music, and lyrics by Jim Jacobs and Warren Casey. Original Off-Broadway production: February 14, 1972. Eden Theatre. Broadway production: Broadhurst Theatre. 3,388 performances. Major Broadway revivals in 1994 and 2007.

The 1958–1959 school year at fictional Rydell High School is the setting for the musical, which is stuffed with names, products, places, and slang of the 1950s. Many of these were already falling into obscurity by 1972, when *Grease* opened on Broadway. The popularity of the musical has made some of the references well known again. Many audience members in 1972 were the right age to remember the 1950s, and the success of the show was often attributed to nostalgia; however, decades have passed since then, and audiences born long after the 1950s continue to embrace *Grease*.

GREASE   *Greasers and their girls were a noticeable part of the 1950s teen scene, but often not as harmless as the ones in the musical.*
Photofest

Expressions, references, names:

Alan Freed: The American disc jockey Alan Freed (1921–1965) was responsible for helping to spread rock 'n' roll music throughout America. He discovered several recording artists and promoted them on the radio and in concerts. In the musical *Grease*, radio DJ Vince says, "I think you'll like this little ditty from the city, a new group discovered by Alan Freed."

American Bandstand: Dick Clark's *American Bandstand* television show came out of Philadelphia and was carried nationally on ABC-TV from 1957 to 1963. Both popular and promising singers lip-synced to their records while the teenage audience in the studio danced. At the high school hop in *Grease*, Cha-Cha complains about the "crummy decorations," and Kenickie says, "Where'd ya think you were goin', *American Bandstand?*"

Annette: In the song "Look at Me, I'm Sandra Dee," Rizzo sings, "Would you pull that stuff with Annette?" The most famous of the Mouseketeers, Annette Funicello (1942–2013) appeared in *The Mickey Mouse Club* on TV and in several Disney movies and "beach" movies. She always retained a wholesome image in her many performances.

Asiatic flu: A pandemic of influenza in 1957–1958 was dubbed the Asiatic flu because it was first identified in China. In the United States the flu killed about seventy thousand people. In the song "It's Raining on Prom Night," Sandy and the radio voices sing, "All I got was a runny nose and the Asiatic flu."

beans: One of the many slang terms for money, a bean usually meant $100. Referring to the hubcaps he stole, Roger says, "They must be worth two beans apiece easy."

Ben-Gay: Advertised as the "Greaseless Muscle & Joint Pain Relief Cream," Ben-Gay was brought to North America in 1898 from France, where it was developed by the French pharmacist Dr. Bengue. Patti tells the greasers that Danny was so mad at the track coach, "he smeared Ben-Gay in the team captain's athletic supporter."

the chicken . . . the stroll: Two of the popular dances in the late 1950s were the chicken and the stroll. Dancers put their hands into their underarms and flapped them like a chicken while wiggling their hips and/or shoulders in the chicken. (This is not to be confused with a later version called the chicken dance that was popular in the 1970s.) The stroll was a slow rock 'n' roll dance in which two lines of dancers face each other, moving in place to the music. In the song "Shakin' at the High School Hop," the chorus sings, "My baby does the chicken and she does the stroll."

chromers . . . dodgem car: In the 1950s, every car had removable hubcaps which were also given the slangy name chromers. Dodgem cars, better known as bumper cars, were an attraction at amusement parks and carnivals. The ride featured small electrically powered automobiles that the patrons drove, trying to bump other cars while avoiding being bumped by them. Roger asks the greasers, "Who the hell would put brand-new chromers on a secondhand dodgem car!"

cooties: A fictional disease that was all too real to teens was called cooties, often referring to body lice. There were no symptoms, but cooties was considered unhealthy and gross. Marty says to Sandy, "Just drink it out of the bottle, we ain't got cooties."

crew cut . . . flat top: Two popular hairstyles for men in the 1950s and early 1960s were the crew cut and the flat top, both of which can still be seen today. A haircut that is trimmed very close to the head but left slightly longer at the front and top was called a crew cut. For a flat top, the hair is cropped short so that it bristles up into a flat surface. When Danny joins the track team, Kenickie says, "Jeez, next thing ya know he'll be gettin' a crew cut," to which Doody says, "He'd look neater with a flat top."

CYO: At the high school hop, Cha-Cha tells Eugene, "I'm gonna teach ballroom at the CYO." An acronym for the "Catholic Youth Organization," the CYO was originally for competing sports teams from different Catholic schools. By the late 1950s, they were more social groups with classes of instruction.

"Dear Abby": The most famous advice column syndicated in national newspapers was "Dear Abby," founded in 1956 by Pauline Phillips under the pen name Abigail Van Buren. In the song "Beauty School Dropout," Teen Angel and an Angel Chorus tell Frenchy to go back to high school, saying, "Betcha Dear Abby'd say the same."

Debbie Reynolds: The bubbly American actress and singer Debbie Reynolds (1932–2016) was known in the 1950s for her movies. Frenchy says, "I wish I had one of those Guardian Angels things like in that Debbie Reynolds movie."

dice: A popular 1950s and 1960s icon was a pair of large foam dice that were hung from a car's rearview mirror. Doody has stolen a pair and says, "Hey, how much can we get for these dice?"

Doris Day . . . Rock Hudson: In the song "Look at Me, I'm Sandra Dee," Rizzo sings, "Rock Hudson lost / His heart to Doris Day." The blond actress-singer Doris Day (1922–2019) and the dashing Rock Hudson (1925–1985) were two of the most popular movie stars in Hollywood in the 1950s and 1960s. Both had long and distinguished careers but are most remembered today by some fans for a series of light comedies they made together in the 1960s.

Fabian: Reading a fan magazine, Frenchy says, "Hey, it says here that Fabian is in love with some Swedish movie star and might be gettin' married." A one-name teen idol of the late 1950s and early 1960s, Fabian (b. 1943) became nationally famous after singing on *American Bandstand.*

Gidget: A fictional teenager who was played by various actresses on film and television, Gidget was introduced in Frederick Kohner's 1957 novel *Gidget, The Little Girl with Big Ideas.* No matter who played her, Gidget was a wholesome, chipper teen who spent most of her time with her surfing friends on the beach in Malibu. Referring to Sandy, Rizzo says to Danny, "Awww, you're all broke up over little Gidget."

Good Humor truck: Soon after World War II ended, Good Humor ice-cream trucks started appearing in suburban neighborhoods across America. An early version of a food truck, the Good Humor truck announced its arrival by a bell or music and sold chocolate-coated ice cream bars. When Rizzo sees Kenickie's used car, she says, "It's about as cool as a Good Humor truck."

greaseball: At first a derogatory term for an unkempt person with greasy hair, *greaseball* evolved into "greasers," used to describe teens with slicked-back hair. Danny and the Burger Palace Boys are proud to be known as greasers.

hand jive: A very popular dance of the 1950s was the hand jive, usually done to rhythm-and-blues music. It involved hand moves and claps at various parts of the body, sometimes followed by vocal sounds imitating percussion instruments. At the high school hop, Johnny Casino sings "Born to Hand Jive," and the teens dance to it.

Hit Parade: Advertised with the phrase "Pleasure up your smoking," Hit Parade cigarettes were very popular in the late 1950s. Rizzo, trying to get Sandy to smoke her first cigarette, says, "Go on, try it. It ain't gonna kill ya. Give her a Hit Parade!"

Howdy Doody: A goofy-looking cowboy puppet named Howdy Doody was the star of the children's television program *The Howdy Doody Show,* which was on the air from 1947 to 1960. The human host was Buffalo Bob, and the kids in the TV studio sat in the "peanut gallery." Kenickie insults Doody when he says to Sonny, "Nice rumble! A herd of Flaming Dukes against you, me, and Howdy Doody."

Hully Gully contest: Danny tells Sandy, "I won a Hully Gully contest at the *Teen Talent* record hop." A forerunner of the twist, the hully gully was a vigorous dance favored by young people up until the early 1960s.

lettermen: A high school or college jock who has been awarded an emblem, in the shape of the initial letter of their school's name, is known as a letterman. To make Danny jealous, Sandy says, "I'm just dying to make a good impression on all those cute lettermen."

Little Lulu: When Rizzo sees Patty coming toward the Pink Ladies' table, she says, "Hey, look who's comin'. Patty Simcox, the Little Lulu of Edgebrook Heights." *Little Lulu* was a comic strip that debuted in the *Saturday Evening Post* in 1935 and was still well-known in the 1950s. The character of Lulu Moppet was an odd-looking girl with loopy curls and a mischievous nature.

Maidenform: In the song "It's Raining on Prom Night," Sandy and the radio voices sing, "It's wilting my quilting in my Maidenform." A best-selling manufacturer of women's underwear was Maidenform Brands. They were particularly known for making shapely bras that appeared on attractive females in newspaper and magazine ads.

The Mickey Mouse Club: The original *Mickey Mouse Club* television program began airing in 1955 and was an immediate sensation. Appealing to kids and teens, the program featured the singing-dancing Mouseketeers. Roger says to the Burger Palace Boys, "Hey, you guys wanta come over to my house to watch the Mickey Mouse Club?"

Mouseketeers: All three incarnations of the *Mickey Mouse Club* television program, from 1955 to 2017, featured the Mouseketeers, a talented group of adolescents who became wholesome ideals of American youth. Danny says, "Hey, we was just goin' to check out the Mouseketeers."

Mr. Clean: In the mocking alma mater at the beginning of the musical, the greasers sing, "If Mr. Clean, Rydell, had seen Rydell / He'd just turn green and disappear." One of the most familiar and long-running icons of commercial advertising was Mr. Clean, a brawny, bald he-man in a white T-shirt who battled dirt and grime. He was the spokesman for Procter & Gamble's all-purpose cleaner.

p.g.: A coy slang term for pregnant; Marty asks Rizzo, "You think maybe you're p.g.?"

Pat Boone: The clean-cut, wholesome singer and actor Pat Boone (b. 1934) was a heartthrob favorite for two decades, selling more than forty-five million records and featured in a dozen Hollywood films. At the high school hop, Danny tells Eugene, "Betty Rizzo thinks you look like Pat Boone."

Paul Anka: The Canadian-born singer and songwriter Paul Anka (b. 1941) has had a long and successful career but was perhaps at his most popular in the late 1950s and early 1960s. When Marty is taking out photos to show the Pink Ladies a picture of her marine, she says, "Oh, here it is . . . Next to Paul Anka."

pedal pushers: Also called clam diggers, pedal pushers were calf-length trousers that women favored in the 1950s. Sometimes they were cuffed and worn tight to the skin, a forerunner of Capri pants. In the song "Freddie, My Love," Marty sings about "Those pedal pushers with the black leather patches."

Petunia Pig: The female significant other to Porky Pig was the animated Petunia Pig, featured in Looney Tunes and Merrie Melodies cartoons from Warner Bros. She looks much like Porky, but she wears a dress and has pigtailed black hair. When Jan says she can eat meat on Friday because she's a Lutheran, Roger says, "Yeah, that's the nice thing about bein' Petunia Pig."

Princess Grace: Grace Kelly (1929–1982) was a stunningly beautiful American actress who became Princess of Monaco by marrying Prince Rainier III in 1956. She was considered one of the world's great beauties and was a symbol of perfect poise and behavior. When Marty starts to put on airs, Rizzo says, "Okay, Princess Grace."

Ricky Nelson: Frenchy says, "Hey Sonny, don't maul that magazine. There's a picture of Ricky Nelson in there I really wanna save." The handsome singer-songwriter Ricky Nelson (1940–1985) grew up on television. From the age of eight, he starred with his family in the radio and television series *The Adventures of Ozzie and Harriet.* He started singing on the TV show as a teenager before going on to a successful recording and concert career.

Ringtails: The school mascot in *Grease* is the ringtail, a mammal of the raccoon family found in the dry regions of North America. A ringtail is hardly a noble or fierce creature, but all the same, the cheerleaders enthusiastically sing, "Hit 'em again, Rydell Ringtails!"

Robert Hall: One of the prizes that Miss Lynch gives out at the high school hop is "A coupon worth ten dollars off at Robert Hall." The American retailer Robert Hall Clothes, Inc., known simply as Robert Hall, flourished from 1938 to 1977.

Rydell High School: The name of fictional Rydell High School is probably a nod to teen idol singer-actor Bobby Rydell (1942–2022), who mainly performed rock 'n' roll and traditional pop music.

Sal Mineo: Best known for his role as "Plato" Crawford in the film drama *Rebel Without a Cause* (1955), Sal Mineo (1939–1976) was an American actor, singer, and director who died tragically young. In Rizzo's song "Look at Me, I'm Sandra Dee," she sings "No, no, no, Sal Mineo, / I would never stoop so low."

Sandra Dee: The actress Sandra Dee (1942–2005) typified the all-American teen in a series of movies in the 1950s and 1960s. Throughout *Grease*, Rizzo mocks Sandy and calls her Sandra Dee, "lousy with virginity," as in the song "Look at Me, I'm Sandra Dee."

Shelley Fabares: Going through a fan magazine, Sonny says, "I was just lookin' at Shelley Fabares's jugs." Best known for her television role as the teenage daughter Mary Stone on the sitcom *The Donna Reed Show* (1958 to 1963), Shelley Fabares (b. 1944) was sometimes billed as "Shelly Farberay" during her singing and acting career.

sock hop: When school dances were held in gymnasiums and students were requested to remove their shoes, the dance was called a sock hop. In the second act of *Grease*, most of the characters assemble at the sock hop hosted by DJ Vince Fontaine.

Troy Donahue: The American film and television actor-singer Troy Donahue (1936–2001) was a youthful sex symbol in the 1950s and 1960s. In the song "Look at Me, I'm Sandra Dee," Rizzo sings, "As for you, Troy Donahue, / I know what you wanna do."

v.d.: Slang for any venereal disease; in the mocking alma mater at the beginning of *Grease*, the greasers sing, "Is it v.d., Rydell? Could be Rydell."

Vogue: A fashionable brand of cigarettes that was marketed and sold primarily to women in the 1950s. The distinctive design of the packaging symbolized elegance and refinement. Marty says, "Hey, anybody want a Vogue?" and Frenchy asks, "You got any pink ones left?"

zip gun: A crude homemade pistol is called a zip gun. It typically consists of a metal tube taped to a wooden stock and firing a .22-caliber bullet. Sonny brings a zip gun that he made in shop class to the rumble, and Kenickie asks, "Hey, Sonny, what Cracker Jack box 'ja get that zip gun out of, anyway?"

GUYS AND DOLLS

Libretto by Abe Burrows and Jo Swerling, based on the stories by Damon Runyon. Music and lyrics by Frank Loesser. Original Broadway production: November 24, 1950. 46th Street Theatre. 1,200 performances. Broadway revivals in 1955, 1965, 1976, 1992, and 2009.

This "musical fable of Broadway" takes place in a cockeyed New York City that never existed. Damon Runyon's stories about funny and harmless gamblers, gangsters, chorus girls, and con men were published in the 1930s, but most take place during the previous decade, when Prohibition was in force. The tales are filled with New York slang and original Runyonisms—both are heard in the musical's libretto and lyrics—but there are also many product names that were well known when *Guys and Dolls* opened in 1950 that no longer exist.

Expressions, references, names:

A & P: The Great Atlantic & Pacific Tea Company, better known as the A & P, was an American chain of grocery stores that operated from 1859 to 2015. Adelaide has written to her mother that her husband, Nathan, is "the assistant manager of an A & P."

according to Hoyle: Sky threatens the crap shooters with, "Anybody who does not conduct himself according to Hoyle will answer to Sky Masterson personally." The seventeenth-century British writer Edmond Hoyle wrote extensively on the rules of card games. Over the years, "according to Hoyle" referred to any kind of rules or expected behavior.

Biloxi: In the song "Guys and Dolls," Nicely-Nicely sings, "He sacrifices ev'rything / And moves all the way to Biloxi." The city of Biloxi is located in southern Mississippi, very far from the doings in New York City.

Blossom Time: The 1921 operetta *Blossom Time* was still being performed in the 1940s but was considered very old-fashioned. Detective Brannigan looks at the assembled gamblers and says, "This looks like the male chorus from *Blossom Time.*"

Bromo fizz: Bromo-Seltzer was an antacid in the 1930s and 1940s, similar to today's Alka-Seltzer. In "Adelaide's Lament," she sings, "With the vitamin A and the Bromo fizz."

Brooks Brothers type: The wealthiest New Yorkers bought men's clothing from Brooks Brothers. In the song "I'll Know," Sky Masterson teases Sarah Brown about her ideal man, singing he is "the breakfast-eating Brooks Brothers type."

crap game: Much of *Guys and Dolls* centers on craps or crap games, played with a pair of dice in which players bet on dice rolls. Popular in casinos, craps was illegal in social gatherings where large amounts of money were wagered. Nathan Detroit operates a "floating crap game," one that moves from one location to another in order to outwit the cops.

dulce de leche . . . Bacardi: A popular mixed drink in the 1920s was a dulce de leche, Spanish for "sweet [made] of milk." It usually consists of chocolate liqueur, rum, and condensed milk. When Sarah Brown requests a milkshake in the Havana restaurant, Sky Masterson orders her a dulce de leche. He tells her it is filled with a "kind of native flavoring," which he admits is actually Bacardi. Rum from the Caribbean was first manufactured by Bacardi Limited in 1862 and is still a familiar brand of the sugar-based alcohol.

Elkton . . . Pimlico: The small city of Elkton, Maryland, was a favorite spot for eloping couples because one could easily and quickly get a marriage license. When he finds out Nathan and Adelaide want to elope, Detective Brannigan says, "You can drive down to Maryland. What's the name of that town?" to which Benny answers, "Pimlico?" Brannigan answers, "Elkton." The horse-racing track in Baltimore, Maryland, known as Pimlico is the home of the Preakness Stakes, the second leg of the Triple Crown.

Emily Post: The American author and socialite Emily Post (1872–1960) was famous for writing about etiquette. When Nathan tells Big Jule that it is "a breach of etiquette" to change dice in the middle of a craps game, Harry the Horse says, "Show me where it says that in Emily Post."

Equipoise: In the song "Fugue for Tinhorns," the three gamblers mention various fictional racehorses; Rusty Charlie sings, "It says the great-grandfather was Equipoise." Equipoise (1928–1938) was an actual American Thoroughbred racehorse and sire. Between 1930 until 1935, Equipoise ran fifty-one times and won twenty-nine races. Today "equipoise" has two very different meanings. It can refer to a state of equilibrium or the ability to maintain balance in sports; it is also the name of a steroid used to boost testosterone in animals, particularly horses.

fish-eye: A scowling or menacing look with an unblinking expression is known as the fish-eye, probably because fish do not have eyelids. In "Adelaide's Lament," she sings about being "tired of getting the fish-eye / From the hotel clerk" because he suspects she and Nathan are not married.

Gideon Bible: When Sky Masterson quotes a passage from the Bible to Sarah and she is surprised, he tells her: "There are two things in every hotel room in the country. Sky Masterson and the Gideon Bible." The religious organization called Gideons International has made it a mission to place a copy of the Bible in every hotel room. These became known as Gideon Bibles.

a grand . . . G's: Slang for one thousand dollars is a grand, as well as a G, a K, or a stack. In the song "The Oldest Established," Nicely-Nicely sings: "But we ain't got a grand on hand." Sky Masterson uses the short form when he says, "I beat 'em for fifty G's at blackjack."

Guy Lombardo: In the song "Marry the Man Today," Adelaide recommends things that she will introduce to Nathan in order to make him respectable, and she includes music by Guy Lombardo. The Canadian-American bandleader Guy Lombardo (1902–1977) formed the Royal Canadians in 1924, and they were soon one of the most popular bands in the nation, particularly famous for their playing "Auld Lang Syne" on New Year's Eve.

guys . . . dolls: Although today the word *guys* refers to a group of men, women, or both, a "guy" used to be only masculine, and was a slangy word suggesting a rough or less-sophisticated male, as opposed to a "man" or a "gentleman." Also slangy was the word *doll*, which hinted at a coarse and less-refined kind of woman. Calling Sarah Brown a doll, for example, shows a lack of respect. Both words were used a lot by Damon Runyon in his stories and are ideal for the title of the musical.

Hollanderize it: In the song "Take Back Your Mink," Adelaide sings about returning such expensive presents as furs to the men: "And tell them to / Hollanderize it / for some other dame." In the past, Hollanderizing was a cleaning process for many types of furs, using sawdust to remove the winter's grime.

Holy Rollers: This slang term is used for any Charismatic, Pentecostal, or other church that involves worship in a frenetic or out-of-control manner. Detective Brannigan has caught the gamblers two nights in a row rolling dice in the Save-a-Soul Mission. He observes, "I never saw crap shooters spend so much time in a mission. Maybe that's what they mean by Holy Rollers."

Howard Johnson's: The name today means hotels and motels, but in the 1940s and 1950s, "Howard Johnson's" referred to the hundreds of restaurants that operated across America. Although they were popular, a Howard Johnson's eatery was not considered fine dining. That is why when Sarah Brown refuses to dine at his favorite restaurant in Havana, Sky Masterson asks her, "Where do you want to eat? Howard Johnson's?"

la grippe: An old-fashioned term for the flu is *la grippe*. The expression started during the Spanish flu epidemic of the 1910s and was used for decades after. In the song "Adelaide's Lament," she sings about how her failure to get married could lead to her developing "la grippe."

lettuce: This was one of the many slang terms for money used a lot in the early decades of the twentieth century. The crap shooters sing, "There are well-heeled shooters / Ev'rywhere—and an awful lot of lettuce" in the song "The Oldest Established."

marker: A signed slip of paper that stated how much money was owed, by whom, and to whom, a marker was a kind of pledge of honor among gamblers. One could not "welch" on such an IOU and retain his reputation. Several markers are exchanged in *Guys and Dolls*, such as Big Jule's marker to Nathan for one thousand dollars, or Sky's marker to Sarah for "twelve sinners."

Mesentheorum: There is no such word, yet Harry the Horse uses it when referring to the flower in his buttonhole: "I paid half a buck for this Mesentheorum." Most likely he means chrysanthemum.

Mindy's: Lindy's was a legendary deli and restaurant in Midtown Manhattan for many years, founded by Leo "Lindy" Lindemann in 1921. Because it was still in operation in 1950, the librettists for *Guys and Dolls* changed it to Mindy's. At one point, Nathan Detroit tells Benny to "run into Mindy's Restaurant and ask Mindy how many pieces of cheesecake he sold yesterday, and also how many pieces of strudel."

New Rochelle: When asked if Sky Masterson will have any luck taking Sarah Brown to Havana, Nicely-Nicely replies, "Havana! He couldn't take this doll to New Rochelle!" The suburb known as New Rochelle is in Westchester County, New York, but still a short distance from Manhattan.

Niagara: The honeymoon destination for millions of couples for many decades was Niagara Falls in northwest New York State. Adelaide has long planned a honeymoon with Nathan Detroit at the Falls. In "Adelaide's Lament," she sings, "When they get on the train for Niagara / And she can hear church bells chime."

no-goodnik: In the song "Sue Me," Nathan Detroit refers to himself as a "no-goodnik." The expression is an English-Yiddish hybrid word meaning a worthless person.

Ovaltine: Although the hot milk concoction known as Ovaltine still exists, it was very popular in the postwar decades. In the song "Marry the Man Today," Adelaide lists Ovaltine as one of the things that she will introduce to Nathan to make him respectable.

parlay: Sky Masterson tells Sarah, "I once won five G's on a parlay, Shadrach, Meshach, and Abednego." A gambling term that means "raising the stakes with each bet using the winning of the previous bet" is known as a parlay. In the biblical book of Daniel, Shadrach, Meshach, and Abednego were three men who refused to bow down to King Nebuchadnezzar's image, so they were put in "the fiery furnace." Sky knows this bit of biblical trivia because he spends so much time in hotel rooms with Gideon Bibles.

peck: Adelaide and the Hot Box Girls sing the song "A Bushel and a Peck," which uses farm measurements in its lyrics. A peck is used for measuring dry foods and is equal to eight dry quarts, or a quarter of a bushel. So when they sing, "I love you a bushel and a peck," it means "even more than a bushel."

platinum folderol: Any useless ornament or accessory can be called folderol. Platinum is the pricey, silvery-white metallic element used in jewelry and other items. In the song "Guys and Dolls," Benny sings, "He's still lifting platinum folderol," meaning the guy is shoplifting expensive trinkets for his "doll."

***Reader's Digest*:** For many years, *Reader's Digest* was the best-selling consumer magazine in the United States. It contains stories, articles, and condensed versions of longer works. Sarah includes *Reader's Digest* on her list of things she will introduce to Sky to make him more domestic.

Rogers Peet: Rogers Peet was a fashionable men's clothing company that was founded in 1874 and existed until the mid-1980s. Rogers Peet is one of the things Sarah Brown plans to introduce to Sky Masterson, according to the song "Marry the Man Today."

Roseland: From the 1920s into the 1960s, the Roseland Ballroom in Manhattan was a popular dance hall where celebrities rubbed shoulders with members of the underworld. It was also known for hot jazz, marathon dances, sneezing contests, and prizefighting (for men and women). When the crap shooters arrive at the Save-a-Soul Mission, Sky Masterson orders them to behave, saying, "This is a mission, not Roseland."

Roxy: Operated by movie showman S. L. "Roxy" Rothafel and dubbed "The Cathedral of the Motion Picture," the Roxy was one of the largest and most opulent movie palaces in New York. In the song "Guys and Dolls," Nicely-Nicely sings, "I'll tell you what's playing at the Roxy."

Saratoga: Saratoga, New York, is home to the famous Saratoga Race Course. The train from New York City to Niagara Falls runs through Saratoga. In "Adelaide's Lament," she sings of her disappointment when she and Nathan head for a honeymoon at the Falls but "get off at Saratoga / For the fourteenth time."

Scarsdale Galahad: Sky Masterson suggests that Sarah's ideal man is a rich and antiquated bore in the song "I'll Know" when he sings, "You have wished yourself a Scarsdale Galahad." The historically wealthy community of Scarsdale, New York, is one of the most affluent suburbs in the nation. Galahad is a legendary knight in King Arthur's court and a symbol of chivalry.

scratch sheet: Horse-race devotees use a scratch sheet to learn more about the horses and the races coming up. Gamblers sometimes refer to it as "the dailies" or "the reports." Sky Masterson tells the gathered sinners at the Save-a-Soul Mission, "Maybe the Bible don't read as lively as the scratch sheet, but it is at least twice as accurate."

Sears and Roebuck: Before Sears and Roebuck was a department store chain, it was better known as a mail-order catalog company. It was founded by Richard Warren Sears and Alvah Curtis Roebuck in 1892. When Nathan Detroit gets Big Jule's gun away from him, he tosses it to Benny and says, "Kindly return this to Sears and Roebuck."

sheep's eye . . . lickerish tooth: In the Irish ballad "More I Cannot Wish You," Sarah Brown's grandfather Arvide sings to her, "Gazing at you / With the sheep's eyes / And the lickerish tooth." To be wide-eyed, pure, and innocent is to have the "sheep's eye." *Lickerish* is an archaic word for "lecherous." Arvide means she is both beautiful and desirable.

streptococci: Streptococci are bacteria that can lead to a variety of illnesses. In "Adelaide's Lament," she sings of her chronic cold, "You can spray her wherever / You figure the streptococci lurk."

The Telegraph: A newspaper founded in 1845 and still in circulation in 1950 was the *New York Telegraph*. In the song "Fugue for Tinhorns," horse-race gambler Rusty sings, "According to this here / In *The Telegraph*," referring to the racing news.

ten C's: A "C" or a C-note is slang for one hundred dollars. Telling a story about Sky Masterson, Nathan says, "He wouldn't take penicillin on account he had bet ten C's that his temperature would go to 104."

Vitalis and Barbasol: In the song "Guys and Dolls," Benny sings about a lovesick guy who "smells of Vitalis and Barbasol." Vitalis was a brand of men's hair cream meant to keep one's hair shiny and in place. Barbasol is a brand of shaving cream and aftershave still on the market.

Wanamaker's . . . Saks . . . Klein's: John Wanamaker Department Store was one of the first department stores in the United States, founded in 1876 by John Wanamaker in Philadelphia. A major force in the early retail industry, Wanamaker's was the first store to use price tags. The New York store was located at Broadway and Ninth Street. Saks Fifth Avenue, originally A. Saks & Co., is an American luxury department store chain. The first store was founded by Andrew Saks in Washington, DC, in 1867. Since 1924, Saks' flagship store has been located on Fifth Avenue in Midtown Manhattan. S. Klein on the Square, or simply S. Klein, was a popular priced department store chain based in New York City. The flagship store was located on Union Square East in Manhattan. Boasting that the company was honest and "on the square" gave rise to the name S. Klein on the Square. Of these three famous Manhattan department stores, only Saks Fifth Avenue survives. In the song "Marry the Man Today," Adelaide sings: "At Wanamaker's and Saks and Kleins . . . you can't get alterations on a dress you haven't bought."

GYPSY

Libretto Arthur Laurents, based on Gypsy Rose Lee's autobiography. Lyrics by Stephen Sondheim. Music by Jule Styne. Original Broadway production: May 21, 1959. Broadway Theatre. 702 performances. Broadway revivals in 1974, 1989, 2003, and 2008.

Gypsy takes place in various cities throughout the United States from the late 1920s into the 1930s. When Rose started promoting her kids in show business, vaudeville was very popular, and there were several "circuits" that booked acts. A circuit was a string of theaters owned by the same company, and performers who were booked on that circuit had steady work, going from one city to another. But as the Great Depression slowly but surely killed off vaudeville and the circuits, one of the few alternatives left for performers was burlesque. The distinction between vaudeville and burlesque is among the things that need explaining in *Gypsy*.

Expressions, references, names:

Beau Brummel: A flamboyant figure in Regency England, Beau Brummell (1778–1840) set the tone for men's fashion for many years. In the song "All I Need Is the Girl," Tulsa sings, "This bum'll / Be Beau Brummel."

born with a caul: A caul (or cowl) is a membrane that can cover a newborn's head and face. Being born with a caul is rare, occurring in fewer than one out of eighty thousand births. The caul is harmless and is immediately removed upon birth of the child. Rose tells young Louise, "You were born with caul. That means you got powers to read palms and tell fortunes and wonderful things are going to happen to you."

Charleston: Perhaps the most popular dance of the 1920s was the Charleston, named after the South Carolina city. The Charleston involves the vigorous swinging of the legs and vivacious arm movements. In the song "All I Need Is the Girl," Tulsa sings to Louise, "Now Charleston right!"

dinna ken: In the Scottish dialect, "did not" or "didn't" comes out as "dinna." Also Scottish is the word *ken*, which means "to know." At the talent show auditions, Uncle Jocko says, "Uncle Jocko dinna ken there were so many talented bairns [children] right here in Seattle."

Elks: The Benevolent and Protective Order of Elks, often simplified to Elks, is a civic group that is social but also philanthropic. Rose tries to shame Jocko with saying, "Have you no loyalty to the Elks?"

Fanny Brice: In the song "If Momma Was Married," June sings, "I'm not Fanny Brice." In vaudeville, on Broadway, and on the radio, there were few stars bigger than Fanny Brice (1891–1951), an American comedian and singer who remained popular from the 1920s into the 1940s. Brice was the subject of the musical *Funny Girl* (1964).

G–string: Standard costume for a striptease artist, the G–string was a garment consisting of a narrow strip of cloth that covers the genitals and is attached to a waistband. Variations of it are worn as underwear today, but in the past they were seen in any burlesque theater. Tessie says to Agnes, "I paid six bucks for that G–string. Back where you found it."

Harris Tweed: Harris Tweed is a high-quality tweed cloth that was handwoven by islanders at their homes in the Outer Hebrides of Scotland. The wool material is still highly valued. In the song "All I Need Is the Girl," Tulsa sings, "My wardrobe is a wow: Paris silk, Harris Tweed."

Knight of Pythias: The Knights of Pythias is a fraternal organization and secret society founded in Washington, DC, in 1864. It is one of the oldest such organizations in America. Rose assumes that Uncle Jocko is a member, but Jocko insists, "I am not a Knight of Pythias!"

the Lunts: The most famous acting couple on Broadway from the 1920s into the 1950s was Lunt and Fontanne, familiarly called the Lunts. American Alfred Lunt (1892–1977) and the English actress Lynn Fontanne (1887–1983) married in 1922, and from that time on, each rarely performed without the other. In the song "If Momma Was Married," Louise sings, "We aren't the Lunts."

Minsky's: While many of the burlesque houses across the country were tawdry and low-class affairs, Minsky's flagship burlesque theatre in New York City was an elaborate and high-quality venue with lavish production numbers, high-quality comics, and famous striptease artists. So when Louise becomes the top-billed Gypsy Rose Lee at Minsky's, she is at the top of her profession.

Odd Fellows Hall: The Order of Odd Fellows is an independent fraternal and benevolent society that originated in England in the eighteenth century. Many American cities had a chapter and met at the local Odd Fellows Hall. Rose says to Jocko, "When I first saw your sensitive face at the Odd Fellows Hall . . ."

Pantages Circuit . . . Orpheum Circuit: Two of the top vaudeville booking companies in the 1920s were the Pantages and the Orpheum Circuits. Alexander Pantages (1867–1936) was a Greek-American vaudeville impresario and early motion-picture producer. He created the lucrative Pantages Circuit of theaters across the western United States and Canada. At the height of his empire, he owned or operated eighty-four theaters. Producer Martin Beck (1868–1940) started the Orpheum Circuit of vaudeville and motion-picture theaters. He also built the Palace Theatre in New York, which, from 1913 to 1932, was the premiere vaudeville house in the United States. Rose says to Herbie, "I promised I'd get her on the Pantages Circuit and I did. I promised I'd get her on the Orpheum Circuit and I did."

Shriners: One of the largest fraternal orders in the United States, the Shriners are highly visible through their community humanitarian efforts, such as children's hospitals. In the song "Some People," Rose sings about "All those Shriners I said hello to."

***Variety*:** Dubbed the "Show Business Bible," *Variety* is a weekly trade magazine for the American entertainment business. When it was founded, *Variety* featured news, box-office grosses, and jobs for vaudeville (or variety, as it was sometimes called). By 1933, vaudeville was nearly gone, and the magazine featured news about movies and theatre. Today television takes up most of the weekly. When Herbie asks Rose, "Don't you know there's a Depression?" Rose answers, "Of course I know! I read *Variety*."

vaudeville . . . burlesque: The most popular form of entertainment in the first two decades of the twentieth century was vaudeville. The name and the idea came from France at the end of the 1800s. Vaudeville is a theatrical genre that emphasized a variety of different acts: singers, dancers, comics, kiddie acts, animal acts, magicians, and so on. The offerings (known as "the bill") changed weekly, so repeat business was essential. Vaudeville was offered at popular prices (whereas theatre and opera could be very expensive), and appealed to families.

Burlesque also came from Europe, but its American version in no way resembled the foreign genre. In Italy, a play that mocked or satirized something or someone was called *burleschi*. The program was a sort of popular opera with dancing, comics, and other acts. When the Depression hit the United States, vaudeville floundered, and astute producers offered programs of raunchy humor and ribald song and dance, which they named burlesque. When burlesque performer Mae Dix absentmindedly began removing her costume before reaching the wings of the stage, the strip-tease was born. American burlesque included comics, dancers, and miscellaneous acts, but it was the striptease artists whom audiences came to see. Burlesque thrived in the 1930s and into the 1940s, until city governments closed it down for moral reasons.

In *Gypsy*, the act is booked into a burlesque theater, and Rose tells Louise, "They say when a vaudeville act plays in burlesque, that means it's all washed up." Later, Tessie tells Rose, "There ain't any vaudeville left except burlesque."

Vogue: Haute couture fashion, beauty, culture, and fine living were among the topics covered in the American monthly magazine *Vogue*. Since starting up in 1892, *Vogue* has featured numerous actors, musicians, models, athletes, and other prominent celebrities. When Rose is shocked that Louise is going to be photographed in the bathtub, Louise says, "It's for *Vogue*."

wee bairn . . . wee laddie: The kiddie-show host Uncle Jocko uses several Scottish words in his one scene. Uncle Jocko says to the girl covered with balloons, "Uncle Jocko promised the wee bairn would be a winner, and she will." Then he says to the boy with an accordion, "Okay, let's have the first wee laddie in Uncle Jocko's Kiddie Show." In Scottish jargon, "wee" means small, and a "bairn" is a child. Any boy up until a certain age can be addressed as "laddie."

Ziegfeld: The celebrated American impresario Florenz Ziegfeld (1867–1932) was most known for his series of theatrical revues, the *Ziegfeld Follies*, which appeared on Broadway from 1907 to 1931. Herbie says to Rose, "Once upon a time there was a prince named Ziegfeld."

HAIR

Libretto and lyrics by Gerome Ragni and James Rado. Music by Galt MacDermot. Original Off-Broadway production: October 29, 1967. Public Theatre. 94 performances. Original Broadway production: April 29, 1968. Biltmore Theatre. 1,472 performances. Broadway revivals in 1977, 2004, 2009, and 2011.

When it premiered, *Hair* was a very contemporary, bold, and in-your-face rock musical about Vietnam and other events in the news. Enough time has passed that it has become a period piece when performed today. The time is 1967, and most of the action takes place in Manhattan's East Greenwich Village. If ever a musical was firmly set in a specific point in American history, *Hair* is that musical. Many of the names and references may be lost today, but the power of the musical has not diminished. There is more than just one authorized script for *Hair*, and even the songs can vary from one version to another. References from all versions are discussed here.

HAIR   *The counterculture of the late 1960s included a variety of types, but their hair and clothes were what distinguished them.*
Photofest

Expressions, references, names:

Alan Burke: From 1966 to 1969, the conservative television and radio talk show host Alan Burke (1922–1992) was heard on the air, primarily in New York City. In the musical, Jeanie says, "I'm gonna say something I always wanted to say. Alan Burke sucks."

Aquarius: The cup bearer to the ancient Greek gods was Aquarius, better known as a winter constellation in the northern hemisphere. Aquarius is also one of the signs of the zodiac. In the opening number, the Tribe sings, "This is the dawning of the Age of Aquarius."

Barney's Boys' Town: The popular New York City discount clothing retailer Barney's began in 1923 as Barney's Boys' Town. It is located at 17th Street and Seventh Avenue and remains a favorite for city shoppers. Jeanie asks Claude, "Where did you get that sari? Barney's Boys' Town?"

Betty Crocker coupons: The fictional character Betty Crocker is one of the most recognized icons of American advertising for food and recipes. Since 1920, Crocker has been the face of General Mills products. In the 1950s and 1960s, there were even Betty Crocker coupons. Customers would collect points on the General Mills packages and redeem them for merchandise. Claude says to Mom, "You save . . . Betty Crocker coupons."

Billy Graham . . . Prince Philip . . . Joe Louis . . . Cardinal Spellman: Berger divides the pills into piles and says, "One for Billy Graham, one for Prince Philip, and one for Joe Louis. One for Cardinal Spellman." Billy Graham (1918–2018) was a very popular American evangelist and an ordained Southern Baptist minister who was known internationally. The friend of many politicians, he was conservative and rarely controversial. Prince Philip (1921–2021), the Duke of Edinburgh, was the late husband of Queen Elizabeth II of Great Britain. Joe Louis (1914–1981) was the US heavyweight boxing champion known as the Brown Bomber. He was heavyweight champion of the world from 1937 to 1949. Cardinal Francis Spellman (1889–1967) was archbishop of New York City for twenty-five years.

Daddy Warbucks: The fictional character of Daddy Warbucks was featured in the long-running comic strip *Little Orphan Annie*. Warbucks was a multimillionaire who adopted the title orphan, Annie. He is best known today from the musical *Annie* (1977). Sheila says to Claude, "I'll scream bloody murder if you touch me, Daddy Warbucks!"

Dr. Spock: The most famous physician in America in the 1950s and 1960s, Dr. Benjamin Spock (1903–1998) was a pediatrician and liberal political activist whose book *Baby and Child Care* (1946) is one of the best-selling books of the twentieth century. Berger says to the school principal, played by Dad, "Call me Dr. Spock."

Eartha Kitt: The Black singer and dancer Eartha Kitt (1927–2008) was known for her sultry vocal style and slinky movements. In 1968, Kitt was at a White House luncheon where she publicly criticized the Vietnam War and drew the disfavor of President and Mrs. Johnson. Sheila says to Claude, "From President Johnson's bedroom window, Eartha Kitt waved to Sheila Franklin," suggesting Kitt was LBJ's lover, and she waved to Sheila from the president's bedroom.

Fellini . . . Antonioni . . . Roman Polanski: In the song "Manchester, England," Claude sings, "it's groovy / To hide in a movie / Pretends he's Fellini / And Antonioni / And also his countryman Roman Polanski." The Italian film director/screenwriter Federico Fellini (1920–1993) was a genius at blending fantasy and earthiness in his very unique movies. Michelangelo Antonioni (1912–2007) was also an Italian movie director, best known for his very modern, very metaphysical art films. The Polish-born Roman Polanski (born 1933) is internationally known for his puzzling but fascinating films and for his tabloid-fodder personal life.

Governor Reagan: President of the United States during the 1980s, actor-turned-politician Ronald Reagan (1911–2004) was the governor of California from 1966 to 1974. Dad says to the audience, "Governor Reagan says turn the schools into concentration camps."

Horn & Hardart: In the song "Colored Spade," Hud, who is Black, lists jobs that Black Americans were stuck with, including "Shoe Shine Boy, Elevator Operator, Table Cleaner at Horn and Hardart." An innovation in food service at the turn of the twentieth century was the "automat," in which patrons purchased various food items from coin-operated glass vending machines. The most famous of the automats was Horn & Hardart, which had famous eateries in Philadelphia and New York City.

John W. Booth . . . Calvin Coolidge . . . Clark Gable . . . Scarlett O'Hara . . . Colonel Custer: During Claude's acid trip, Ulysses S. Grant reads off a roll call that includes the following: John Wilkes Booth (1838–1865), an American stage actor who assassinated Abraham Lincoln at Ford's Theatre; Calvin Coolidge (1872–1933), the thirtieth president of the United States, known for his few words and hands-off policy during the prosperous 1920s; film star Clark Gable (1901–1960), who played the dashing Rhett Butler in *Gone with the Wind* opposite Vivien Leigh, who played the feisty heroine Scarlett O'Hara; and George Armstrong Custer (1839–1876), the US Cavalry officer who was killed, along with all of his men, in a clash with the Sioux Indians at Little Bighorn in Montana.

Johnson . . . 007s . . . Castros . . . Con Edisons . . . Napalm . . . Tuesday Weld . . . Burton-Taylor . . . Andy Warpop: In the song "I Got Life," the Tribe lists people and things then in the news. Lyndon B. Johnson (1908–1973) was the thirty-sixth president of the United States and in office during the most turbulent years of the 1960s. The code number for the fictional spy James Bond was 007. Fidel Castro (1927–2016) was the revolutionary leader who set up a Communist regime in Cuba and ruled over it for many years. Consolidated Edison, Inc., commonly known as Con Edison, or ConEd, is one of the largest investor-owned energy companies in the United States, providing electric and gas service in New York City. Napalm is a highly flammable, sticky jelly used in incendiary bombs and flamethrowers. Its use in Vietnam was very controversial. Tuesday Weld (born 1943) is a pretty and petite movie actress very popular in the 1960s. Welsh stage and film actor Richard Burton (1925–1984) was twice married to British-born movie star Elizabeth Taylor (1932–2011). The Burton–Taylor relationship was fodder for the tabloids in the 1960s. American artist Andy Warhol (1928–1987) was a leading figure in the visual art movement, known as Pop Art; hence, the name "Andy Warpop" in the song.

Kate Smith: The Moms and Dads ask Claude, "What are you going to do with your life? What do you want to be . . . besides . . . disheveled?" He answers, "Kate Smith." The rotund singer Kate Smith (1907–1986) was dubbed "First Lady of the Radio" for her many broadcasts in the 1930s and 1940s. She was most known for singing "God Bless America" for any occasion.

LBJ . . . IRT: In the song "Initials," the Tribe sings, "LBJ took the IRT / Down to 4th Street USA." The familiar LBJ initials are short for President Lyndon B. Johnson (1908–1973). The IRT stands for the Interborough Rapid Transit Company, which operates much of the rapid transit lines in New York City. Today only a few subway lines called IRT are in use.

LSD . . . DMT . . . STP . . . BMT . . . A & P . . . TWA: In the song "Hashish," the Tribe sings a series of acronyms. LSD, DMT, and STP are all potent hallucinogenic drugs. The Brooklyn-Manhattan Transit Corporation (BMT) was an urban transit holding company, based in Brooklyn. The Great Atlantic & Pacific Tea Company, better known as A & P, was an American chain of grocery stores that operated from 1859 to 2015. TWA was the widely used acronym for the now-defunct Trans World Airlines.

Margaret Mead: The anthropologist and social psychologist Margaret Mead (1901–1978) wrote a number of books and articles about primitive cultures as found on remote islands of the Pacific. After Mom bids the Tribe farewell, with "Good-bye all you sweet little flowerpots," they answer sweetly, "Fuck you, Margaret Mead."

Mr. McNamara: Berger says to the school principal played by Dad, "Mr. McNamara, this is 1968, not 1967." The name is a reference to Robert McNamara (1916–2009), who was secretary of the US Department of Defense during much of the Vietnam War.

Medusa . . . Prince Valiant . . . Orphani Annie . . . Veronica Lake: When Dad asks Berger, "Who are your heroes?," various members of the Tribe answer, "Medusa . . . Wonder Woman . . . Prince Valiant . . . Orphani Annie . . . Veronica Lake." In Greek mythology, Medusa was a monstrous Gorgon with living venomous snakes in place of hair. Anyone who gazed into her eyes would turn to stone. The comic strip *Prince Valiant in the Days of King Arthur*, which began in 1937, is an epic adventure set during medieval times. The comic strip *Little Orphan Annie* by Harold Gray ran in newspapers from 1885 to 2010. Berger mangled the title, calling the young heroine Orphani Annie. Veronica Lake (1922–1973) was a sultry blond movie star best known for her femme-fatale roles in film noir movies and her peekaboo hairstyle.

"moon in the seventh house": In astrology, the Seventh House for a zodiacal sign is an indication of love and pleasing interrelationships. In the opening song, "Aquarius," the Tribe sings, "When the moon is in the seventh house."

NYU: Sheila introduces herself with, "Sheila Franklin / Second semester / NYU." New York University is the distinguished undergraduate and graduate school in Manhattan. The campus is located in the Greenwich Village neighborhood of Lower Manhattan.

Peyote . . . Equinol . . . Dexamyl . . . Compozine . . . Kemidrin . . . Thorizene . . . Trilophon . . . Dexedrine . . . Benzedrine . . . Methedrine: In the song "Hashish," the Tribe rattles off a series of drugs popular at the time, many of which are still used today. Peyote is a small cactus that is used to make the drug mescaline. Equinol is a medication used to treat symptoms of anxiety and nervous behavior. Dexamyl was a drug used to suppress appetite and depression, but it was so misused that it ceased to be manufactured in 1982. Compozine is used to treat nausea and vomiting caused by major surgery. Kemidrin is used to treat patients with Parkinson's disease, but it has severe side effects. Thorizene and Trilophon are both prescription drugs used to treat those suffering from schizophrenia and psychotic disorders. Dexedrine stimulates the central nervous system, creating energy and decreasing appetite. It is also used to treat some forms of depression. Benzedrine, also called "bennies," was the first amphetamine prescribed for medical use. It also is a powerful stimulant that increases heart rate, breathing, and blood pressure. Methedrine is used as an appetite suppressant but also affects the nervous system.

pickaninny . . . jungle bunny . . . jigaboo: In the song "Colored Spade," Hud sings, "I'm a colored spade / A pickaninny / Jungle bunny jigaboo." These are all derogatory terms: a *pickaninny* is a racial slur for a Black child; *jungle bunny* is a contemptuous term for Black people, referring to their roots in Africa; and *jigaboo* is a very old expression for Black people, coming from the white man's fear that they were the bogeyman.

Pope Paul: The Italian pope on the throne of St. Peter's from 1963 to 1978 was Pope Paul VI (1897–1978). He is most remembered for presiding over the influential Second Vatican Council in the 1960s. In *Hair*, Dad says, "Pope Paul says stop the Peace Demonstrations."

Pratt: Berger asks Claude, "Didn't you tell them you are going to Pratt next year?" Pratt Institute is an institution of higher education situated in New York City that prepares its students for successful careers through its schools of art, design, architecture, and liberal arts and sciences.

PS 183: In New York City, there are so many public schools that many have numbers instead of names. The initials PS (Public School) are used before the number. Berger makes a toast, saying, "Up PS 183."

Ruby Tuesday . . . Michelle your belle . . . Lovely Rita Meter Maid: To the tune of "The Marine Hymn," the Tribe sings, "You'll forget your Ruby Tuesday, / You'll forget your Michelle your belle, / As for lovely Rita Meter Maid, / Well, she can go to hell." These are references to three popular songs of the 1960s: "Ruby Tuesday" (1966) was by the Rolling Stones (Mick Jagger and Keith Richards); a Beatles song by Paul McCartney and John Lennon, "Michelle," was introduced on their 1965 album, *Rubber Soul*; and "Lovely Rita (Meter Maid)" is also by McCartney and Lennon, and was sung by the Beatles on the 1967 album, *Sgt. Pepper's Lonely Hearts Club Band*.

S&H Green Stamps . . . King Korn Stamps . . . Plaid Stamps: Trading stamps were very popular in the 1960s. The stamps, which were given out with purchases mostly in grocery stores, were collected in stamp books and, when filled, were turned in for products. S&H Green Stamps, the King Korn Stamp Company, and MacDonald Plaid Stamps were three of the major stamp programs; all are gone now. Claude says to Mom, "You save S&H Green Stamps and King Korn Stamps and bloody Plaid Stamps."

Sanpaku: In *Hair*, GI 4 says, "Home of Macrobiotics and Sanpaku." *Sanpaku* refers to a particular appearance of a person's eyes; specifically, when the whites of a person's eyes are visible either below or above the colored portion.

three five zero zero: In the song "Three-Five-Zero-Zero," the Tribe sings about the carnage of the Vietnam War: "It's a dirty little war, / Three five zero zero / Take weapons up and begin to kill." Sections of the song are inspired by (and quoted from) the Allen Ginsberg antiwar poem "Wichita Vortex Sutra." The title number "3500" comes from a 1966 statement by the military command: "Viet Cong losses leveling up three five zero zero per month."

Timothy Leary: In the song "Manchester, England," Claude sings, "Why is life dreary dreary / Answer my weary query / Timothy Leary dearie." The American psychologist and writer Timothy Leary (1920–1996) was known for his strong advocacy of psychedelic drugs.

Tonto: In the long-running *The Lone Ranger* serial on radio, film, and television, the Ranger's companion is the Native American Tonto, who speaks in simple English phrases. The characterization is considered an offensive stereotype today. In *Hair*, Mom says to the audience, "Hello there. This is not a reservation. Tonto!"

Twiggy: Berger throws a branch to Woof and says, "Hey, Woof! Here's Twiggy . . . Twiggy!" Perhaps the most internationally famous fashion model of the 1960s was Lesley Hornby (born 1949), known as "Twiggy" because she was so thin, her arms and legs seemed as thin as twigs. She later enjoyed a successful acting and singing career onstage and in the movies.

Uncle Tom . . . Aunt Jemima . . . Little Black Sambo: In the song "Colored Spade," Hud sings, "I'm Uncle Tom and Aunt Jemima / Voodoo zombie / Little Black Sambo," all stereotypical Black characters. In Harriet Beecher Stowe's 1852 novel, *Uncle Tom's Cabin*, Tom is an old, passive slave who doesn't stand up for himself or others of his race. Over the years, calling someone an Uncle Tom was considered a derisive insult. The fictional Aunt Jemima, a Black woman who wears a bandana, was pictured on pancake mix and syrup from 1889 to 2021. Although the character was modernized from a fat "Mammy" to a slim, more attractive aunt, the stereotype remained, so she was retired in 2021. *The Story of Little Black Sambo* is an 1899 children's book written and illustrated by Scottish author Helen Bannerman. The tale of a little native boy in the jungle delighted children for decades, but fell out of favor in the 1960s.

USO: To the tune of "The Caissons Go Rolling Along," the Tribe sings, "Lift your skirt, point your toe / Volunteer for the USO." The United Service Organizations, Inc. (USO) is an American nonprofit-charitable corporation that provides live entertainment and social activities for members of the United States Armed Forces and their families.

Viet Cong: The Communist guerrilla movement in Vietnam that fought the South Vietnamese government and American troops was known as the Viet Cong. Speaking of Berger's mother, Woof says, "Do they know she's a Viet Cong?"

Village Voice: The nation's first alternative weekly newspaper was the *Village Voice*, founded in 1955 and headquartered in Greenwich Village in New York City. In *Hair*, Berger says, "I got my job through the *Village Voice*."

Waverly: In the song "Frank Mills," Chrissy sings, "I met a boy called Frank Mills . . . Right here in front of the Waverly." The Waverly movie theater has been a landmark in New York City for several decades, showing art films and experimental movies. It was at the Waverly that the first midnight audience-participation screenings of the movie *The Rocky Horror Picture Show* began. In 2005 the old theater was renovated and is now known as the IFC Center.

"What a piece of work is man": Near the end of the musical, the characters of Ronny and Walter sing the song "What a Piece of Work Is Man," in which the lyrics are taken from a speech by Hamlet. As in the Shakespeare text, man is seen as "noble in reason . . . infinite in faculties . . . in action how like an angel . . . in apprehension how like a God." But the speech and the song end on a pessimistic note, the song lyrics concluding that man "appears no other thing to me / Than a foul and pestilent congregation of vapours."

HAIRSPRAY

Libretto by Mark O'Donnell and Thomas Meehan, based on the film by John Waters. Lyrics by Scott Wittman and Marc Shaiman. Music by Marc Shaiman. Original Broadway production: August 15, 2002. Neil Simon Theatre. 2,642 performances.

Hairspray falls between the late 1950s of *Grease* and the late 1960s of *Hair*. It is 1962 in Baltimore, Maryland, and the score for *Hairspray* has the distinctive sound of this transitional period. Many of the references in the musical revolve around television. *The Corny Collins Show* is a local program featuring local talent. Such a program was to be found in several American cities, the most famous one being Philadelphia's *American Bandstand*. The influence of pop music, television, and the movies on teenagers in 1962 was substantial. Tracy says it all: "Welcome to the Sixties."

Expressions, references, names:

Aida: Giuseppe Verdi's 1871 opera *Aida* is set in the Old Kingdom of Egypt and tells a love story that surfaces from the struggles of the conquered Nubians. Arias from the Italian opera were once staples for talent contests. In the song "Miss Baltimore Crabs," Velma sings, "Batons ablaze / While singing *Aida* / And preparing cheese soufflés!"

Candid Camera . . . **Allen Funt:** In its different versions, the television show *Candid Camera* was broadcast intermittently from 1948 until 2014. The gimmick was simple: Unsuspecting people were placed in confusing, embarrassing, ridiculous, or hilarious positions, while their reactions were recorded by a hidden camera. The host of the program for many years was Allen Funt. When things get out of hand at the television studio, Velma asks, "Wait, are we on *Candid Camera*? Okay, where is Allen Funt?"

Castro: In the song "(You're) Timeless to Me," Edna sings to Wilbur, "Fads keep a-fadin' / And Castro's invading / But Wilbur, you're timeless to me." The Cuban revolutionary Fidel Castro (1926–2016), who headed the Communist government in Cuba, was much in the news in the early 1960s, especially during the Cuban Missile Crisis of 1962.

Connie Francis: The American singer-actress Connie Francis (born 1937) was known for her wholesome image and many top-charting female vocal hits. When too much rhythm and blues is heard on *The Corny Collins Show*, Velma asks Corny, "Have you got something against Connie Francis?"

cooties: A slang term for body lice is *cooties*. The word was far from scientific, and teens often used it to describe any imaginary germ said to have infected someone considered socially undesirable. In the song "Cooties," the chorus picks on Tracy, repeating, "She's got cooties!"

The Corny Collins Show: This fictional Baltimore television program is based on the many local dance programs that could be found in different cities at the time of *Hairspray*. The model was *American Bandstand* from Philadelphia, a program that ran nationally from 1952 to 1989, hosted by Dick Clark for most of its tenure. The recipe was the same: Local teens danced to music played by a disc jockey, or, if you were lucky, by the actual artist lip-syncing to a record.

Debbie Reynolds . . . Eddie Fisher: The tabloid story of the era burst on the scene when singer Eddie Fisher (1928–2010) left his wife, singer-actress Debbie Reynolds (1932–2016), to marry the movie star Elizabeth Taylor (1932–2011). Edna tells her daughter, "But you and I are going to have a talk about crooners. You can learn a lot from the mistakes of Miss Debbie Reynolds." Later, when Link walks out on Tracy, Edna says, "It's just Eddie Fisher all over again."

Detroit sound: Upset over the rhythm-and-blues music heard on the TV program, Velma tells Corny Collins, "None of that Detroit sound today." A nickname for Detroit is Motown (taken from Motor Town), and that word was used to describe the new, innovative music and the Black artists coming from Detroit. Motown Records was founded in 1959 by Berry Gordy, who discovered and promoted such artists as the Supremes, Stevie Wonder, and Marvin Gaye.

Doris Day . . . the Apollo: The American blond singer-actress Doris Day (1922–2019) had a long career in movies, and during the 1960s she was known mostly for playing virginal, wholesome women. The Apollo Theater was established in 1913 in Harlem and became famous for the Black artists who performed there. One would never see the likes of Doris Day at the Apollo, yet in the song "Without Love," Seaweed sings to Penny, "Without love / Life is Doris Day at the Apollo."

Eva Marie . . . Saint: American film and television actress Eva Marie Saint (born 1924) is a stunning blonde who never played dumb blondes. In *Hairspray*, the newscaster on the radio says, "In entertainment news, Eva Marie is no saint."

Frankie Avalon . . . Mouseketeer: Heartthrob teenage singer Frankie Avalon (born 1940) had many hit records, but he's most remembered for a series of beach movies he made with Annette Funicello (1942–2013), the former Mouseketeer from TV's *The Mickey Mouse Club*. Funicello was the most popular of all the Mouseketeers. In the song "It Takes Two," Link sings, "Just like Frankie Avalon / Has his favorite Mouseketeer."

Gabor sisters: The Hungarian beauty Zsa Zsa Gabor (1917–2016) and her sisters, Eva (1919–1995) and Magda (1915–1997), were actresses in movies and on television, but they were in the news more often because of their many marriages. Edna jokes about the sisters' many lawyers when she tells Tracy, "You need a top-shelf professional. Who handled the Gabor sisters? Well, who didn't?"

Geritol: In the song "(You're) Timeless to Me," Edna sings to Wilbur, "Hey! Pass that Geritol." A widely advertised dietary supplement for senior citizens in the 1960s, the product even suggests its clientele in its name, which comes from "geriatric." Geritol consists of several vitamin complexes plus iron, and comes in both liquid form and tablets. The supplement used to be recommended for people over forty, so there were always plenty of Geritol jokes at one's fortieth birthday party.

Gidget: A fusion of the words "girl" and "midget" (although this is considered offensive today), Gidget was a fictional teenage girl with plenty of spunk and wholesome enthusiasm. The character appeared in a TV series and in movies, such as *Gidget Goes to Rome*. Corny Collins says on the air, "Now don't forget, guys and Gidgets." Later in the musical, Amber sings, "But now I'm just like Gidget / And I gotta get to Rome!"

Glenn Miller . . . Chubby Checker: One of the Big Band greats in the 1940s, Glenn Miller (1904–1944) was a jazz trombonist and bandleader. Chubby Checker (born 1941) is an American rock 'n' roll singer and dancer, widely known for popularizing many dance styles, particularly the Twist. Miller and Checker could not be further apart musically, but in the song "(You're) Timeless to Me," Edna sings to Wilbur, "Glenn Miller had class / That Chubby Checker's a gas / But they all pass eventually."

Hindenburg disaster: On May 6, 1937, the German dirigible *Hindenburg* caught fire while attempting to dock in Manchester Township, New Jersey, and was destroyed as the newsreel cameras were rolling, capturing it all on film. In the song "(You're) Timeless to Me," Wilbur sings to Edna, "Yeah, Edna, you're like the *Hindenburg* disaster."

Jackie Gleason: The film and television comic Jackie Gleason (1916–1987) was known to most Americans in the 1950s and 1960s because of his TV programs, *The Honeymooners* and *The Jackie Gleason Show*. One of his signature phrases was "Hommina, hommina, hommina!" Corny Collins tells the kids at the high school dance, "Let's make it like Jackie Gleason— hommina, hommina, hommina!"

Jezebel: Edna says to Tracy about her big hairdo, "All ratted up like a teenage Jezebel." In the Bible, the Phoenician wife of Ahab who tried to force the cult of Baal on the Israelites was named Jezebel. Ever since, the word has been used to describe a shameless or wicked woman.

Khrushchev has his shoes off: The premier of the USSR from 1958 to 1964 was Nikita Khrushchev (1894–1971), a Soviet who made no secret of his disdain for the Western world. While attending a meeting of the General Assembly at the United Nations in 1960, Khrushchev was not getting the attention he wanted, so he took off one of his shoes and banged it on the desk. When Penny calls Edna to the TV set, Edna says, "Don't tell me Khrushchev has his shoes off again!"

Liz . . . Dick: The romance and two marriages of Welsh actor Richard Burton (1925–1984) and British-born movie star Elizabeth Taylor (1932–2011) filled the tabloids in the 1960s. They were so famous at the time that all one had to do was say "Liz" or "Dick," and everyone knew whom you meant. In the song "It Takes Two," Link sings, "Romeo had Juliet / And Liz, she has her Dick."

Lollobrigida: In the song "Welcome to the Sixties," Edna sings, "Tell Lollobrigida to step aside!" The beautiful and busty Italian movie star Gina Lollobrigida (1927–2023) was an international sex symbol in the 1960s.

Mamie Eisenhower: First Lady Mamie Eisenhower (1896–1979), the wife of Dwight ("Ike") Eisenhower, the thirty-fourth president, had a matronly look, with her old-fashioned hair and clothes. Edna tells Tracy, "I haven't been out of this apartment since Mamie Eisenhower rolled her hose and bobbed her bangs."

Metrecal: In the early 1960s, the low-calorie, powdered diet drink Metrecal was introduced, and was very popular for a time. Amber says that Tracy is "the before in the Metrecal diet ad!"

NAACP: In the song "You Can't Stop the Beat," Penny sings, "And if they try to stop us, Seaweed / I'll call the NAACP." The National Association for the Advancement of Colored People (NAACP) is a civil rights organization formed in 1909 to advance justice for Black people.

Orange Crush: While Orange Crush sounds like a healthy carbonated drink made from fruit, it was actually loaded with sugar and, consequently, very popular in the 1960s. Before he goes back to his shop, Wilbur says, "I'm grabbin' an Orange Crush."

Perry Como: In the song "Without Love," Tracy sings to Link, "Without love / Life's just making out to Perry Como." During a career spanning more than half a century, singer Perry Como (1912–2001) recorded many hit records and was frequently seen on television. He was known for his warm, easy-listening style of singing.

***Peyton Place*:** Demonstrating a dance step he has invented, Seaweed tells Tracy, "I call this one Peyton Place after Midnight. I use it to attract the opposite sex." Grace Metalious's 1956 bestseller *Peyton Place* was about the scandalous doings behind closed doors in a picture-perfect little town. *Peyton Place* was also a successful movie and TV soap opera. Today the term *Peyton Place* means a place or a group of people with much to hide.

Rock Hudson: Link says about his fans' attraction to him, "I don't know how Rock Hudson stands it." Dashing movie star Rock Hudson (1925–1985) was the idol of moviegoers in the 1950s and 1960s.

Rosa Parks: In many ways, the civil rights movement began in 1955, when Rosa Parks (1913–2005) refused to give up her bus seat to a white man in Montgomery, Alabama, an act that led to a bus strike and nationwide attention. Little Inez says, "We'll set off sparks, like Rosa Parks!"

Sammy Davis: The versatile dancer-actor-singer Sammy Davis Jr. (1925–1990) was the Black member of the celebrated "Rat Pack" of the 1960s. In the song "Velma's Revenge," Velma sings, "Look, I love Sammy Davis / And he's Black and a Jew."

Shirley Temple: The most famous and most beloved child star in the history of the movies was Shirley Temple (1928–2014), who rose to fame during the Great Depression. Velma was also a child performer in the 1930s, and in the song "Miss Baltimore Crabs," Velma sings, "When that damn Shirley Temple / Stole my frickin' act."

"Teen Angel": The 1959 ballad "Teen Angel" by Jean Dinning and Red Surrey, recorded by Mark Dinning, was a tear-jerking hit. It told of a teenage girl who died when her car was stuck in the path of an oncoming train. After Tracy is hurt during a game of dodgeball in gym class, Link asks her, "You better? For a second there it looked like 'Teen Angel' time."

Wilt the Stilt: The Basketball Hall of Famer Wilt Chamberlain (1936–1999) was a Black basketball player known as Wilt the Stilt because he was seven feet, one inch tall. Corny Collins tells the kids at the high school dance, "Take it to the basket like Wilt the Stilt."

HELLO, DOLLY!

Libretto by Michael Stewart, based on the play *The Matchmaker* by Thornton Wilder. Music and lyrics by Jerry Herman. Original Broadway production: January 16, 1964. St. James Theatre. 2,844 performances. Broadway revivals in 1975, 1978, 1995, and 2017.

Although the musical is set in the 1880s, the so-called Gilded Age, most of the characters are working-class folks who can only imagine the frills of the age's millionaires. The action begins and concludes in Yonkers, New York, a village north of Manhattan. The rest of the musical is set in a fairy tale–like New York City, full of color and activity. Michael Stewart and Jerry Herman include many real New York landmarks and period expressions in the libretto and lyrics.

Expressions, references, names:

Ada Rehan: The statuesque American actress Ada Rehan (1857–1916), one of the most popular stage stars of her day, had a striking profile. Dolly Levi refers to it when she tells Ambrose, "I do those silhouettes with scissors and black paper; here's one of Ada Rehan looking the other way."

Astors . . . Tony Pastor's: The American capitalist John Jacob Astor (1763–1848) made a fortune in fur trading and founded the family dynasty. It was the women in the Astor family who dictated fashion and determined who could be admitted into a very selective society. Tony Pastor (1837–1908) was an American impresario who established American vaudeville as a wholesome entertainment for the whole family. His theater was patronized by a wide range of society, although it was unlikely to see the Astors there. All the same, the residents of Yonkers sing, "We'll join the Astors at Tony Pastor's" in the song "Put on Your Sunday Clothes," as they set off by train to New York City.

Barnum's Museum: P. T. Barnum's American Museum on lower Broadway was one of the main attractions of New York City, offering scientific finds and sometimes-bogus curiosities. Both Cornelius and Barnaby want to see "the stuffed whale at Barnum's Museum," and they mention it several times throughout the musical. Alas, they never get there.

bowler brim: In the song "Put on Your Sunday Clothes," the chorus sings, "Beneath your bowler brim the world's a simple song." A hard felt hat with a rounded crown is called a bowler, fashionable headgear for men at the time of *Hello, Dolly!*

brilliantine: A hair-grooming product intended to soften men's hair, including beards and mustaches, brilliantine gave a man's hair a glossy, well-groomed look. Cornelius sings, "Get out the brilliantine and dime cigars" in the song "Put on Your Sunday Clothes."

Castle Garden: In the song "Dancing," Barnaby gets carried away with his athletic footwork and sings, "I might join the chorus of the Castle Garden show." Castle Clinton, or Fort Clinton, in Lower Manhattan's Battery Park was previously known as Castle Garden, and entertainments were presented there once the immigration station was moved to Ellis Island.

corset: A corset is a support garment commonly worn to hold and train the torso into a desired shape. Although they were mostly associated with women, there were male corsets as well. When Cornelius asks Irene if he can put his arm around her waist, she says yes, but "I might as well warn you, a corset is a corset."

cravat: Any scarf or band of fabric worn around the neck as a tie could be termed a *cravat*. The French invention has always stood for casual sophistication. In the song "Put on Your Sunday Clothes," the chorus sings, "Put on your silk cravat" as they board the train for New York.

damn the torpedoes: During the climax of the silly patriotic "Motherhood" march, Dolly cries out, "Damn the torpedoes, full steam ahead!" During a Civil War naval battle, the Union officer David Farragut, when told there were mines called torpedoes in the waters ahead, is said to have exclaimed, "Damn the torpedoes!"

Delmonico's: The citizens of Yonkers sing, "We'll see the shows at Delmonico's" in the song "Put on Your Sunday Clothes." Delmonico's was an exclusive and expensive eatery in New York City during the Gilded Age, believed to be the first American restaurant to offer French cuisine. The Fifth Avenue establishment introduced the cut of meat still known as Delmonico steak.

garter: A band worn to hold up a stocking or sock; the word also applies to a band worn to hold up a shirt sleeve. Ernestina refers to a garter worn out of sight when she tells Vandergelder that she doesn't wear a money belt, but keeps two dollars hidden away, "Only it's in my garter!"

hack: When Irene and Minnie suggest to Cornelius and Barnaby that they take a hack to the restaurant, Cornelius informs them, "Nowadays really elegant people never take hacks." Short for "hackney" carriage, a hack is a horse-drawn vehicle for hire.

hootchy-kootchy: Usually performed in a carnival sideshow or a burlesque theater, the hootchy-kootchy is a sexual and exaggerated form of belly dance. When dancing commences at the elegant Harmonia Gardens Restaurant, Ernestina says to Vandergelder, "Tell [the bandleader] to play something refined . . . I'm going to do the hootchy-kootchy!"

hothouse peaches: A hothouse flower, vegetable, or fruit is one not hardy enough to grow outside, but must be grown in a greenhouse, or hothouse. At the Harmonia Gardens Restaurant, Cornelius orders "Champagne, and Neapolitan ice cream, and hothouse peaches."

J. P. Vanderbilt . . . Diamond Jim Morgan: Barnaby gets three millionaires mixed up when he says that "J. P. Vanderbilt [and] Diamond Jim Morgan" were among those who take streetcars. Known for his love of diamonds, the American businessman, financier, and philanthropist Diamond Jim Brady (1856–1917) was one of the most colorful celebrities of the Gilded Age. J. P. Morgan (1837–1913), who created General Electric and the US Steel Corporation, was one of the richest men in the world. Cornelius Vanderbilt (1794–1877), nicknamed "the Commodore," was an American business magnate who built his wealth in railroads and shipping.

Irene sings, "We are out with Diamond Jims tonight"; Minnie sings, "Vanderbilt kowtows to us"; and Cornelius sings, "J. P. Morgan scrapes and bows to us" in the quartet "Elegance."

Jenny Lind: Known as "the Swedish nightingale" for the crystal clarity of her voice, the Swedish soprano Jenny Lind (1820–1887) was a sensation when P. T. Barnum brought her to America. Exaggerating the devil-may-care personality of Cornelius, Dolly says to Irene, "Who took the horses out of Jenny Lind's carriage and pushed her through the streets?"

ladyfingers: A small finger-shaped sponge cake is known as a ladyfinger. Ernestina orders expensive items at the Harmonia Gardens and ends the list with "ladyfingers."

millineress: A person who makes or sells women's hats is a milliner. Irene, who runs her own millinery shop, tells Minnie, "All millineresses are suspected of being wicked women."

***non compos mentis* . . . a garnishee:** Dolly arranges for Cornelius to take Irene out to dinner by threatening him with legal double talk. She tells Irene, "You've got grounds for at least two writs, a *non compos mentis*, and a garnishee." A writ is a written command in the name of a court or other legal authority to require a specific action. *Non compos mentis* is a Latin legal phrase that translates to "of unsound mind," and means one has no control over one's mind. A garnishee is a third party who is served notice by a court to surrender money in settlement of a debt or claim.

patent leathers: In the song "Put on Your Sunday Clothes," Dolly sings, "Get out your feathers / Your patent leathers." Using lacquer to give a hard glossy surface to leather or imitation leather is to "patent" it. Commonly done to shoes, patent leathers came to mean shiny leather shoes.

sheep dip: Sheep dipping is the process of dunking a sheep into a vat of water containing insecticides and fungicides. It is quite a smelly concoction, which is why Vandergelder tells Cornelius, "And don't forget to put the lid on the sheep dip."

slickers . . . flannel knickers: A *slicker* is another name for a raincoat that is made of smooth and water-resistant material. Knickers are loose-fitting trousers gathered at the knee or calf. *Knickers* can also refer to a lady's undergarment. In the song "Put on Your Sunday Clothes," the chorus sings, "Get out your slickers, your flannel knickers!"

"Sweet Rosie O'Grady": A song from the 1890s that was a huge success on both sides of the Atlantic, the Irish-flavored "Sweet Rosie O'Grady" was written by Maude Nugent, though some believe it was written by her husband, William Jerome. Dolly tells Vandergelder that Miss Money will meet him at the Harmonia Gardens Restaurant, where she'll be "humming an old-fashioned tune, yes, Sweet Rosie O'Grady."

washing and blueing and shoeing the mare: Using a strong mixture of soap and blue coloring to wash clothes was known as blueing. An adult female horse is a mare. When Vandergelder sings, "washing and blueing and shoeing the mare" in the song "It Takes a Woman," he pictures his future wife cleaning and putting horseshoes on his livestock.

weaning the Guernsey: In the song "It Takes a Woman," Vandergelder sings, "It takes a female for setting the table / And weaning the Guernsey." The process of weaning means to gradually introduce an infant human or another mammal to an adult diet while withdrawing the supply of its mother's milk. A Guernsey is a breed of dairy cattle originally from the isle of Guernsey.

HOW TO SUCCEED IN BUSINESS WITHOUT REALLY TRYING

Libretto by Abe Burrows, Jack Weinstock, and Willie Gilbert, based on Shepherd Meade's book. Music and lyrics by Frank Loesser. Original Broadway production: October 14, 1961. 46th Street Theatre. 1,417 performances. Broadway revivals in 1995 and 2011.

This satire on business, ambition, and love took a very modern approach and was quite contemporary when it opened in 1961. Because both the libretto and the score are so firmly set in the early 1960s, most productions since have kept the original time and place. The action takes place in the sparkling new Park Avenue office building of the World Wide Wicket Company, Inc., in New York City. Some of the references are now obscure or have changed meaning over the years. As for "wickets," no one in the company seems to know exactly what they are.

HOW TO SUCCEED IN BUSINESS WITHOUT REALLY TRYING *The women in this very 1960s musical are far from liberated and are often the playthings of men, such as Hedy LaMarr (Maureen Arthur) and J. B. Biggley (Rudy Vallée).*
Photofest

Expressions, references, names:

blitz: To "blitz" something means to destroy it; in fact, any kind of heavy attack can be called a blitz. In the song "The Company Way," Mr. Twimble sings about playing golf with Mr. Bratt, and that "he blitzes me / In ev'ry game, like that!"

cigarette girl at the Copa, head: The Copacabana Club, or The Copa, was a New York City nightclub hot spot for several years, catering to the rich and famous. A cigarette girl was an attractive female who went from table to table selling cigarettes and cigars. Hedy says her last job was as "head cigarette girl at the Copa."

Elks . . . Shriners: In the song "Brotherhood of Man," Finch sings, "You may join the Elks, my friend, / And I may join the Shriners." The Elks Club (the Benevolent and Protective Order of Elks) and the Shriners, a fraternal order that is an auxiliary of the Masons, are civic groups known for their charitable causes.

FAO Schwarz: FAO Schwarz was the most famous toy shop in New York City, beginning operation in 1870. In the song "A Secretary Is Not a Toy," Bud Frump sings, "You'll find nothing like her / At FAO Schwarz!"

gavotte: A French peasant dance marked by raising rather than sliding the feet is known as a gavotte. The music for a gavotte is usually a rapid 4/4 time. In the song "A Secretary Is Not a Toy," the businessmen and secretaries sing, "The secretary y'got / Is definitely not / Employed to do a gavotte."

gin and vermouth: In the song "I Believe in You," Finch sings to (and about) himself in the mirror about his "Slam, bang, tang / Reminiscent of gin and vermouth." The main ingredients of a martini cocktail are gin (or vodka) and dry vermouth, usually garnished with an olive or a twist of lemon.

Helena Rubenstein . . . Betty Crocker: The cosmetics entrepreneur Helena Rubenstein (1872–1965) was the founder and eponym of Helena Rubinstein Incorporated cosmetics company, which made her one of the world's richest women. The fictional character of Betty Crocker is still used in advertising campaigns for food and recipes put out by General Mills. In the 1960s, she represented the ideal housewife. Hedy La Rue thinks Crocker is a real person, and tells Mr. Biggley, "I thought you were going to help me be a big businesswoman, like Helena Rubenstein or Betty Crocker."

Judith Anderson: The Australian-born Judith Anderson (1897–1992) was a renowned stage and film actress, mostly known for her severe, spinsterish villains. When Rosemary sees Biggley's secretary, the formidable Mrs. Jones, coming, she says to Finch, "Uh-oh. Here comes Judith Anderson."

Lionel on her caboose: The company Lionel LLC is an American firm that designs, builds, and imports toy trains and model railroad items. The *caboose*, the last car in a train, is a slang term for one's buttocks. Bub Frump, in the song "A Secretary Is Not a Toy," sings about a sexy secretary who has "the name Lionel on her caboose."

members of the Diners: Before credit cards, businessmen joined the Diners Club, which allowed members to pay for things using a card, settling their account at the end of each month. These charge cards were used mostly in restaurants when the Diners Club started in 1950, but eventually they were used for all kinds of purchases. In the song "Brotherhood of Man," Finch sings of men who "carry cards / As members of the Diners."

Metrecal: When Smitty is called out of her office by Rosemary, Smitty says, "Good God, Rosemary, you could at least have let me finish my Metrecal." Introduced in the early 1960s, Metrecal was the brand name for a variety of diet foods. Although Metrecal was not very tasty, it was popular with those trying to lose weight.

mimeograph: Before there were photocopiers, a mimeograph machine was the only way to duplicate documents. It worked by making copies from a stencil, but was never as sharp or clear as the original. When the ladies at the cocktail party find that they are all wearing the same "Paris Original" dress, they sing, "Suddenly I've gone / Into mimeograph."

New Rochelle . . . White Plains: Two of the closest and most desirable suburbs of New York City in the 1960s were New Rochelle and White Plains, New York. Rosemary fantasizes about marrying Finch and living in "New Rochelle . . . or maybe White Plains. No . . . New Rochelle."

Old Ivy . . . groundhog: In the college fight song "Grand Old Ivy," Biggley sings, "Grr-roundhog! Grr-roundhog! . . . Ree-rip! Rip! Rip the Chipmunk / Off the field!" There is no such school as Old Ivy College. The name suggests that it belongs to the Ivy League, a group of long-established colleges and universities in the eastern part of the nation having high academic and social prestige. Most colleges have a mascot that is celebrated in song. Old Ivy has the groundhog, and the rival college has the chipmunk, both silly choices for a sports mascot.

pad: A slang term in the 1960s for an apartment or any other living place was "pad." Secretaries used a "steno pad" to take down dictation. In the song "A Secretary Is Not a Toy," three secretaries sing, "Her pad is to write in / And not spend the night in."

particulars: An old way of referring to facts or details was to call them "particulars." The director of personnel, Mr. Bratt, says to Hedy, "If you will come in here with me, I'll get your particulars." She thinks he means her measurements, and says, "Thirty-nine, twenty-two, thirty-eight."

personnel: Any group of people employed in the same organization is called "personnel," and most companies used to have a personnel office. (Today the term *human resources* is more common.) In the musical, Mr. Bratt is head of personnel, and Smitty is his secretary.

popcorn stitch: In crocheting, a popcorn stitch is made with a number of loose stitches fastened in a common base so that the yarn puffs up, looking much like a piece of popcorn. Biggley proudly shows Finch his knitted golf club covers, saying, "I made the covers for those golf clubs. See? Popcorn stitch."

Stouffer's: Known today for its frozen foods, Stouffer's was first a series of restaurants going back to 1924. Smitty suggests to Rosemary and Finch, "There's a yummy Friday Special at Stouffer's."

three-button suit: Finch sings in the title song, "How to commute in a three-button suit." The fashion for businessmen in the 1960s was the three-button suit, meaning three buttons in the jacket. The style was to leave the middle button unfastened.

Tinker Toy: In 1914 the Tinkertoy Construction Set was introduced, designed to let children create structures with wooden rods and spools. The toy is still sold today. The businessmen and the secretaries sing, "A secretary is not . . . a Tinker Toy" at the end of the song "A Secretary Is Not a Toy."

Vassar: This small but renowned liberal arts college was for many years a women's college, not going coed until 1969. After Finch and Biggley sing a reprise of "Grand Old Ivy," two scrubwomen come to clean up. One wonders what college that song is from, and the other woman picks up Finch's knitting and suggests, "I'd say Vassar."

Wildroot Cream Oil: Wildroot Cream Oil was introduced during Prohibition because it contained no alcohol, using lanolin instead. The hair tonic was out-of-date by the 1960s, yet Bud Frump enters the executive washroom and asks, "Has anybody seen my Wildroot Cream Oil?"

win the pool: A slang term for a betting activity is a "pool." Each member in a group chooses a number or a score and puts money into the pool, the one with the correct answer taking all the winnings. Mostly used with sporting events, the pool in this musical is for the businessmen to guess the physical measurements for the sexy Hedy La Rue. When she tells Mr. Bratt, "Thirty-nine, twenty-two, thirty-eight," Bud Frump happily announces, "I win the pool!"

IN THE HEIGHTS

Libretto by Quiara Alegría Hudes. Music and lyrics by Lin-Manuel Miranda. Original Broadway production: March 9, 2008. Richard Rodgers Theatre. 1,184 performances.

Broadway's first truly Latinx musical, *In the Heights* is set in the present and takes place over a period of a few hot summer days in the Washington Heights neighborhood of Upper Manhattan. The George Washington Bridge is the local landmark and seems to overshadow the area. People from Puerto Rico, the Dominican Republic, Cuba, and other Latin lands fill the musical, so there is a great deal of Spanish, both spoken and sung. Yet *In the Heights* is very accessible to non-Spanish-speaking audience members. Here are some of the expressions and places to be found in the musical.

Expressions, references, names:

abuela: "Grandmother" in Spanish; the character of Abuela Claudia is not Usnavi's real grandmother, but, as he sings in the title song, "She practically raised me."

aguinaldo: In several Latin American countries, Christmas is celebrated with folk songs called *aguinaldo*. These are traditional Spanish Christmas carols, or villancicos, sung throughout the holiday season. In the song "Carnaval del Barrio," Daniela sings, "As we sang the aguinaldo, / The carnaval would begin to grow."

apagón: *Apagón* is the Spanish word for "blackout." When the lights go out, the Piragua Guy sings, "Vino el apagón," meaning, "The blackout has come."

A train: When Usnavi describes how to get to Washington Heights in the opening number, he says, "You take the A train / Even farther than Harlem to northern Manhattan and maintain. / Get off at 181st and take the escalator." Ever since 1941, New York City's subway line known as the A train has linked Midtown with Harlem and points north. The train became famous through the Billy Strayhorn song "Take the A Train," which became Duke Ellington's theme song.

bandera: The word in Spanish for a flag or national banner is *bandera*. In the song "Carnaval del Barrio," the company sings, "Alza la bandera," meaning "Lift the flag." Then the flags from the Dominican Republic, Puerto Rico, Mexico, and Cuba are raised and sung about.

barrio: The Spanish-speaking quarter or neighborhood in a city or town is called a *barrio* by the residents. In the opening song, Usnavi sings about "The Rosarios / They run the cab company, they struggle in the barrio."

Bennett Park: The highest point of land in New York City is Bennett Park, located in Fort Washington in northern Manhattan. In the song "When You're Home," Nina recalls, "Now back in high school when it darkened / You'd hang out in Bennett Park."

Big Pun: The Latino hip-hop artist Christopher Lee Rios (1971–2000) became a celebrated rap singer under the stage name Big Pun. In the finale of the musical, Usnavi sings, "The nights in Bennett Park blasting Big Pun tapes."

bodega: In the opening number, Usnavi sings, "Times are tough on this bodega." A small grocery store in a Latinx urban area specializing in ethnic groceries was called a bodega. Usnavi runs a bodega in Washington Heights. Today the word *bodega* can mean any small grocery store in an urban neighborhood.

the Bronx: The northernmost borough of New York City is the Bronx, the last stop going north on the NYC subway map. Once a lower- and middle-class neighborhood, today it has sections that are considered the poorest and most dangerous in the city. In the song "When You're Home," Usnavi sings, "I used to think the Bronx was a place in the sky."

calor: The Spanish word for "hot" or "heat" is *calor*. The Piragua Guy ends the song "Piragua" by singing, "Qué calor, Qué calor, Qué calor, Qué calo-o-or!"

Castle Garden: In the song "When You're Home," Nina asks Benny, "Are we going to Castle Garden?" The circular sandstone fort located in Battery Park at the southern tip of Manhattan has gone by different names over the years: Castle Garden, Castle Clinton, or Fort Clinton.

Chita Rivera: When Vanessa asks Sonny if Usnavi can dance, he replies, "Like a drunk Chita Rivera." The celebrated singer-dancer-actress Chita Rivera (born 1933) is one of the first Latinx performers to become a mainstay Broadway star.

Cole Porter: A distinguished and unique Broadway and Hollywood songwriter (1892–1964); among his many famous songs is "Too Darn Hot" from the musical *Kiss Me, Kate* (1948). Usnavi says about the heat, "Oh my God, it's gotten / Too darn hot, like my man Cole Porter said."

con leche: Café con leche is a coffee beverage common throughout Spain and Latin America. It consists of strong coffee mixed equally with scalded milk. Usnavi tells Claudia, "Abuela, my fridge broke. I got café but no con leche."

Dominican Republic: In the title song, Usnavi sings, "I emigrated from the single greatest / Little place in the Caribbean / Dominican Republic. / I love it." The Dominican Republic is the second-largest nation in the Antilles, with a population of approximately 10.8 million people. One third of the Dominicans live in the capital city of Santo Domingo.

East Secaucus: In the song "Carnaval del Barrio," Usnavi asks, "In fact, can we sing so loud and raucous / They can hear us across the bridge in East Secaucus?" East Secaucus is a New Jersey municipality located about thirteen miles from Washington Heights.

Frodo: Frodo Baggins is a fictional character in J. R. R. Tolkien's *The Lord of the Rings* and other writings. In the song "96,000," Benny sings, "Keep the bling, I want the brass ring like Frodo!" Later in the song, Usnavi sings to Benny, "As for you, Mr. Frodo of the Shire / Ninety-six g's ain't enough to retire."

GWB: Local slang for the George Washington Bridge in New York City. Opening in 1931, the GWB is a suspension bridge spanning the Hudson River, connecting the Washington Heights neighborhood in the borough of Manhattan in New York City to Fort Lee, New Jersey. In the song "Breathe," Nina sings, "Just me and the GWB asking, 'Gee, Nina what'll you be?'"

the Heights: Usnavi begins the musical singing, "Lights up on Washington Heights." Washington Heights is a neighborhood in the uppermost part of the New York City borough of Manhattan. Locals just refer to the area as the Heights. It is named for Fort Washington, a fortification constructed during the American Revolutionary War.

the hydrants are open: During sweltering summer heat in urban centers, the city's fire hydrants are uncapped and residents cool off in the pulsating water. In the finale, Carla sings, "The hydrants are open. Cool breezes blow."

inútil: The Spanish word *inútil* means "useless" or "unusable." Kevin remembers his past in the song "Inútil," singing, "Just like my father was before me: / Inútil. Useless."

La Vibora: The most populated barrio in Havana, Cuba, is La Vibora. In the song "Paciencia y Fé," Claudia sings, "It was hotter at home in La Víbora, / The Washington Heights of Havana."

LaGuardia: Fiorello La Guardia (1882–1947) was the very popular mayor of New York City from 1934 to 1945. In the song "Paciencia y Fé," Claudia fantasizes about the past when she sings, "I remember / Dancing with Mayor La Guardia."

linda . . . vieja . . . sucia . . . cabrona: At the hair salon, the women sing the song "No Me Diga" ("You Don't Say"), in which they alternate compliments with insults: "Gorgeous! . . . Linda! . . . Vieja! . . . Sucia! . . . Cabrona!" *Linda* means "beautiful" or "cute" in Spanish. *Vieja* is an old woman. *Sucia* refers to literally being dirty, but is often used to describe an immoral woman. *Cabrona* is a woman who has been treated badly by her male partner; the word is an insult to the woman.

9 train: In the New York subway system, the 9 train once operated during rush hour on the same tracks as the 1 train. This practice was discontinued in 2005, when the 9 train was eliminated. In the song "When You're Home," Usnavi sings, "And the 1-slash-9, climbed a dotted line to my place," then Benny reminds him, "There's no 9 train now."

No me diga: A popular Spanish colloquialism used to express disbelief; when someone shares gossip, saying "No me diga" means "You don't say." When Usnavi and Carla hear that Julio has been caught in bed with "José from the liquor store," they both exclaim, "No me diga!" The phrase is later used as the title of a song sung by Daniela, Carla, Vanessa, and Nina.

paciencia y fé: The Spanish for "patience and faith" is *paciencia y fé*, a familiar expression that goes with a wish. Claudia kisses the pair of lottery tickets, holds them up to the sky, and says, "Paciencia y fé." She later sings about her past in a song titled "Paciencia y Fé."

parcha . . . china . . . mamey: The Piragua Guy is selling different flavors of iced treats called piraguas. He sings, "Ice-cold piragua! Parcha. China. Cherry. Strawberry. Just for today I got mamey!" *Parcha* is a Puerto Rican term for "passion fruit." *China* is the name used in Puerto Rico and the Dominican Republic for "orange." *Mamey* comes from a tree found in

Cuba and Central America whose sweet fruit is used to make milkshakes and ice cream.

piragua: In the opening number of *In the Heights*, the Piragua Guy sings, "Ice cold piragua!" A popular summer treat from Puerto Rico is a piragua. Similar to a snow cone, shaved ice is piled up and topped with fruit-flavored syrup. Piraguas are usually sold from small pushcarts by vendors known as piragüeros.

Playa Rincón: Playa Rincón in the Dominican Republic has been rated as one of the world's most beautiful beaches. Legend has it that Christopher Columbus landed on Playa Rincón when he reached the Caribbean. In the song "Hundreds of Stories," Usnavi sings, "There's a little beach named Playa Rincón."

pregunta: The Spanish word for "question" is *pregunta*. In the song "96,000," Carla asks Daniela, "What would you do with ninety-six g's," and she replies, "Esa pregunta es tricky!"

Puerto Plata: On the northeast coast of the Dominican Republic is the province of Puerto Plata. In the song "96,000," Usnavi sings, "Just fly me down to Puerto Plata, I'll make the best of it."

Salud . . . L'Chaim!: In the number "The Club," Usnavi and Benny sing, "To killing the mood. Salud!" Later in the song, they sing, "To doing shots on a weekend. As long as you buy 'em, L'Chaim!" *Salud* is a Spanish word that literally means "health," and is used when one toasts before drinking. The Hebrew term for the same expression is *L'Chaim*, which literally means "to life."

Vega Alta: Located on the northern coast of the island of Puerto Rico. In the song "Carnaval del Barrio," Daniela sings, "When I was a little girl / Growing up in the hills of Vega Alta / My favorite time of year was Christmastime."

Wepa!: "Wepa!" is a Latin-American Spanish slang exclamation used to express joy, excitement, and congratulations. An equivalent phrase in English might be "That's awesome!" In the number "The Club," the company keeps singing, "Wepa, Vanessa!"

THE KING AND I

Libretto by Oscar Hammerstein, based on Margaret Landon's novel *Anna and the King of Siam*. Lyrics by Oscar Hammerstein. Music by Richard Rodgers. Original Broadway production: March 29, 1951. St. James Theatre. 1,246 performances. Broadway revivals in 1977, 1985, 1996, and 2015.

The first Rodgers and Hammerstein musical with no American characters, *The King and I* is based on real people, but the story has been dramatized with fictional touches. The chilling finale, in which the King dies and Anna is there to see the young Prince come to power, is fiction; the real Anna left Siam a year before the King died. But the clash of different cultures is true. Most of the action takes place inside the Royal Palace in Bangkok, and the story unfolds from 1862 to 1867. References are made to President Abraham Lincoln and to some British customs, but *The King and I* is really about an exotic Eastern world as seen through the eyes of a Westerner.

Expressions, references, names:

Anna Leonowens: The real Anna Leonowens (1831–1915) was a British travel writer and social activist as well as an educator. During her busy life, she lived in Australia, Singapore, the United States, Canada, and Germany. In 1862, Leonowens was hired by the court of King Mongkut of Siam as teacher and advisor, and she remained in Bangkok for five years. Around 1870, Leonowens wrote a memoir of her time as teacher, *The English Governess at the Siamese Court*. In 1944, author Margarest Landon took this work and, using interviews with Leonowens's descendants, created a more-fictionalized account, the novel *Anna and the King of Siam*. There is some controversy over just how much influence Leonowens had on Prince Chulalongkorn, who succeeded to the throne in 1868, a year after she left Siam.

Bangkok: As the ship enters the harbor, Captain Orton tells Louis, "See that cluster of lights jutting out into the river? That's it. That's Bangkok." The capital, and the most populous city in Siam, was Bangkok, which remains the capital of Thailand today. It is located on the delta of the Chao Phraya River, about twenty-five miles from the Gulf of Thailand.

THE KING AND I   *Both the King (Yul Brynner) and Miss Anna (Gertrude Lawrence) are based on real people, and their relationship was perhaps as complex as the one in the musical.*
Photofest

Burma: Before 1989, the current nation of Myanmar was called Burma. The country is located in the western portion of mainland Southeast Asia. The Burmese language has been known as Myanma since the thirteenth century. Siam and Burma share a long border, but in the nineteenth century, the two nations were not allies. When the King is told that Tuptim is a present from the Prince of Burma, he says, "Am I to trust a ruler of Burma? Am I to trust this present they send me, or is she a spy?"

"evil eye": In many cultures, there is a superstition known as the evil eye. It is the belief that a wicked or jealous look can bring harm to another person. When one of the wives sees Edward's monocle, she cries out, "Oh, evil eye! Evil eye!" and runs away.

gaols: The British spelling of "jail" is *gaol*, but it is pronounced the same. In the song "Shall I Tell You What I Think of You," Anna sings, "I am from a civilized land called Wales, / Where men like you are kept in county gaols."

King of Siam: The fourth monarch of Siam under the House of Chakri was King Mongkut (1804–1868), who ruled from 1851 to 1868. Before becoming king, Mongkut was a Buddhist monk. The first monarch to feel the pressures from the outside world, he embraced Western innovations and initiated the modernization of his country, both in technology and culture. In his nation, Mongkut is known as "The Father of Science and Technology." He is so revered in Thailand that the government thought *The King and I* was a disrespectful treatment of the King, and initially both the play and the movie were banned there.

King Simon of Legree: The main antagonist in the novel *Uncle Tom's Cabin* is Simon Legree, an extremely cruel plantation slave driver who subjects the workers to beatings in order to break their spirits. In Tuptim's theatrical presentation, "The Small House of Uncle Thomas," Simon is turned into a king, and the parallels between the novel and her own slave situation are made clear. Tuptim narrates the tale, saying, "House is in Kingdom of Kentucky, ruled by most wicked King in all America—Simon of Legree."

Kralahome: The prime minister in Siam was called the *Kralahome*. He was a very powerful advisor to the King and was sometimes a sorcerer as well. The Kralahome in *The King and I* is suspicious of Western influences and doesn't like "Missus Anna." In the first scene, Captain Orton warns her, "That man has power, and he can use it *for* you or *against* you."

O-hee-o: The Siamese characters in *The King and I* pronounce Ohio as "O-hee-o." During the presentation of "The Small House of Uncle Thomas," Tuptim says, "This King has sold her lover / To a faraway province of O-hee-o."

protectorate: When one nation is controlled and protected by another nation, it is defined as a *protectorate*. Lady Thaing tells Anna that "Greedy eyes are on Siam. They describe the King as a barbarian, and suggest making Siam a protectorate."

Siam: When Anna looks at Siam on the map, she tells the women and children, "For many years, before I came here, Siam was to me that little white spot. Now I have lived here for more than a year. I have met the people of Siam. And I am learning to understand them." Today's Thailand was historically known as Siam up until 1939. Siam was a monarchy in the nineteenth century and remains one today. The king of Thailand is the head of state and leader of the ruling Royal House of Chakri. In *The King and I*, the monarch was King Mongkut of this same House of Chakri.

Singapore: The Republic of Singapore is a sovereign island country and city-state in maritime Southeast Asia. During the nineteenth century, Singapore grew to become one of the busiest shipping and trading ports in the world. Anna and Louis have arrived in Bangkok on a ship from Singapore. Captain Orton tells them, "If you wish to stay on my ship and return to Singapore, ma'am . . ."

slavery: Anna offers Tuptim *Uncle Tom's Cabin* and tells the King, "A very wonderful book, Your Majesty. All about slavery . . ." The King says, "Ha! President Lingkong against slavery, no? Me, too. Slavery very bad thing." The slavery system in nineteenth-century Siam differed from that in the United States, with no racial distinction between slaves and free persons. Slavery in Thailand was sometimes a voluntary alternative for individuals to be rid of social and financial obligations. One could be punished for torturing slaves in Siam, and some slaves could buy their freedom. Some Western scholars and observers have expressed the opinion that Siamese slaves were treated better than English servants were. The real Anna Leonowens claimed that her conversations with Prince Chulalongkorn about human freedom, and her relating to him the story of *Uncle Tom's Cabin*, inspired him to abolish slavery forty years later.

twenty pounds . . . sterling: In the British monetary system, the pound is the main unit of sterling, and the currency itself may be referred to as pound sterling. One pound sterling is subdivided into 100 pence sterling. The King complains about how much Anna costs, saying, "Do not ever let me hear of not believing teacher, who I have bring here at great expense—twenty pounds—each month. Twenty English pounds! Sterling!"

Uncle Tom's Cabin: The full title of Harriet Beecher Stowe's 1852 book is *Uncle Tom's Cabin; or, Life Among the Lowly*. It was a powerful, widely read abolitionist novel, and its depiction of slavery in the American South was one of the factors that led to the Civil War. The real Anna Leonowens introduced the book to Prince Chulalongkorn, but in the musical, it is the slave Tuptim who adapts the novel into the theatrical presentation "The Small House of Uncle Thomas."

KISS ME, KATE

Libretto by Samuel and Bella Spewack, based on Shakespeare's *The Taming of the Shrew*. Music and lyrics by Cole Porter. Original Broadway production: December 30, 1948. Winter Garden Theatre. 1,077 performances. Broadway revivals in 1952, 1999, and 2019.

Kiss Me, Kate is unique in that it has two distinct plots: Shakespeare's comedy *The Taming of the Shrew* and the story of actors putting on a musical version of that play. The way the two plots overlap and support each other is one of the marvelous things about this classic musical. The setting is a Baltimore theater in 1948, and the libretto is filled with 1940s names and expressions. But the setting is also the Italian Renaissance, and there are many words and phrases that Shakespeare used in his play that might need explaining.

Expressions, references, names:

Aeschylus . . . Euripides: In the introduction to the song "Brush Up Your Shakespeare," the two gangsters sing about impressing "girls today in society," and suggest that "to win their hearts, one must quote with ease / Aeschylus and Euripides." The ancient Greek playwrights Aeschylus (c.

524–c. 455 BCE) and Euripides (480–406 BCE) are two of the giants of early tragedy.

Aly Kahn: Prince Ali Salman Aga Khan (1911–1960), known as Aly Khan, was a Pakistani diplomat and a wealthy playboy. When Lilli is showing off her ring from her fiancé, Fred asks if it is "Aly Kahn's emerald."

Araby: An expression for Arabia that goes back to the Middle Ages, "Araby" is often used in poetry. In the song "I Hate Men," Katharine sings about suitors who might bring "perfume from Araby."

Backa Bay: A prosperous residential and commercial area of Boston is the Back Bay. In the song "Always True to You in My Fashion," Lois sings of a Boston beau who was "middle class and notta Backa Bay."

Barter Theatre: The regional Barter Theatre in Abingdon, Virginia, opened in 1933, and to deal with the Depression, allowed patrons to buy theater tickets with crops or food they couldn't sell. When Lilli recalls the time she and Fred played a season at the Barter, she notes, "They gave you a ham," sarcastically commenting on his acting.

Big Frost . . . . Dick Tracy: *Dick Tracy* is an American comic strip by Chester Gould featuring Dick Tracy, a tough and intelligent police detective. One of the many villains who battled Dick Tracy in the comics was Big Frost. When Fred is imagining Lilli's future life with Harrison Howell, he says, "You'll discuss this and that, topics of the day. Will Big Frost escape Dick Tracy?"

bonny: In the Scottish jargon, *bonny* means physically attractive or appealing, and the use of the word spread throughout the British Isles. Petruchio flatters Katharine when he calls her "bonny Kate," until the end of the play, when he means it.

borscht: In Eastern and Central Europe, a soup made with beets, and usually served with sour cream, is called borscht. It is a working-class or peasant food and far from gourmet. When Lilli is on the phone to the president, Fred loudly asks, "Is it true, Mr. President, that you are serving borscht at the White House?"

breeches: In Elizabethan wear, breeches were the short pants that covered the hips and thighs and fit snugly at the knees. Bianca describes Petruchio's outfit at the wedding: "A pair of breeches thrice turned [inside out]!"

chattels: Chattels are any item of tangible movable (or immovable) property except real estate and things (such as buildings) connected with real property. After marrying Katharine, Petruchio declares, "She is my goods, my chattels, my horse, my ox, my ass, my anything!"

cheat: When an actor is speaking to another actor onstage, it is customary to "cheat" out; that is, turn slightly toward the audience when delivering the lines. In the first scene of *Kiss Me, Kate*, the director-star Fred Graham explains to Lois, the newcomer to the stage, how to "cheat" out.

Civic Repertory: Founded in 1926 by Eva Le Gallienne, the Civic Repertory Theatre was one of New York's most distinguished companies, offering new and classic plays at low admission prices. Fred tries to convince Harrison Howell that the two gangsters are graduates of "the Civic Repertory."

Copa canary: The Copacabana was a popular New York City nightclub that opened in 1940 and was known for its chorus line, the Copacabana Girls. Lilli refers to Lois, who used to sing at the Copacabana, as "that Copa canary."

coxcomb: A jester's cap adorned with a strip of red was called a coxcomb. The word later came to mean a conceited, foolish man. Katharine asks Petruchio of his family crest: "What is your crest? A coxcomb?"

crowns: A British coin worth five shillings was called a crown. Baptista offers Petruchio "thirty thousand crowns" as Katharine's dowry.

dinna ken: In the Scottish dialect, "dinna ken" means "don't know." The expression was soon found throughout the British Isles. In the song "I Hate Men," Katharine sings, "Their worth upon this earth I dinna ken."

dolt: In Middle English, a stupid person, or a dunce, was known as a "dolt." When Petruchio is locked out of his bedroom by Katharine, he says, "In faith, the woman has shot her bolt! She has performed while I did act the dolt!"

dowry: In arranged marriages, a dowry is property or money given by a bride to her husband on their wedding day. Petruchio asks Baptista, "What ʻdowry shall I have with her to wife?"

duomo: An Italian cathedral is often called a duomo. In the song "Where Is the Life That Late I Led?," Petruchio recalls a former lover named Momo who sold "those pictures of the scriptures in the duomo."

Equity: Actors' Equity Association (AEA), commonly referred to as Actors' Equity, or simply Equity, is an American labor union founded in 1913 representing those who work in live theatre. When Lilli threatens to leave the show mid-performance, Fred tells her, "I'll have you up on charges at Equity!"

farthingales: A farthingale is a hooped petticoat or circular pad of fabric around the hips, formerly worn under women's skirts to extend and shape them. Petruchio tells Katharine that when they return to her father's house, she will be dressed "with best silken coats, and caps and golden rings, with ruffs and cuffs and farthingales and things."

fie: A Middle English exclamation of disapproval or disgust. Bianca is outraged at Katharine's obedience to her husband and says, "Fie! What foolish duty call you this?"

Firenze: The Italian name for Florence is *Firenze*. In the song "Where Is the Life That Late I Led?," Petruchio recalls a former lover when he sings, "And in Firenze, where are you, Alice?"

Gable: The popular movie star Clark Gable (1901–1960) is mentioned in the song "Always True to You in My Fashion," when Lois sings, "Mr. Gable, I mean Clark / Wants me on his boat to park."

Gadzooks: An archaic expression of surprise or wonderment, "Gadzooks" is probably derived from "God's hooks," referring to the nails of the Crucifixion. Petruchio sings, "Gadzooks, completely mad you are" in the song "I've Come to Wive It Wealthily in Padua."

GI: Because uniforms had the initials *G.I.* marked on them, for "General Issue," American soldiers became known as GIs in foreign lands. In the song "Too Damn Hot," the men sing "A GI / For his cutie pie" is not interested in sex when the weather is "sizzling hot."

Mr. Gob: *Gob* is slang for a sailor. The men sing that "Mr. Gob" is not interested in sex when it's "Too Damn Hot."

going to whoops: A slang expression for making a mistake is "whoops." Fred uses it more as an illness or losing control when he says, "Now, Lilli, you're not going to whoops?" She later tells him, "I'm not nervous. I'm not going to whoops."

gone with the wind: In "Where Is the Life That Late I Led?," Petruchio sings, "Where is the fun I used to find? / Where has it gone? Gone with the wind." This is a reference to the popular 1936 novel and 1939 movie *Gone with the Wind*. But because Cole Porter uses the Elizabethan pronunciation of the word "wind" to rhyme to "find," the nod to *Gone with the Wind* is often missed.

Group: Founded in 1931, the Group Theatre was one of the most ambitious companies of stage craftsmen, known for demanding social drama. Fred tells Harrison Howell that the two gangsters are "two of the most promising graduates of the Group."

Harvard Club: The Harvard Club is a distinguished gathering place in Washington, DC, for alumni of Harvard University. Lois reminds Harrison Howell of when they met "in front of the Harvard Club."

***He Who Gets Slapped*:** A 1915 play by the Russian dramatist Leonid Andreyev has a title that translates as *He Who Gets Slapped*. After Lilli has slapped Fred onstage, he says to her backstage, "May I remind you, Miss Vanessi, the name of this piece is *The Taming of the Shrew*, not *He Who Gets Slapped*."

Homer: The legendary poet-author of *The Iliad* and *The Odyssey*, Homer (c. 850–701 BCE) is among the poets one may quote, according to the song "Brush Up Your Shakespeare," but he is not as effective as quoting from the Bard of Avon.

Hope Diamond: When Lilli is admiring the ring her fiancé gave her, Fred asks her sarcastically, "What is it? The Hope Diamond?" The Hope

Diamond is a large blue diamond that was mined in India in the seventeenth century and has been world-famous ever since. Today the diamond is on display at the Smithsonian in Washington, DC.

jade: Middle English slang for a broken-down or worthless horse is a jade. Katharine insults Petruchio when she says, "No such jade as bear you."

jerkin: A sleeveless jacket in Elizabethan wear was called a jerkin. After the wedding ceremony, Bianca laughs at what Petruchio wore to the church: "And in such garb! An old jerkin!"

Jungfrau: Translated literally as "young maiden," the Jungfrau is one of the tallest mountains in the Swiss Alps. In the song "Wunderbar," Fred sings, "gazing down on the Jungfrau," which is ridiculous, since there is nothing nearby that is taller.

Kinsey Report: In 1948, a book by Alfred Kinsey and others titled *Sexual Behavior in the Human Male* was the talk of the town and was referred to as the "Kinsey Report." In the song "Too Darn Hot," Paul and the guys sing, "According to the Kinsey Report / ev'ry average man" prefers to make love when it's cool rather than when it is too hot.

kowtow: To act in an excessively subservient manner to someone or something is to "kowtow" to them. The two gangsters sing in "Brush Up Your Shakespeare" how women "will all kowtow" to you if you quote the Bard to them.

Lassie: In the song "I Hate Men," Katharine sings that it is ridiculous to admire a man just because "He may have hair upon his chest, but sister, so has Lassie!" Lassie is a fictional female Rough Collie dog who has appeared in radio, television, film, toys, comic books, animated series, juvenile novels, and other media.

L. B. Mayer: Louis B. Mayer (1884–1957) was a famous film producer and co-founder of Metro-Goldwyn-Mayer studios (MGM), in 1924. In the song "We Open in Venice," Lilli sings, "Not stars like L. B. Mayer's are we."

Louella Parsons: When Fred inquires what Lilli plans to do with Harrison Howell, she replies, "You are not Louella Parsons and I don't care to discuss my private life with you." Louella Parsons (1881–1972) was an American movie gossip columnist who was very powerful because she was retained by publishing tycoon William Randolph Hearst.

Max Factor Number Two: After Lilli slaps Fred on the face, he looks to see if there is blood but realizes it is "Max Factor Number Two." Max Factor & Company is a line of cosmetics founded in 1909 that makes a variety of colors of makeup for actors.

mutton: A low-grade cut of meat that comes from a sheep, mutton was a staple of the less-wealthy Elizabethans. Petruchio complains to his servants about the mutton: "'Tis burnt, and so is all the meat!"

odds-bodkins: An antiquated phrase expressing surprise, "odds-bodkins" might be a euphemism for "God's body!" When the two gangsters sing "Brush Up Your Shakespeare," they declare, "Thinks thou / Odds-bodkins."

palazzo: The Italian for any palatial building or mansion is *palazzo*. In the song "Where Is the Life That Late I Led?," Petruchio wonders if his old flame Venetia is still "drinkin' in her stinkin' pink palazzo."

pate: A Middle English term for one's head; Katharine sings to Petruchio in the title song, "I'll crack your pate."

patrician: An archaic term for an aristocrat or nobleman, going back to the Roman word. In the song "Tom, Dick, or Harry," Hortensio sings, "I come to thee a thoroughbred patrician."

pitch some woo: The slang for sweet-talking, particularly to a loved one; Paul sings, "I'd like to pitch some woo with my baby tonight" in the song "Too Darn Hot."

Pitti Palace: A famous mansion in Florence is the Pitti Palace, an Early Renaissance palazzo begun in 1440. In the song "Where Is the Life That Late I Led?," Petruchio recalls an old love named Alice who lived "in [her] pretty, itty-bitty Pitti palace."

Pompeii: Pompeii was the ancient Roman city southeast of Naples that was one of four cities buried by an eruption of Mount Vesuvius in AD 79.

Petruchio sings of "the scandalous doin's in the ruins of Pompeii" in the song "Where Is the Life That Late I Led?"

Ponte Vecchio: The famous bridge across the Arno River in Florence is the Ponte Vecchio, or "old bridge." In the song "Where Is the Life That Late I Led?," Petruchio wonders if his old love Becky was still "cruising that amusing Ponte Vecchio."

porringer: When inspecting Katharine's new clothes, Petruchio complains to the haberdasher about the cap looking like "it was molded on a porringer." A porringer is a small bowl, typically with a handle, used for soup, stew, or similar dishes.

Prince of Potsdam: One of the most popular operettas at the turn of the twentieth century was called *The Prince of Pilsen* (1903), which was revived many times. Fred recalls, "that flop revival of the *Prince of Potsdam*," a nod to the famous operetta.

quaff carouses: The Middle English term to drink or imbibe alcohol with relish is to "quaff carouses." When Petruchio is determined to woo Katharine, Gremio says, "Let's quaff carouses to this gentleman!"

Ritz: The name of the luxury hotels founded by César Ritz (1850–1918), the Ritz in various cities was the peak of ostentatious display. In the song "Always True to You in My Fashion," Lois sings about Mr. Fritz, who "often moved me to the Ritz."

Sanka: Sanka is a brand of instant decaffeinated coffee, sold around the world, and was one of the earliest decaffeinated varieties. When Bill sings the song "Bianca" to Lois, he says, "I would gladly give up / Coffee for Sanka, / Even Sanka, Bianca."

Sarah Bernhardt: The world-renowned French actress Sarah Bernhardt (1844–1923) was known on both sides of the Atlantic in the late nineteenth and early twentieth centuries. Later the name was used to denote any actress, usually in a sarcastic manner. Bill Calhoun teases Lois when he greets her with, "Hiya, Sarah Bernhardt!"

Schlitz: The Joseph Schlitz Brewing Company produced a popular American brew, "the beer that made Milwaukee famous." By 1902, Schlitz was the largest beer producer in the nation. When singing about her past loves in "Always True to You in My Fashion," Lois recalls, "Mr. Fritz is full of Schlitz and full of play."

Shelley . . . Keats . . . Pope: In the introduction to "Brush Up Your Shakespeare," the two gangsters sing, "Unless you know Shelley and Keats and Pope, / Dainty debbies will call you a dope." Percy Bysshe Shelley (1792–1822), John Keats (1795–1821), and Alexander Pope (1688–1744) were among the foremost English Romantic poets.

Shuberty: The Shubert brothers were theatrical managers and producers of the largest theater empire in the twentieth century. In "Where Is the Life That Late I Led?," Petruchio sings that his pursuit of girls was "like a show that's typically Shuberty" in order to rhyme with "puberty."

Sophocles . . . Sappho: In their introduction to the song "Brush Up Your Shakespeare," the two gangsters suggest that one ought to quote "Sophocles—also, Sappho-Ho." The playwright Sophocles (c. 497–405 BCE) is one of three ancient Greek tragedians whose plays have survived. Sappho (c. 630–c. 570 BCE) was an Archaic Greek who lived on the island of Lesbos and is known for her lyric poetry. Because of the strong affection for women found in the poems, the word *Sappho* has been associated with female homosexuality, and the word *lesbian* comes from her native island.

sup: An archaic word meaning to eat and drink during the evening meal; in the song "Too Darn Hot," Paul sings, "I'd like to sup with my baby tonight."

Svengali: In George du Maurier's 1894 novel *Trilby*, a young girl falls under the spell of Svengali, a villainous musician and hypnotist. The name later was used for any person who manipulates or exerts excessive control over another. Lilli tells Fred, "You're not going to hypnotize me, Svengali."

Theatre Guild: The Theatre Guild was a prestigious theatrical society founded in 1918 and the home of high-class, distinguished productions. In the song "We Open in Venice," Fred sings, "No Theatre Guild attraction are we." Later he tries to convince Harrison Howell that the two gangsters are graduates of "the Guild Theatre, Inc."

thine: The archaic form of "yours," it is also used for the thing or things belonging to or associated with "thee." Petruchio sings to Katharine, "Were thine that special face."

thou: The word for "you" or "yours" in Middle English; Shakespeare uses "thou" throughout his works, but in *Kiss Me, Kate*, the word pops up backstage as well, as when Lilli calls Fred "Thou jerk!"

thy: The archaic or dialect form of "your" in poetic works; Katharine tells Petruchio, "Thy message is not for me."

trousseau: The personal possessions that a bride brings to a marriage—usually including clothes, accessories, and household linens and wares—is called a trousseau. Harrison Howell tells Lilli, "That'll give you just enough time to assemble a trousseau."

Vesuvius: Mount Vesuvius is the volcanic mountain in Italy that erupted in AD 79 and destroyed the Roman cities of Pompeii, Herculaneum, Oplontis, and Stabiae. Petruchio sings, "If she fume like Vesuvius" in the song "I've Come to Wive It Wealthily in Padua."

virago: A domineering, violent, or bad-tempered woman is sometimes called this Italian word. In the song "Where Is the Life That Late I Led?," Petruchio calls his ex-lover Fedora a "wild virago."

Waldorf: The Manhattan luxury hotel Waldorf Astoria is often simply called "the Waldorf." In making his wedding plans on the phone, Harrison Howell says, "Wedding reception at the Waldorf."

Washington Heights dream: Washington Heights is a neighborhood in the uppermost part of Manhattan named for the colonial Fort Washington. In the song "Brush Up Your Shakespeare," the two gangsters sing, "If your goil [girl] is a Washington Heights dream," one should quote from *A Midsummer Night's Dream*.

Woolworth's: A popular five-and-dime store chain that sold a variety of items and offered reasonably priced food at their lunch counter. Fred recalled how in their early days of marriage, he got a job "demonstrating shaving soap in Woolworth's."

Wunderbar: *Wunderbar* is the German word for "wonderful." Fred and Lilli recall an operetta they performed in once, and sing a mock love duet titled "Wunderbar" from the show. It is one of Porter's very few waltzes.

Zed: An expression for the letter *Z* that goes back to the twelfth century, "Zed" is still used in Europe today. In the song "I Hate Men," Katharine sings about the male species, noting, "Oh, I hate men / From all I've read, alone in bed, from A to Zed, about 'em."

"Zounds!": A mild oath or exclamation in Middle English, "zounds" is most likely a euphemism for "God's wounds!" Petruchio sings, "Zounds, a loathsome lad you are" in the song "I've Come to Wive It Wealthily in Padua."

LITTLE SHOP OF HORRORS

Libretto by Howard Ashman, based on the screenplay by Charles Griffith. Lyrics by Howard Ashman. Music by Alan Menken. Original Off-Broadway production: May 6, 1982. WPA Theatre. 2,209 performances. Broadway revival in 2003.

Roger Corman's 1960 cult film *Little Shop of Horrors* may not have been likely material for a musical, even an Off-Broadway musical, but Howard Ashman's libretto and lyrics struck the right tone, mixing comedy and horror so masterfully. Just as Alan Menken's music echoes the sound of the early 1960s, so, too, do the script and lyrics pastiche the vernacular of that time period. There are many references to products, names, and television shows of the 1950s and 1960s, already considered nostalgic when *Little Shop of Horrors* opened in 1982.

Expressions, references, names:

Betty Crocker . . . Donna Reed: In the song "Somewhere That's Green," Audrey sings, "I cook like Betty Crocker / And I look like Donna Reed." Two icons of the white, middle-class American home were Betty Crocker and Donna Reed. Betty Crocker was a fictional character created by General Mills in 1936 as a symbol of the ideal housewife and mother. She graced the boxes of cake mixes and other products and, for a time, even had an advice column in the newspapers and a television show, *Betty Crocker Star Matinee*. Donna Reed (1921–1986) was a real person, an

American actress with forty films to her credit. But she is most remembered as the ideal wife and mother in the film *It's a Wonderful Life* (1946), and in the TV series *The Donna Reed Show*, which ran from 1958 to 1966.

DDS: A certified doctor of dental surgery puts the initials "DDS" after his or her name. Audrey introduces Orin to Seymour, saying, "This is my boyfriend, Orin Scrivello," then adds, "DDS."

December Bride . . . Father Knows Best . . . Howdy Doody: In the song "Somewhere That's Green," Audrey sings, "I'm his December Bride / He's Father, he knows best / Our kids watch Howdy Doody." She is referring to three very popular television shows of the 1950s. *December Bride* was a CBS sitcom about a spry widow, played by Spring Byington, ever hopeful of finding a "December" romance. The show started out as a radio program, and then was on TV from 1954 to 1959. *Father Knows Best* was a domestic series about the wholesome, middle-class Anderson family. It also began as a radio program, and was on television from 1954 to 1960. *The Howdy Doody Show* was a very popular children's program with a Western theme, hosted by Buffalo Bob and featuring a goofy cowboy puppet named Howdy Doody. In the studio, several children sat in a section that was called the "Peanut Gallery," an expression that has remained a popular way to refer to a bunch of kids. It ran from 1947 to 1960 on NBC-TV.

Edgar Allan Poe: The master of mystery and the macabre, fiction writer Edgar Allan Poe (1809–1849) was an early American author whose works have been dramatized many times. Seymour sings, "Something out of Edgar Allan Poe / Has happened!" in the song "Ya Never Know."

FTD: In the song "Mushnik and Son," Mushnik sings, "What business we'll do for FTD." Originally known as Florists' Telegraph Delivery, this large network of florists in the United States and Canada allowed customers to send flowers to far-flung locations using telegraph messages. Today, orders are done online.

George Washington Carver: The most prominent Black scientist of the early twentieth century, George Washington Carver (c. 1864–1943) was an agricultural scientist and inventor who promoted methods such as crop rotation of cotton to prevent soil depletion. In the musical, the Urchins urge Audrey to consider Seymour for a boyfriend, saying he is "A little botanical genius . . . And [we] ain't talkin' about George Washington Carver."

Howard Johnson's: The largest restaurant chain in the United States during the 1960s and 1970s, Howard Johnson's began in 1925 and eventually had over one thousand restaurants known for their reasonably priced meals. While the restaurants are gone, a chain of hotels survives. Seymour tells Audrey, "I don't even know what it's like to fly in an airplane . . . Or eat a fancy dinner at Howard Johnson's."

Hula Hoops: In 1958, the Wham-O toy company introduced the plastic Hula Hoop, and sales skyrocketed. In the musical, the promoter Martin wants to take cuttings of the plant, telling Seymour, "Imagine, boy, Audrey Two's everywhere. Why, with the right advertising, this can be bigger than Hula Hoops."

ironing machine: Mechanical machines used for ironing different fabrics had been in use commercially for decades, but in the early 1960s home versions of an ironing machine were a fad that didn't last long. In the song "Somewhere That's Green," Audrey sings, "A washer and a dryer and / An ironing machine."

Jack Paar . . . Hedy Lamarr: In the song "Feed Me," the Plant sings, "Would you like a Cadillac car? / Or a guest shot on Jack Paar? / How about a date with Hedy Lamarr?" Jack Paar (1918–2004) was an American talk show host on radio and then television. He became host of *The Tonight Show* in 1957, and quickly grew very popular with viewers. Hedy Lamarr (1914–2000) was an Austrian-born American film actress, considered one of the great beauties of the silver screen. Years later it was learned that Lamarr was also an astute inventor.

James Dean: A cultural icon of teenage angst, the film actor James Dean (1931–1955) made only three films before his premature death, but he still remains a movie idol and a symbol of social estrangement. In the song "Feed Me," Seymour wishes for a "Harley machine" and wants to go "toolin' around like I was James Dean."

juniah: In the song "Mushnik and Son," Seymour sings, "Thanks to you, sweet petunia / Mushnik's takin' . . . a juniah." This is not a Yiddish word but just Seymour's pronunciation of the word "junior."

laissez-faire: The French phrase *laissez-faire* literally means "allow to do." The phrase is used internationally for the attitude or policy of letting things take their own course without interference. In the song "Now (It's Just the Gas)," Seymour looks at Orin suffocating and sings, "I can finish him with simple / laissez-faire."

Leader of the Plaque: A number-one pop hit in 1964 for the American girl group the Shangri-Las was "Leader of the Pack," written by George "Shadow" Morton, Jeff Barry, and Ellie Greenwich. It told of a teenage tragedy involving motorcycles. Ronette plays off of the popular song title when she says about the dentist Orin, "Here he is, girls, the Leader of the Plaque."

Levittown: After World War II, there was a housing shortage, and a village in central Long Island called Levittown was created, with hundreds of modestly priced "cookie-cutter" houses. There were also Levittowns in New Jersey, Pennsylvania, and Puerto Rico. Audrey dreams of a life in the suburbs, saying, "Not fancy like Levittown."

***Life* magazine:** Published weekly from 1883 to 1972 and monthly from 1978 until 2000, *Life* magazine was a wide-ranging, general-interest magazine known for its photography. In the song "The Meek Shall Inherit," Mrs. Luce sings to Seymour, "We want your face on the cover / Of the December third issue of *Life*. / Yes, the front of *Life* magazine."

Lucy: One of the most-watched TV sitcoms of all time was *I Love Lucy*, which ran on CBS from 1951 to 1957. The farcical domestic series starred Lucille Ball; her husband, Desi Arnaz; Vivian Vance; and William Frawley. In the song "Somewhere That's Green," Audrey sings, "We snuggle watching Lucy / On our big, enormous / Twelve-inch screen."

Marquis de Sade: The French revolutionary politician, philosopher, and writer, the Marquis de Sade (1740–1814) was famous for his literary works dealing with blatant sexuality. The words *sadism* and *sadist* come from the Marquis' sensual-painful fiction. The Urchins say about the dentist Orin, "Who wants their teeth done by the Marquis de Sade?"

matchbox: A small and often cheaply built house that looks like all the others in the neighborhood has been called a matchbox, or a matchbox house. The expression arose with the building of so many suburbs (such as

Levittown) after World War II. In the song "Somewhere That's Green," Audrey sings, "A matchbox of our own."

mensch: The Yiddish expression for a good person, "mensch" is usually used to indicate the type of person one would hope to have for a trusted friend or colleague. In the song "Mushnik and Son," Mushnik sings to Seymour, "I used to think you left a stench / But now I see that you're a mensch."

Pine-Sol: In the song "Somewhere That's Green," Audrey sings, "In the Pine-Sol-scented air, / Somewhere that's green." In 1929, the Clorox Company introduced a household cleaning product called Pine-Sol, which contained pine oil to help clean grease and heavy soil stains. Today Pine-Sol doesn't use pine oil, as it's too expensive.

Ritz: The Ritz Hotels in London and Paris are still among the world's most prestigious hotels. The name *Ritz* has become so associated with luxury and elegance that the word *ritzy* is used to denote something that is ostentatiously stylish, fancy, or fashionable. In the song "Feed Me," the Plant sings, "How's about a room at the Ritz?"

shiner: An expression for a black eye, or any dark bruise near the eye, is a shiner. Audrey is often physically abused by her boyfriend, Orin, and has the facial marks to prove it. When she comes in to work, Mushnik asks her, "Andrey, where'd you get that shiner?"

Skid Row: Originally "skid row" was a slang term meaning the area of shacks along the side of the railroad tracks outside of town. Today Skid Row is the name given to an area of town that houses the city's poorest or most disreputable people. Mushnik says to Audrey and Seymour, "Not that we had a customer. Who has customers when you run a flower shop on Skid Row?"

Sominex: A popular brand of the drug diphenhydramine hydrochloride, Sominex was used as a sleep aid in the 1950s and 1960s. In the song "Sominex/Suppertime," Audrey sings, "I couldn't sleep / I took a Sominex."

status quo: Latin for "state in which," *status quo* has been used in English since the early 1800s to mean the existing state of affairs, especially regarding social or political issues. In the song "Skid Row (Downtown)," Seymour sings, "Downtown / Where depression's jes' status quo!"

sturm and drang: Referencing a literary and artistic movement in Germany in the late eighteenth century, *Sturm und Drang* literally means "storm and stress." The expression is used internationally for strife and frustration. In the title song, Chiffon sings, "Shang-a-lang / Feel the sturm and drang / In the air!"

terrazzo: A composite flooring material consisting of chips of marble or granite set in concrete and polished to give a smooth surface; in the song "Skid Row (Downtown)," the Urchins sing, "Uptown you cater to a million whores / You disinfect terrazzo on their bathroom floors."

urchins . . . ragamuffins: A mischievous young person, especially one who is poorly or raggedly dressed, can be called an urchin or a ragamuffin. Mushnik says to Chiffon, Ronette, and Crystal, "You! Urchins! Off the stoop! It ain't bad enough I got winos permanently decorating the storefront? I need three worthless ragamuffins to complete the picture?"

Vitalis: A popular hair tonic for men in the 1950s and 1960s, Vitalis was used in large quantities to get the "greased" look. Crystal says to Orin, "Why don't you get lost, Vitalis-brains?"

Wolfman: Robert Weston Smith (1938–1995) was an American disc jockey who became famous as Wolfman Jack. His distinctive gravelly voice was heard on national radio and in a handful of films. After Seymour is interviewed on the radio, Chiffon tells him, "You sounded sexier than the Wolfman!"

MAME

Libretto by Jerome Lawrence and Robert E. Lee, based on their play *Auntie Mame* and the book by Patrick Dennis. Music and lyrics by Jerry Herman. Original Broadway production: May 24, 1966. Winter Garden Theatre. 1,508 performances. Broadway revival in 1983.

The misadventures of Auntie Mame are spread across three decades, from the Roaring Twenties to the jitterbugging 1940s, and various locations, from Manhattan to the Deep South. Because Mame Dennis gets involved

MAME   *The fun-loving Mame Dennis (Angela Lansbury, center) is right at home in the Roaring Twenties, but she keeps kicking up her heels in the 1930s and 1940s.*
Photofest

in show business, the art world, and other cultural activities, there is a lot of name-dropping and references to people in the news. There are also many literary references and names ranging from mythology to recent history. Young Patrick has been given a notebook by his auntie Mame in which he writes down words and phrases that he doesn't know; some are not well-known today. *Mame* is rich with period details that help to re-create the world of 1928 to 1946 onstage.

Expressions, references, names:

Algonquin: The bar-lounge of the Algonquin Hotel on West 44th Street was famous in the 1920s as a gathering place for Manhattan's literary and theatrical celebrities. Mame must drop in on the group on occasion, for she tells one of her party guests, "See you Tuesday at the Algonquin."

alligator pear: A slang term for an avocado, so dubbed because of its coarse texture and dark skin. The Southern matriarch Mother Burnside can't understand why Beauregard "would go hankerin' after some Northern alligator pear," meaning Mame.

Amos 'n' Andy: A famous radio show comedy in the 1930s and 1940s featuring two Black friends, *Amos 'n' Andy* was voiced by white actors using a thick "Negro" dialect that audiences today find offensive. Mame and Vera compare their friendship to that of Amos 'n' Andy in the song "Bosom Buddies."

antediluvian: Near the end of the musical, Mame says to her great-nephew Peter, "I hope you won't be as antediluvian as your father." Literally meaning "before the flood," *antediluvian* can refer to a time before the biblical Noah's flood, or to any person or custom that is very old and out-of-date.

avant-garde: Literally translated from the French as "advance guard," the term *avant-garde* refers to anything new and unusual or experimental, particularly in the arts. When the decorator Pegeen hangs a mobile in Mame's apartment, Patrick complains, "That's pretty avant-garde for the Upsons."

Bears and Bulls: Stock market terms for the way the prices of stock vary are "bear" and "bull." A bull market is when the buyers are optimistic about the rise in the prices of the shares. A bear market is when the buyers are pessimistic about the rise in the prices of the shares, and the sellers outnumber the buyers in the market. Vera doesn't understand the economics, and when the stock market crashes in 1929, she says, "The Bears have done something terrible to the Bulls—or vice versa."

Beekman Place: Beekman Place is a small street located in the Turtle Bay neighborhood on the East Side of Manhattan. It is an out-of-the-way neighborhood and as unconventional as Mame Dennis, who lives there.

Bohemian Delilah: A Bohemian is a socially unconventional person, especially one who is involved in the arts. In the Bible, Delilah is the woman who betrayed Samson to the Philistines by cutting his hair and causing him to lose his strength. The name *Delilah* has come to mean any seductive female. The banker Mr. Babcock calls Mame a "deceitful Bohemian Delilah" because of her wild, carefree lifestyle.

bootlegger: During Prohibition, a person who made, distributed, or sold alcohol illegally was called a bootlegger. Agnes says that there were only thirteen cocktail parties over the past two weeks because "the bootlegger was sick that day."

bully: While today a bully is a person who intimidates or harms someone vulnerable, the term *bully* was coined by Theodore Roosevelt at the turn of the twentieth century as an admirable fellow who is hardy and strong. The conservative banker Mr. Babcock is so out-of-date that he is still quoting Roosevelt, telling young Patrick, "Well, you look like a bully little chap."

cakewalk: In the song "Mame," the chorus of Southerners sing, "You brought the cakewalk back into style!" The cakewalk is a strutting dance for couples that was popularized by minstrel shows in the nineteenth century and was still popular in the twentieth century. The dance got its name because originally it was a Black dance contest with a cake as the prize.

Charlotte Brontë: The British author Charlotte Brontë (1816–1855) wrote *Jane Eyre* (1847) and other novels. Patrick teases Mame when she decides to write her memoirs, calling her Charlotte Brontë.

chemise: In the song "The Man in the Moon," Vera sings, "That isn't a nightgown, / It's a Saturn [satin] chemise." A popular dress in the 1920s, a chemise (French for "shirt") hung straight from the shoulders and gave the figure a uniform shape. It later came to mean a woman's loose-fitting undergarment or nightdress, typically made of silk or satin, with a lace trim.

crinoline: The stiffened or hooped petticoat worn to make a long skirt stand out, the crinoline was particularly popular in Southern women's dresses. In the song "Mame," the male chorus sings of "a beautiful bevy / Of crinolined ladies."

Damon and Pythias: In ancient times, the legendary fourth-century Syracusan Damon risked his life to save his friend Pythias. Vera refers to her friendship with Mame, asking, "What's the female equivalent to Damon and Pythias?"

Daphnis and Chloe: The poet Daphnis in Greek mythology falls in love with the maiden Chloe, and both undergo terrible hardships before they are finally united. Mame says her friendship with Vera is like Daphnis and Chloe, but Vera says, "I think one of 'em was a fella."

Dictaphone: A small recording device used to take down speech for transcription at a later time; Mr. Lindsay Woolsey says he bought Mame a Dictaphone to use to write her memoirs.

Flaubert . . . *Madame Bovary*: The French writer Gustave Flaubert (1821–1880) wrote the novel *Madame Bovary* (1857), which was about a bored wife in a small provincial French village who was unfaithful to her husband and met a tragic end. When Vera teases Mame about how slow she is in writing her memoirs, Mame replies, "Flaubert spent thirteen years on *Madame Bovary*!"

Gertrude Stein . . . Alice B. Toklas: In the song "Bosom Buddies," Vera refers to Gertrude Stein and Alice B. Toklas when naming famous pairs that compare to her friendship with Mame. The influential American writer Gertrude Stein (1874–1946) lived in Paris during the 1920s and 1930s with her companion and secretary, Alice B. Toklas (1877–1967), patronizing young and brilliant writers and artists.

the gin's in the bathtub: During Prohibition (1920–1933), when alcohol was outlawed, many people made various spirits on their own, the bathtub being a convenient receptacle for concocting homemade recipes. In the first scene, Mame says, "The gin's in the bathtub" as a reason to celebrate with the song "It's Today!"

Hotsy Totsy Club: There was a speakeasy bar on Broadway that was named the Hotsy Totsy Club. It was a notorious hangout for Legs Diamond and other gangsters and bootleggers. Young Patrick hears the club mentioned at a cocktail party and tells Mame that he has added it to his notebook.

Jezebel: A decadent Phoenician princess who lived in the ninth century BCE, the term *Jezebel* later referred to any shameless or immoral woman. Mr. Babcock tells Mame, "You're no more fit to raise a child than Jezebel."

jitterbuggin' and lindy hoppin': In the song "That's How Young I Feel," Mame sings about "lindy hoppin' and jitterbuggin'." The jitterbug was a fast dance popular in the 1940s, performed chiefly to swing music. The lindy hop is a wild, athletic American dance that came out of Harlem and was danced to jazz and swing music in the first half of the twentieth century.

Jumpin' Jehovah: A mild oath or cry of surprise going back to 1866 is "Jumpin' Jehoshaphat!" From this came the expression "Jumpin' Jehovah." In the song "The Man in the Moon," Vera sings, "The cow that jumped ovah / Cried, 'Jumpin' Jehovah.' "

Karl Marx: The German philosopher, political theorist, and socialist revolutionary Karl Marx (1818–1883) is best known as the author of the Communist manifesto *Das Kapital.* Young Patrick heard Marx's name at one of Mame's parties and tells her he put it in his notebook.

knickers: A short form of "knickerbockers," the short pants gathered at the knee that boys wore during the first decades of the twentieth century were called knickers. Mr. Babcock tells young Patrick to be ready to go off to boarding school in the morning, adding, "And, kid, you better be wearing knickers!"

Mr. Lindbergh: When young Patrick wakes Mame with his toy airplane, Mame tells him, "I just didn't expect Mr. Lindbergh to land on my bed before breakfast." She is referring to the American aviator Charles A. Lindbergh (1902–1974), who made his famous nonstop flight from New York City to Paris in 1927.

mint julep: A favorite mixed drink in the South, a mint julep consists of bourbon, crushed ice, sugar, and fresh mint, typically served in a tall, frosted glass. In the song "Mame," the Southerners sing, "You give my old mint julep a kick . . . Mame!"

Mother Cabrini . . . Lent: When Mame accuses Vera Charles of having no motherly instincts, Vera claims (probably falsely) that "once in Pittsburgh I played Mother Cabrini. During Lent." The first American to be canonized as a saint by the Roman Catholic Church was Frances Xavier Cabrini (1850–1917), a missionary nun called Mother Cabrini. Lent is the period from Ash Wednesday to Easter, as observed by several Christian denominations. It is a time of penitence and fasting; many theaters used to close during Lent.

No Man's Land: During World War I, the unoccupied and deadly area between opposing armies was called No Man's Land. When Mame declares that fighting to keep Patrick in her care will be "war," Vera climbs into bed and says, "If you need any help, I'll be right here in No Man's Land."

on the horn: Antiquated slang for the telephone; when a call comes in for Patrick, Junior Babcock tells him, "Hey, Dennis. On the horn. Long distance. It's the overseas operator."

Pago Pago: The chief port of American Samoa is Pago Pago on Tutuila Island. Pago Pago is one of the exotic locales Mame and Beauregard visit on their honeymoon.

peckin' and bunny huggin': In the song "That's How Young I Feel," Mame sings, "I feel like peckin' and bunny huggin'." Antiquated slang for kissing is "pecking." The dance known as the bunny hug was a favorite of young people in the early decades of the twentieth century. It was very physical and was usually danced to ragtime music.

Peg o' My Heart . . . **Lady Macbeth:** In the song "Bosom Buddies," Mame insults her actress friend Vera by saying she is too old to play Peg o' My Heart, and that Lady Macbeth is more her type. The character of Peg in J. Hartley Manners's play *Peg o' My Heart* is a young, saucy Irish girl. The queen in Shakespeare's *Macbeth* who urges her husband to kill the king, Lady Macbeth is known as one of the most cold-blooded characters in all of the Bard's works.

Reflected Glory . . . **Tallulah Bankhead:** George Kelly's 1936 comedy *Reflected Glory* was a star vehicle for Tallulah Bankhead (1902–1968), the flamboyant American stage and screen actress who was a popular but controversial figure for several decades. When Gloria Upson first meets Vera Charles, she tells Vera how good she was in *Reflected Glory*, getting her mixed up with Bankhead.

Rhett Butler: The dashing fictional Rhett Butler in the novel and movie *Gone with the Wind* is a symbol of a masculine, romantic Southerner. After

Beauregard Jackson Pickett Burnside offers to take Mame and the household out to dinner, she says, "I never expected Santa Claus to look so
much like Rhett Butler."

Robert E. Lee: During the Civil War, General Robert Edward Lee
(1807–1870) led the Confederate States Army. Greatly revered in the
South forever after, Lee was a symbol of courage and fortitude. Beauregard
tells Mame, "You've done more for the South than anyone since Robert
E. Lee!" This is also an inside joke, for one of the authors of both the play
Auntie Mame and the musical *Mame* is the Ohio-born Robert E. Lee.

Romulus and Remus: In Roman mythology, the twin brothers Romulus and Remus founded the city of Rome. In the song "Bosom Buddies," Mame sings to Vera, "We're the greatest team since Romulus and
Remus," unaware that it is believed that Romulus killed his twin brother.

Rudy Vallée: The American singer-actor Rudy Vallée (1901–1986) was
one of the first modern pop stars of the teen-idol type, and girls were
known to squeal with delight at hearing his voice. Mame sings about
"giving out with a Rudy Vallée squeal" in the song "That's How Young
I Feel."

rumble seat: A folding seat in the rear of an automobile was called a
rumble seat. It often had the association of being a place where young
couples made love. In the song "That's How Young I Feel," Mame sings
"[I] wanna ride in the rumble seat—Sheldon's got the Chevy."

St. Bridget: One of the patron saints of Ireland, St. Brigid (or Brigit or
Bridget) lived in the sixth century AD. Agnes Gooch sings a hymn to St.
Bridget at the beginning of *Mame* as she and young Patrick look for the
address where his auntie Mame lives.

salaam . . . Sahib: In Arabic-speaking and Muslim countries, a *salaam*
is a gesture of greeting or respect, done with a low bow of the head and
body, with the hand or fingers touching the forehead. Mame has taught
little Peter how to salaam, and he demonstrates it for his parents, adult
Patrick and Pegeen. Mame compliments Peter on his salaam bow with,
"Ahh, very good, Sahib." In the Arabic culture, *Sahib* is a polite title or
form of address for a man.

Schlitz: The most popular beer in America for a time was Schlitz, from the Joseph Schlitz Brewing Company in Milwaukee. Patrick's fiancée, Gloria, has told Mame about washing her hair in beer, so later Mame refers to her as "little Miss Schlitz-head" to Patrick.

sowbelly . . . hominy . . . tripe: In the song "Mame," the chorus sings, "There's sowbelly, hominy, catfish, and tripe!" Sowbelly is pork or bacon that is heavily salted. Hominy is coarsely ground-up corn that is used to make the Southern favorite, grits. Tripe is the less-desirable portion of a cow that is used as food.

Speed-o: The name of a popular shorthand class in the 1930s was Speed-o. The word came from "speedometer," and its students were supposedly the fastest stenographers. When Mr. Lindsay Woolsey asks Agnes if she will be able to take down Mame's dictation, she replies, "Oh, Speed-o won't let anybody out who can't do at least a hundred words a minute."

spinet: In the song "We Need a Little Christmas," Mame sings, "Candles in the window, / Carols at the spinet." This term refers to both an early form of the piano—a small harpsichord with the strings set in the keyboard, a very popular instrument in the eighteenth century—as well as a type of small upright piano produced through the 1990s.

The Spirit of St. Louis: Because Charles Lindbergh's plane was financed by businessmen in St. Louis, Missouri, he named his aircraft *The Spirit of St. Louis*. Young Patrick has given his model airplane the same name.

stinko: A 1920s slang expression for being extremely drunk is "to be stinko." It is one of the words young Patrick heard at a party and has put in his notebook.

Tiffany's . . . Walgreen's: Known for its luxury goods, Tiffany & Co. in New York City sells jewelry, sterling silver, china, crystal, stationery, fragrances, watches, personal accessories, and leather goods. The popular drugstore Walgreen's still exists, though the stores no longer have food-counter service. Mame buys an inexpensive wristwatch at Walgreen's and gives it to Ito as a Christmas gift, apologizing, "It's not Tiffany's, Ito. It's Walgreen's."

the Village: The district of New York City in Lower Manhattan is named Greenwich Village, but is often just called the Village. The neighborhood was long associated with writers, artists, and musicians. In *Mame*, Ralph Devine runs his advanced school, The Laboratory of Life, "down in the Village."

Mr. Woollcott . . . yardarm: Young Patrick makes Mr. Babcock a martini in the morning, explaining, "Mr. Woollcott says *somewhere* in the world the sun is just below the yardarm." Alexander Woollcott (1887–1943) was a theatre critic, radio personality, and renowned wit in the 1920s and 1930s. In sailing terms, the *yardarm* is the outer extremity of a ship's sail. The common expression "The sun is below the yardarm" meant it was the proper time to start drinking cocktails.

MAN OF LA MANCHA

Libretto by Dale Wasserman, based on Cervantes's novel *Don Quixote*. Lyrics by Joe Darion. Music by Mitch Leigh. Original Broadway production: November 22, 1965. ANTA Theatre. 2,328 performances. Broadway revivals in 1972, 1977, 1992, and 2002.

Rarely do big, epic novels make for good musicals, but Dale Wasserman found a way of dramatizing *Don Quixote* by having its author, Cervantes, onstage, telling the tale. The wandering Quixote uses words from the golden age of chivalry, when the medieval knights had strict religious, moral, and social codes. Often he is not understood by the other characters; sometimes the audience doesn't know his references. Quixote lived in a fantasy and saw things no one else saw, from dreaded ogres to virginal maidens. The libretto and lyrics for *Man of La Mancha* conjure up some of this fantasy, even as the musical is raw and realistic at times.

Expressions, references, names:

barber: In "The Barber's Song," the itinerant barber sings, "You can use me as a doctor, / For I also cure the sick." Before surgeons were accepted as respectable professionals in the mid-1700s, barbers were the physicians on whom most people depended. In addition to cutting hair and shaving customers, barbers could bleed people in order to release evil toxins in the blood.

Castellano: The noble or lord of a castle in Spain was given the dignified title of Castellano. Upon arriving at the inn, Quixote asks, "Is the lord of the castle at hand? . . . I say, is the Castellano here?"

charlatan: A person falsely claiming to have a special knowledge or skill is known as a fraud, but the more antique expression is *charlatan*. The Knight of Mirrors tells Quixote, "Now hear me, thou charlatan! Thou art no knight, but a foolish pretender."

chatelaine: Among the upper classes of Castellan society, the mistress of a household or of a large establishment was called a chatelaine. Quixote addresses the muleteers and then the innkeeper's wife with, "Gentle knights! Fair Chatelaine!"

dub: Quixote confesses to the Innkeeper, "I have never actually been dubbed a knight." The French word *adober* means "to equip with armor." From this we get the word *dub*, which is a placing of the sword on the shoulder of a prospective candidate and "dubbing" him a knight.

gauntlet: In the song "I, Don Quixote," he sings, "A knight with his banners all bravely unfurled / Now hurls down his gauntlet to thee!" In the times of chivalry, heavy mailed gloves called gauntlets were worn with a suit of armor to protect the hands. To challenge or confront someone, one of the gloves was thrown down to issue a challenge or invitation to a fight or competition. Long after medieval armor was no longer used, the expression "throw down the gauntlet" continued to mean a challenge.

gossamer: In the autumn, cobwebs spun by small spiders create a lacy, fragile material called gossamer. The word later came to mean any delicate and finely woven fabric. When Sancho presents Quixote with a filthy rag from Aldonza and says it is the token handkerchief he requested, Quixote takes it carefully and says, "Sheer gossamer."

the Inquisition: Between 1478 and 1834, Spain was ruled (and terrorized) by the Spanish Inquisition. This body of religious leaders sought out heresy or threats to the Catholic Church, often using infamously brutal methods to obtain confessions from suspected offenders. Cervantes and his assistant have been accused of heresy by the Inquisition and must stand trial. Cervantes asks the Captain about the other prisoners: "Do they all await the Inquisition?"

kitchen scullion: An archaic term for a servant employed to do rough household work; when Aldonza tells Quixote her name, he replies, "My lady jests! . . . [It is] the name of a kitchen scullion."

knight-errant: In the Middle Ages, a medieval knight wandering in search of chivalrous adventures was termed a *knight-errant*. The word comes from the Latin *errant* ("they wander"), and goes back to the fourteenth century. Cervantes tells the other prisoners about Alonso Quijano, who imagined himself "a knight-errant" who sallies forth "into the world to right all wrongs."

missive: An antiquated term for a handwritten communication on paper is missive, from the Latin word *missus*, meaning "to send." None of the characters in the musical know the word except Quixote. Continuing his narration, Cervantes tells the prisoners, "Don Quixote, having discovered his lady, sends his faithful squire to her with a missive."

Moors . . . scurvy lot: The Christian Europeans called all peoples from North Africa, Malta, and Sicily "Moors," though the word was never used by the people themselves. Scurvy is a disease caused by a lack of vitamin C and characterized by spongy gums, loosening of the teeth, and bleeding into the skin and mucous membranes. It was once prominent among sailors who were lacking food on board with vitamin C. Later, *scurvy* was used to describe anything worthless or contemptible. When a group of Moors approach, Sancho says to Quixote, "Moors! Let's make a wide track around them, for they're a scurvy lot."

muleteers: The men who drove pack mules from place to place were known as muleteers. Cervantes describes to the prisoners the kind of men staying at the inn as "Rough men—muleteers—fifteen miles on the road today."

poxy goat: The word *poxy* can be used to describe anything of poor quality, or deemed worthless. It comes from the disease known as the "pox," used to describe an illness that manifests itself with sores or bumps, such as syphilis or smallpox. Tending to the wounded muleteers, Aldonza says to Pedro, "Turn over, you poxy goat."

right of sanctuary: To avoid arrest or other dangers, one could take refuge in a sacred place, such as a church, and be safe. This was known as the "right of sanctuary." When Quixote and Sancho return to the inn after all their goods have been stolen, the Innkeeper refuses to let them in. So Quixote says, "What, sir? Deny the right of sanctuary?"

shaving basin: A bowl used when shaving was a shaving basin, a circular tin or metal object with a section cut out so the basin fits around the front of the neck. When Quixote insists that the Barber hand over the "Golden Helmet," the Barber tells him, "Why this is nothing but a shaving basin!"

squire: In the song, "I, Don Quixote," Sancho sings, "I tell all the world proudly / I'm his squire, / I'm his friend." While training to become a knight, a young nobleman acting as an attendant to a knight was called a squire. After the days of knighthood, *squire* came to mean a man of high social standing who owns and lives on an estate in a rural area.

Woeful Countenance: When Quixote insists on a new name to go with his knighthood, the Innkeeper sings, "Hail, Knight of the Woeful Countenance . . . Wherever you go / People will know / Of the glorious deeds of the Knight of the Woe— / —Ful Countenance!" An old-fashioned expression for a person's face or facial expression is *countenance.* "Woeful" can be used to describe anything causing sorrow or misery.

THE MUSIC MAN

Libretto by Meredith Willson and Franklin Lacey. Music and lyrics by Meredith Willson. Original Broadway production: December 19, 1957. Majestic Theatre. 1,375 performances. Broadway revivals in 1965, 1980, 2000, and 2022.

Perhaps no other American musical has as many obscure references and expressions than *The Music Man.* The story takes place during the summer of 1912 in the fictional town of River City, Iowa, so it is removed from audiences today by time, and, for most of us, place. Yet when the musical premiered in 1957, those first audiences probably didn't recognize these odd words and phrases much more than audiences do today. Only the oldest playgoers at that time would have had memories of 1912, and then, they would have had to have grown up in a Midwestern rural community for some of these expressions to sound familiar. The remarkable thing about Willson's words in *The Music Man* is that one can thoroughly enjoy the show without knowing the meaning of everything. River City is like a foreign place in a distant time. As audience members, we enter this strange and funny town and are charmed and entertained.

THE MUSIC MAN   *Harold Hill (Robert Preston) and Marian Paroo (Barbara Cook) demonstrate the cakewalk, a nineteenth-century dance still popular at the turn of the twentieth century.*
Photofest

Expressions, references, names:

balkline game: In the song "(Ya Got) Trouble," Professor Harold Hill speaks proudly of the game of billiards; it is pool that he says is evil. A balkline game is one in which a straight line is indicated on a billiards table and the surface is divided into "balks," or rectangles. Hill sings, "It takes judgment, brains, and maturity to score in a balkline game."

beefsteak pounded: Among the signs of corruption Hill points out in the song "Trouble" is "never mind getting the beefsteak pounded." Often beefsteak was a thick slice of lean beef that needed to be pounded with a mallet or the back of a knife in order to get it tender. It was hard and tedious work, so neglecting it, according to Hill, was a sign of sloth.

Bevo . . . Cubebs . . . Tailor Mades: Hill warns the parents of River City in the song "Trouble" that their young ones will be "tryin' out Bevo, tryin' out Cubebs, tryin' out Tailor Mades like Cigarette Feends [fiends]!" Sometimes called "near beer," Bevo was a nonalcoholic malt beverage brewed by the Anheuser-Busch company beginning in the early twentieth century. The dried, unripe berries of the cubeb, a kind of pepper, was used for medicinal purposes, but it was also used to flavor cigarettes. Tailor Mades was a brand of machine-made cigarettes. Most smokers rolled their own tobacco, but Tailor Mades introduced a pre-rolled cigarette.

billiards: A general term for various games played on a billiard table is billiards; in most versions, cue sticks are used to strike balls against each other, or into pockets around the edge of the table. Hill advocates billiards, but not the American form of billiards known as "pool."

Black Hole of Calcutta: In 1756, 146 English prisoners were confined overnight in a narrow dungeon in Calcutta, India; by morning, most of them were dead. The expression "the black hole of Calcutta" was thereafter used as an example of a very dismal place. Zaneeta tells Tommy that she is tired of meeting him in awful places and wonders, "Where will you meet me after that? In the Black Hole of Calcutta?"

Buster Brown: Buster Brown is a comic strip character created by Richard F. Outcault. Adopted as the mascot of the Brown Shoe Company in 1904, Buster Brown was well known to the American public in the early twentieth century. The character's name was also used to describe a popular style of suit for young boys, the Buster Brown suit. Hill insults the reformed Marcellus with "Listen, Buster Brown!"

buttonhooks: At a time when buttonholes and buttons could be very small, a metal object called a buttonhook was used to drive the buttons into the holes. In the opening "Rock Island" number, a salesman says, "Cash for the merchandise—cash for the buttonhooks."

Cap'n Billy's Whiz Bang: In the song "Trouble," Hill asks the parents if their sons are "memorizing jokes out of *Cap'n Billy's Whiz Bang?*" This was a very popular and notorious humor magazine during the early decades of the twentieth century, appealing particularly to boys.

Capulets: In Shakespeare's *Romeo and Juliet*, Juliet's family is the Capulets, and it is their rivalry with the Montagues that causes so much bloodshed. Zaneeta scolds her father, "It's Capulets like you [who] make blood in the marketplace."

Chaucer . . . Rabelais . . . Balzac: In the song "Pick-a-Little, Talk-a-Little," Mrs. Shinn and some of the ladies of River City tell Hill that the librarian "advocates dirty books . . . Chaucer . . . Rabelais . . . Balzac!" Geoffrey Chaucer (c. 1340s–1400) wrote *The Canterbury Tales*, some of which are very ribald. François Rabelais (1494?–1553) was a French Renaissance writer who was known for his satire, grotesque prose, and bawdy jokes and songs. Honoré de Balzac (1799–1850) was a French novelist and playwright whose works were a bit too realistic and graphic for American readers. Marian also refers to Balzac in the duet she sings with her mother, "Piano Lesson."

cistern: This underground tank for storing water is opened when it rains and fills with potable water for cooking and drinking. Hill's warning in the song "Trouble" of "the cistern empty on a Saturday night" means someone has been careless and not opened the cistern, therefore there is no water.

COD: The townspeople singing "The Wells Fargo Wagon" wonder if a package will be "a prepaid surprise or COD." The abbreviation *COD* stands for "Cash on Delivery." It means one does not pay for mail-order goods until they arrive.

Dan Patch: Hill is not opposed to a trotting horse race but is appalled at the idea of a jockey actually sitting on a horse in a race. In the song "Trouble," he sings, "Like to see some / Stuck-up jockey boy / Settin' on Dan Patch? / Make your blood boil? Well, I should say!" Dan Patch was a racehorse, known as an American Standardbred pacer, who was a celebrity when harness racing was one of the most popular sports in the nation.

DAR: An acronym for the Daughters of the American Revolution, the DAR is a patriotic organization for women founded in 1890. Originally only women related to the Colonial fighters in the Revolution could be members, but later it included all female patriots. Waiting for the Wells Fargo wagon, the townspeople sing that "the DAR have sent a cannon for the courthouse square."

Delsarte: Frenchman François Delsarte (1811–1871) was a renowned teacher of acting and singing known for his ideas of movement, which are considered the origin of modern and contemporary dance. Hill tells the mayor's wife that "every move you make, Mrs. Shinn, bespeaks Delsarte."

Diana: The mythological virgin goddess of the hunt, Diana had a rapport with animals. Hill sings to Marcellus in "The Sadder But Wiser Girl" that "for no Diana do I play fawn," meaning he will not waste his time with virginal women.

dime novel . . . corncrib: During the song "Trouble," Hill asks the parents if there is "a dime novel hidden in the corncrib?" Dime novels were cheaply printed paperback books, usually about romance or adventure. They were very popular among young readers but were frowned upon by educated adults. Ears of corn were stored until needed in a bin or ventilated space called a corncrib.

double boiler: A particular saucepan that has a detachable upper compartment, a double boiler is heated by boiling water in the lower compartment. This keeps food in the upper compartment from burning while it heats. One of the townspeople is hoping the Wells Fargo wagon will bring her a "double boiler."

Egad!: The archaic exclamation "Egad!" or "Egads!" is a mild oath or expression of surprise, probably a euphemism for "Oh God!" The mayor's daughter Zaneeta is always saying "Egads!" in every situation.

Frank Gotch . . . Strangular Lewis: Mayor Shinn says, "I haven't seen Iowa people get so excited since the night Frank Gotch and Strangular [Strangler] Lewis lay on the mat for three and a half hours without moving a muscle!" Frank Alvin Gotch (1877–1917) is credited with popularizing professional wrestling in the United States. His reign as World Heavyweight Wrestling Champion (from 1908 to 1913) is one of the longest in the history of professional wrestling. Robert H. Friedrich (1891–1966) was better known in the ring as Ed "Strangler" Lewis. He was a four-time World Heavyweight Wrestling Champion.

fritterin': An antiquated term for reducing something or squandering time doing nothing is to *fritter*. To be frittering implies doing something lazy or sinful. In the song "Trouble," Hill tells the townsfolk that their "Youth'll be fritterin' away, / I say your young men'll be fritterin'!"

Gilmore . . . Liberatti . . . Pat Conway . . . Great Creatore . . . W. C. Handy . . . John Philip Sousa: In his introduction to "Seventy-Six Trombones," Hill says, "You'll feel something akin to the electric thrill I once enjoyed when Gilmore . . . Liberatti . . . Pat Conway . . . the Great Creatore . . . W. C. Handy . . . and John Philip Sousa all came to town on the same historic day!" The Irish-born composer and band conductor Patrick S. Gilmore (1829–1892) was one of the most popular bandleaders in America from the 1850s to the 1870s. Alessandro Liberatti (1847–1927) was a noted cornet virtuoso, bandmaster, and composer who conducted bands throughout Italy, and then came to North America and played in bands all over English-speaking Canada. Patrick Conway (1865–1929) and his band of professionals were as famous as John Philip Sousa's band, playing throughout the country for state fairs, expositions, and concert series. The Italian-born bandmaster Giuseppe Creatore (1871–1952) was so famous in America that he was dubbed the Great Creatore, and also rivaled Sousa's fame. W. C. Handy (1873–1958) is the American composer and musician known as the Father of the Blues. Celebrated composer and band director John Philip Sousa (1854–1932) was known as "The March King" for his many famous march compositions; when he was a young man, Meredith Willson played in Sousa's band.

Grecian urn: Cremation ashes have often been placed in containers called urns, and a Grecian urn has come to symbolize romanticized death because of John Keats's poem "Ode to a Grecian Urn." Mrs. Shinn titles her tableau at the picnic after Grecian urns, unaware of their morbid connotation.

Hector Berlioz: When Marcellus interrupts Hill and Marian at the footbridge, Hill remarks, "I'm expecting a cable from Hector Berlioz." Louis-Hector Berlioz (1803–1869) was a French Romantic composer and conductor, long dead in 1904. His output includes orchestral works, choral pieces, and operas. In the movie version of *The Music Man*, the composer was changed to "Rudy Friml," the popular operetta composer Rudolf Friml (1879–1972).

Hester: In the song "The Sadder But Wiser Girl," Hill wants "Hester to win just one more A." He is referring to Hester Prynne, the protagonist of Nathaniel Hawthorne's novel *The Scarlet Letter*, who is forced to wear the letter *A* as a sign of her adultery. Although Hester is condemned by her Puritan community, Hill is hoping she will sin again (possibly with him).

hogshead, cask, and demijohn: In the "Rock Island" number, one of the salesmen laments, "Gone with the hogshead, cask, and demijohn." A hogshead is a large container for wine or beer. A cask is a similarly large vessel used to store liquids, usually alcohol. A demijohn is a bottle with a narrow neck and a wicker cover that can hold up to ten gallons of liquid, usually spirits.

"In the Gloamin'": The old English love song "In the Gloaming" goes back to the mid-nineteenth century and was still very popular in America at the turn of the twentieth century. In "My White Knight," Marian sings about a schoolteacher who used to sing "In the Gloaming."

iron-clad leave: In the game of billiards, if one "leaves" an impossible setup for his opponent, they say it is iron-clad. The expression "iron-clad lead" is also used. Hill uses the phrase "iron-clad leave" in the song "Trouble."

Jeely Kly: The regional oath or declamation "Jeely Kly!" is probably a euphemistic slurring of "Jesus Christ!" Being a tough street kid, Tommy Djilas utters "Jeely Kly" a lot. In the film version of *The Music Man*, it was softened to "Great Honk!"

jew's harp: A popular American musical instrument found mostly in rural areas, a jew's harp is a small lyre-shaped device held between the teeth and struck with a finger to create a twanging sound. Having been told how Harold Hill sells instruments for a boys' band, one of the salesmen in the

"Rock Island" number says, "I know you can't make a livin' sellin' big trombones . . . Mandolin picks perhaps . . . here and there a jew's harp."

knickerbockers: In American jargon, any loose-fitting trousers gathered at the knee or calf are called knickerbockers. In the song "Trouble," Hill asks the parents of River City, "The moment your son leaves the house, does he rebuckle his knickerbockers below the knee?," trying to look as if they are wearing long trousers.

The Last Days of Pompeii: This 1834 novel by Edward Bulwer-Lytton is about the cataclysmic destruction of the city of Pompeii by the eruption of Mount Vesuvius. River City names its fireworks display "The Last Days of Pompeii" without realizing its disastrous meaning.

libertine men: A libertine is one who is without moral principles and engages in sexual pursuits without any sense of responsibility. Hill describes "libertine men" dancing at the Armory in the song "Trouble." It is possible he means "liberty men," referring to military personnel on leave who are looking for sex, alcohol, gambling, or other immoral activities.

mackinaw: A short coat or jacket made of a thick, heavy woolen cloth, usually with a plaid design. A woman waiting for the Wells Fargo wagon to arrive sings of another delivery she received from the wagon: "In March I got a gray mackinaw."

masher: American slang back in the day for a man who makes unwanted sexual advances, often in public places, and usually to females he does not know. Marian tells her mother in the song "Piano Lesson" that the "man with the suitcase" was a "common masher."

Model T Ford: The traveling salesmen on the train in "Rock Island" complain how "the Model T made the trouble, made the people want to git up and go" to the county seat to shop. The Model T Ford, familiarly known as the "Tin Lizzie" or "flivver," was the popular automobile manufactured by the Ford Motor Company between 1908 and 1927. It was the first affordable vehicle, making car travel available to middle-class Americans.

Montgom'ry Ward: During the song "Wells Fargo Wagon," one of the townspeople sings, "Montgom'ry Ward sent me a bathtub and a crosscut saw." Montgomery Ward & Co. was an extremely popular mail-order business that published catalogs filled with all kinds of products. It was later also a chain of department stores.

nicotine stain: In the song "Trouble," Hill asks the parents of River City if their sons have "a nicotine stain on [their] index finger," referring to the yellowish residue on one's hands from holding tobacco or cigarettes.

noggins and the piggins and the firkins: In the opening number, "Rock Island," the salesmen sing, "Cash for the noggins and the piggins and the firkins." While "noggin" is slang for a person's head, "noggins" is a small quantity of liquor, usually a quarter of a pint. A *piggin* is a wooden pail with a handle. A *firkin* is a small container often holding liquids, easy to fill with alcohol and conceal on one's person.

notions: Small items used in sewing and haberdashery, such as needles, buttons, and thread, are called notions. One of the salesmen on the train says, "Credit is no good for a notion salesman."

O'Clarke, O'Mendez, O'Klein: In the characteristic way Hill has of altering words and names, the three notable horn players Herbert L. Clarke (1867–1945), Rafael Méndez (1906–1981), and Emmanuel "Mannie" Klein (1908–1994) are given Irish names to impress Mrs. Paroo. Another inside joke: Meredith Willson had known and performed with all three of these real-life trumpeters.

Paul Bunyan . . . Saint Pat . . . Noah Webster: In the song "Piano Lesson," Mrs. Paroo tells her daughter not to foolishly wait around for a man who is "a blend o' Paul Bunyan, Saint Pat, and Noah Webster." In American folklore, Paul Bunyan is a giant lumberjack with superhuman strength who, with his ox, Babe, performs amazing feats. Saint Patrick is the patron saint of Ireland. The name of the American author and lexicographer Noah Webster Jr. (1758–1843) has become synonymous with "dictionary" in the United States, especially the modern Merriam-Webster dictionary, first published in 1828.

pest house: An antiquated name for a hospital treating persons with infectious or pestilential diseases; Mayor Shinn announces to the crowd that the fireworks display will be "out to Madison Picnic Park in the far meadow, 'cross the crick from the pest house."

pinch-back suit: Hill warns the citizens of River City about their sons, singing, "And the next thing you know, yer son is playin' fer money in a pinch-back suit." Any cheap or poorly made garment that tries to look expensive was said to be "pinch-beck." The term developed into "pinch-back," as Hill uses it in the song "Trouble."

ragtime: Hill sings, "Ragtime! Shameless music!" in the song "Trouble," as the kind of sinful music heard at a "dance at the Armory." Music characterized by a syncopated melodic line and regularly accented accompaniment became known as ragtime. It came from Black musicians in the 1890s, in particular, Scott Joplin, who was considered the King of Ragtime.

Remember the *Maine* . . . Plymouth Rock . . . Golden Rule: Hill conjures up the townspeople's patriotic pride in the song "Trouble" when he sings, "Remember the *Maine*, Plymouth Rock, and the Golden Rule!" The US battleship *Maine* was blown up in the harbor of Havana, Cuba, in 1898, precipitating the Spanish-American War. The rallying cry "Remember the *Maine*!" became a patriotic call to arms, used for many years after. Plymouth Rock is traditionally marked as the site where the Pilgrims landed in Massachusetts in 1620. The Golden Rule is the principle of treating others as one wants to be treated. It is a motto in many religions and cultures, usually expressed with "Do unto others as you would have them do unto you."

rig: Any open vehicle drawn by one or two horses was called a rig. Hill wants to hire a rig from Jacey Squires near the beginning of the musical, and that's how he meets Marcellus.

Sen-Sen: Hill warns River City in the song "Trouble" that the young ones are going to be "braggin' all about how they're gonna cover up a telltale breath with Sen-Sen." Sen-Sen was a "breath perfume" first manufactured in the late nineteenth century. It was used to improve bad breath, but Hill sees it as a way to disguise the tobacco smell on their breath.

Shipoopi: It is believed that Willson created this nonsense word for *The Music Man*, for no previous use has been found. Although Tommy Djilas says it is a dance, its origin is much more scatological. Combining the words *shit* and *poopie*, *Shipoopi* is a naughty word used by the street kids and not understood by the adults. According to the song, the girl who waits until the third date to kiss is "your shipoopi."

stereopticon slides: A stereopticon is a slide projector that uses a candle or lantern to project photographic images onto a screen. Showings of stereopticon slides were popular before the advent of movies. During the Fourth of July festivities, Mayor Shinn thanks Jacey Squires for "the fine stereopticon slides."

tablow: A popular entertainment in the nineteenth and early twentieth centuries was the creation of a tableau—a scene from history or a specific story depicted by using a group of posed models or motionless actors. In *The Music Man*, the members of the school board had planned a tableau (or tablow) for the Fourth of July activities, but the mayor announces that it is canceled, probably because of a "disagreement over the costumes."

tempest fugits: The Latin phrase *tempus fugit* is traditionally translated into English as "time flies." Mrs. Shinn uses the phrase incorrectly, saying "tempest fugits."

three-rail billiard shot: Arguably one of the most difficult maneuvers in pool or billiards, it is when the player bounces the cue ball off three sides of the table. Hill mentions his admiration for the billiards shot in the song "Trouble."

tierce: An antiquated name for a vessel filled with wine is a *tierce*. The salesmen sing about "the tub and the pail and the tierce" in the opening number, "Rock Island."

tintype: An early form of photography, a tintype was a photograph taken as a positive on a thin tin plate, hence its name. The anvil salesman Charlie Cowell uses the familiar expression "not on your tintype" when he talks to Marian Paroo.

Uneeda Biscuits: Introduced in 1898 by the National Biscuit Company (later known as Nabisco), the Uneeda Biscuit was the first cracker to come wrapped in wax paper and inside a cardboard box. Before that, crackers were sold loose from a cracker barrel. One of the traveling salesmen in the opening number says, "It's the Uneeda Biscuit made the trouble . . . Put the crackers in a package . . . Made the cracker barrel obsolete."

walls of Jericho: Hill rouses the citizens of River City with a reference to the biblical city of Jericho, which was destroyed by a blast of horns. In his introduction to "Seventy-Six Trombones," Hill sings, "Remember, my friends, what a handful of trumpet players did to the fabled walls of Jericho!"

Wells Fargo wagon: A common sight in cities and towns as America grew in the nineteenth and early twentieth centuries was the Wells Fargo wagon, which delivered all sorts of goods even to the most faraway places. The arrival of the Wells Fargo wagon in River City is a major event, as expressed in the song "Wells Fargo Wagon."

MY FAIR LADY

Libretto by Alan Jay Lerner, based on George Bernard Shaw's play *Pygmalion.* Lyrics by Alan Jay Lerner. Music by Frederick Loewe. Original Broadway production: March 15, 1956. Mark Hellinger Theatre. 2,717 performances. Major Broadway revivals in 1976, 1981, 1993, and 2018.

Because *My Fair Lady* is so thoroughly British, one forgets that the musical adaptation was written by an American librettist-lyricist and a German-born composer. Alan Jay Lerner and Frederick Loewe did their job so well, capturing the words and music of the English setting so completely that the musical seems like an authentic British creation. While much of the British play *Pygmalion* is quoted in the libretto, the new scenes blend seamlessly into Shaw's original. The action is set in and around London in 1912, during the Edwardian era, so there are several upper- and lower-class terms and expressions that need to be explained, not to mention all the place names, as well.

Expressions, references, names:

abso-bloomin'-lutely: Alan Jay Lerner made up this word in which the expression "bloomin'" was placed in the middle of the word "absolutely." In Great Britain, something "blooming" means "very much" or "extremely so," as in a "blooming idiot" or a "blooming hot day." Also, "blooming" was a polite alternative to the coarse "bloody." In the song "Wouldn't It Be Loverly?," Eliza sings, "so loverly sittin' abso-bloomin'-lutely still."

Aida . . . Götterdämmerung: Colonel Pickering says to Mrs. Higgins, "One night I went to the opera at Covent Garden to hear one of my favorite operas, *Aida . . .* No, they did *Götterdämmerung* instead." Giuseppe

Verdi's 1868 opera *Aida* is about a Nubian princess, set in ancient Egypt. *Götterdämmerung* is the last in Richard Wagner's cycle of four operas titled *Der Ring des Nibelungen* (*The Ring of the Nibelung*). The mythic tale is based on Nordic and German legends.

Ascot: The village of Ascot in south-central England west of London is the home of the Royal Ascot horse races, initiated by Queen Anne in 1711, and held annually each June. It is a very formal and fashionable affair. Mrs. Higgins says to Pickering, "Ascot is usually the one place I can come to with my friends and not run the risk of seeing my son."

balmies: British slang for someone who is crazy, demented, or bonkers, most likely to be used by the lower classes. When Higgins gets excited about turning her into a duchess, Eliza says, "I don't want no balmies teachin' me."

Biarritz: A fashionable beach community on France's southwestern coast, Biarritz was once the vacation spot for nobility. Today it is a popular spot for surfing. The Third Cockney jokingly asks Eliza, "Where're y'bound for this spring, Eliza—Biarritz?"

blackguard: A rude or dishonest man can be called a blackguard in Great Britain. When Doolittle arrives at Higgins's doorstep, Higgins says, "Send the blackguard up."

blighters: Any person or thing that is deemed despicable or irritating; in the song "Show Me," Eliza is fed up with words, and sings to Freddie, "Is that all you blighters can do?"

blimey: The oft-used word *blimey* is a way of expressing surprise at something that is amazing and impressive rather than shocking or upsetting. The Hoxton Man says to Higgins, "Blimey, you know everything, you do."

blinkin' . . . bloomin': Instead of using the crude word "bloody," the British prefer these two less-offensive expressions. Both *bloomin'* and *blinkin'* are mild exclamations of sudden strong emotion, much like the American "gosh" and "heck." Early in the musical, the First Costermonger says about Eliza, "We've got a bloomin' heiress in our midst." In the song "With a Little Bit of Luck," Doolittle sings, "Someone else will do the blinkin' work!"

bolted: A way of saying you're leaving, often in a hurry; when Eliza leaves Higgins's home in the middle of the night, he says to Pickering, "Here's a confounded thing! Eliza's bolted!"

brass farthing: One of the smallest units of currency was the British farthing, worth only one quarter of a penny. The expression *brass farthing* meant anything that is worth very little, next to nothing, or nothing at all. When Doolittle tries to ask Eliza for some money, she cuts him off with, "Not a brass farthing."

Cheltenham . . . Harrow . . . Cambridge: When asked where Pickering comes from, Higgins immediately replies, "Cheltenham, Harrow, Cambridge, and India." Cheltenham is an idyllic town in the Cotswolds region of England. Harrow is a large town in Greater London, but Higgins is referring to the Harrow School, the prestigious independent boarding school for boys in Harrow on the Hill. The University of Cambridge is the second-oldest university in the English-speaking world, and the world's third-oldest surviving university, founded in 1209 and granted a royal charter by Henry III.

copper: A slang term for a British policeman is a *copper*. In America, the word was shortened to *cop*. An angry man shouts to the noisy Doolittle and his pals, "One more sound, so help me, I'll call a copper!"

costermonger . . . Capri: In the song "Wouldn't It Be Loverly?," the Third Costermonger sings, "The missus wants to open up, / The castle in Capri." A coster, or costard or costermonger, is a street seller of fruit and vegetables in Great Britain. Three costermongers in Covent Garden harmonize and sing "Wouldn't It Be Loverly?" with Eliza. Capri is an island located in the Gulf of Naples in Italy. It has been a desirable resort since the time of the ancient Romans.

Covent Garden: In the Edwardian era, Covent Garden was a West End district in London with an extensive fruit and vegetable market. Today it is a popular shopping and tourist site. Also there is the Royal Opera House, known simply as Covent Garden, which is letting out patrons at the beginning of *My Fair Lady*.

dashed: A very British expression, meaning surprised or dumbfounded. When Pickering discovers that Eliza has run off, he says, "I'm dashed!"

Demosthenes: The Greek statesman and orator Demosthenes (384–322 BCE) of ancient Athens had a speech impairment and improved his diction by putting pebbles in his mouth and practicing his elocution. When Pickering asks if putting marbles in Eliza's mouth are necessary, Higgins responds, "If they were necessary for Demosthenes, they are necessary for Eliza Doolittle."

dustman . . . dustbin: In the United Kingdom, a collector of trash or garbage is called a dustman. When he works (which is not often), Alfred Doolittle is a dustman. The butler at Wimpole Street announces to Higgins, "If you please, sir, there's a dustman downstairs." The word *dustbin* is British for a trash or garbage can. When Mrs. Pearce asks Higgins where she is to put Eliza, he replies, "Put her in the dustbin."

governor: When members of the working class in England address employers and such, they use the respectful term "governor." In British slang, this becomes "guv." When Doolittle calls on Higgins, he says, "Morning, governor. I come about a very serious matter, governor."

gutter-snipe: A homeless vagabond, particularly an outcast boy or girl in the streets of a city, is referred to as a gutter-snipe. Deciding to teach Eliza, Higgins boasts, "I'll make a duchess of this draggle-tailed gutter-snipe!"

half a crown . . . tuppence . . . ha'pence: Before the British simplified their monetary system, there were many different kinds of coins. A crown was worth five shillings, or one pound sterling. *Tuppence* is a slang term for two pence, or two pennies. A *ha'pence* refers to half of a penny, a very small amount indeed. When Pickering tells Eliza he hasn't any change to buy a flower, she says, "I can change half a crown. Here, take this for tuppence." Pickering looks again in his pockets, then tells Eliza, "Here's three ha'pence, if that's any use to you."

heighteen pence . . . shilling: Eliza explains to Higgins, "A lady friend of mine gets French lessons for heighteen pence an hour . . . I won't give more than a shilling." A British coin worth eighteen pence (or pennies) was called an eighteen pence, but Eliza pronounces it "heighteen pence." The shilling was a coin worth one-twentieth of a pound sterling.

Hertford . . . Hereford . . . Hampshire: The vocal exercise lesson Eliza repeats in order to pronounce her H's is, "In Hertford, Hereford, and Hampshire, hurricanes hardly ever happen." Hertford is a historic market town in the East Hertfordshire countryside. Hereford is a cathedral town in the county of Herefordshire. Hampshire is the largest county in southeast England, stretching from the coastal beaches in the southwest to London's suburban fringe in the northeast.

Houndslow: Houndslow is a hamlet in the Scottish Borders area of Scotland. When Higgins first hears Doolittle's voice, he tells Pickering, "Born in Houndslow, mother, Welsh!"

Hoxton: Located in London's East End, in an area in the London borough of Hackney. When the Hoxton Man asks Higgins, "Do you know where I come from?," Higgins promptly replies, "Hoxton."

Keats . . . Milton: In the song "I'm an Ordinary Man," Higgins complains, "You want to talk of Keats or Milton; she only wants to talk of love." John Keats (1795–1821) was an English Romantic poet who died of tuberculosis at the age of twenty-five. John Milton (1608–1674) was an English poet and intellectual who is best known for his epic poem, *Paradise Lost* (1667).

Mrs. Langtry: The beloved British socialite and stage actress Lillie Langtry (1853–1929) was born on the island of Jersey and was billed as "The Jersey Lily." She took London by storm and was arguably the most famous woman of her day. At the embassy ball, Karpathy says about Eliza, "She fascinate[s] everyone. Not since Mrs. Langtry came to London . . ."

Lisson Grove: Lisson Grove is a street and district in London's Marylebone neighborhood. In the Edwardian era, the section was rather rundown and mostly industrial. Higgins asks Eliza, "How do you come to be so far east? You were born in Lisson Grove."

"The Owl and the Pussycat": As Eliza struggles to recite a poem with pebbles in her mouth, Pickering says to Higgins, "Why don't you try a simpler [poem], like 'The Owl and the Pussycat'?" For many years, Edward Lear's popular, and rather silly, children's poem, "The Owl and the Pussycat," was memorized by British schoolchildren.

pounds: The British pound, also referred to as pound sterling, is the official currency of the United Kingdom and some of its territories. The pound is subdivided into 100 pence (or pennies). In the Edwardian era, a live-in servant earned only about eight pounds a year. After Eliza offers to pay one shilling per hour for voice lessons, Higgins considers the offer, then says, "Not as a simple shilling but as a percentage of this girl's income, it works out as fully equivalent to sixty or seventy pounds from a millionaire!"

Queen of Sheba: In the Hebrew Bible, the Queen of Sheba brings a caravan of valuable gifts for the Israelite king, Solomon. The expression "Queen of Sheba" has come to mean a wealthy and powerful woman. Higgins boasts to Eliza, "I can pass you off as the Queen of Sheba."

Selsey: In the first scene of the musical, Higgins asks the Selsey Man, "And how are all your people down at Selsey?" Selsey is a seaside town in the county of West Sussex, England.

sixpence: Sometimes known as a tanner or sixpenny bit, sixpence is a coin that was worth six pence, equivalent to one-fortieth of a pound sterling, or half a shilling. A furious Eliza tells Higgins, "Take the whole bloomin' basket for sixpence."

Soho Square . . . aitches: Soho Square was not a fashionable neighborhood in London in the Edwardian era, but today it is a bustling district filled with cafes, bars, clubs, and world-class theaters. In Cockney vernacular, the letter *H* is rarely pronounced. In the song "Why Can't the English?," Higgins refers to the many Cockney-speaking residents when he sings, "Hear them down in Soho Square / Dropping aitches everywhere."

Spanish Inquisition: In the song "I'm an Ordinary Man," Higgins sings, "I'd prefer a new edition / Of the Spanish Inquisition / Than to ever let a woman in my life." The judicial institution known as the Inquisition terrorized Spain from 1478 to 1834, combating heresy in the Catholic country and using infamously brutal methods in its interrogation.

St. George's, Hanover Square: Because of his newfound wealth, Alfred Doolittle is to be married in the distinguished venue of St. George's Church, an Anglican church in central London that sits on the prestigious Hanover Square in Mayfair. Doolittle asks Eliza, "I say, do you want to come and see me turned off this morning? St. George's, Hanover Square."

St. James: Although King Edward resided in Buckingham Palace, St. James's Palace is the most senior royal palace in the United Kingdom. It gives its name to the Court of St. James's, which is the monarch's royal court. In the song "Just You Wait," Eliza sings about how she will "go to St. James so often I will call it St. Jim."

tec: An informal short term for a police detective in Great Britain is *tec*. A Selsey Man says about Higgins, "He ain't a tec. He's a gentleman. Look at his shoes."

Tottenham Court Road: A very busy thoroughfare in London since the late eighteenth century, Tottenham Court Road was a crossroads that saw many different classes collide. Eliza tells Higgins and Pickering, "I want to be a lady in a flower shop 'stead of selling at the corner of Tottenham Court Road."

tub of butter: To "land in a tub of butter" in British slang means to suddenly find good fortune. The neighbor lady Mrs. Hopkins tells Doolittle, "Fallen into a tub of butter, you have."

Wimpole Street: Wimpole Street is a very quiet street in the center of the medical quarter of London. It was (and still is) a very desirable address. Elizabeth Barrett lived at number 50 Wimpole Street. It is where Higgins lives, and he insists that Pickering reside with him there when he says, "You're staying at 27-A Wimpole Street."

Zed: In Great Britain, the letter *Z* is often pronounced "Zed." In the song "Why Can't the English?," Higgins sings, "Every Frenchman knows his language from 'A' to 'Zed.'"

OKLAHOMA!

Libretto by Oscar Hammerstein, based on the play *Green Grow the Lilacs* by Lynn Riggs. Lyrics by Oscar Hammerstein. Music by Richard Rodgers. Original Broadway production: March 31, 1943. St. James Theatre. 2,212 performances. Broadway revivals in 1951, 1953, 1958, 1963, 1965, 1979, 1980, 2002, and 2020.

The first Rodgers and Hammerstein musical is still their most popular work, being produced even more often than *The Sound of Music*.

Hammerstein's libretto indicates that the action takes place at the turn of the twentieth century. Near the end of the musical, everyone is celebrating the news that Oklahoma is to become a new state, which places the time of the musical just before 1907. The location in the libretto is "Indian Territory," but that land was also called Oklahoma Territory. The rural dialect in *Oklahoma!* is pretty thick, and Hammerstein writes it phonetically. Tomatoes become "termayters" and pretty is pronounced "purty." But there are some words and phrases that are not so common today, no matter how you pronounce them.

Expressions, references, names:

beauty spots: When it was fashionable for women to sport a "beauty mark" on their cheek, it was common to apply some dark makeup or even a little dark patch to simulate the mark. These were sometimes called "beauty spots." Curly agrees to take Aunt Eller to the picnic, and tells her, "See that you got yer beauty spots fastened onto you proper, so you won't lose 'em off."

Bell telephone: When early telephones were introduced, they were sometimes referred to as "Bell telephones" after the inventor, Alexander Graham Bell (1847–1922). When singing about "Kansas City," Will Parker says, "I put my ear to a Bell telephone and a strange woman started in to talk!"

bits: When counting money using North American informal speech, "two bits" is the equivalent of twenty-five cents. While a single "bit" is worth twelve and a half cents, the term is only used in even multiples. Four bits, for example, is half a dollar. The actual coinage is the same; *bits* is just a slang way of counting. "Bits" caught on when circus sideshow barkers shouted "Admission, two bits!" Several of the characters in *Oklahoma!* use "bits" in their speech, as at the auction at the Box Social, when Jud offers "Ten dollars and two bits" for Laurey's hamper.

bloomers: The abolitionist and suffragette Mrs. Amelia J. Bloomer (1818–1894) invented a loose-fitting kind of trousers for women so they could move freely when cycling or participating in other sports. The baggy pants became known as "bloomers." Bloomers also referred to a ladies' undergarment, not meant to be seen. Ado Annie tells Will that the story about "losing" her bloomers was just a rumor.

Box Social: A fund-raising event in which box lunches are auctioned off was known as a Box Social, and it was usually in aid of some well-meaning cause. The Box Social in *Oklahoma!* is to raise money for the new school-house. The ladies bring their lunches in hampers or picnic baskets, and the men bid on them.

bull-dogger: Curly tells Aunt Eller that he's "the best bull-dogger in seventeen counties." Bull-dogging in rural America is the ability to wrestle a steer to the ground by holding its horns and twisting its neck. Not only used when getting cattle down for branding, bull-dogging is also a competition event at a rodeo.

burleeque: A burlesque at the time of *Oklahoma!* was a variety show with pretty chorus girls, some of whom might remove articles of clothing as they danced. In "Kansas City," Will sings of going to such a show, using the slang term *burleeque*.

churn: Any mechanism that "churns" ingredients together can be called a churn. In the beginning of *Oklahoma!*, Aunt Eller uses a wooden butter churn, making butter by churning cream or milk.

cowman: A person who owns or is in charge of a cattle ranch was called a cowman, as opposed to the more familiar "cowboy," someone who does the work of herding, branding, and watching over cattle. There is a rivalry in *Oklahoma!* between cowmen and farmers, because the cowmen sometimes drive their cattle onto farmers' property, knocking down fences and destroying crops.

Darby and Jones: A British expression that goes back to the eighteenth century, "Darby and Joan" referred to any old married couple who are living out their final years together and are still in love. The two names are believed to come from an eighteenth-century song. By the nineteenth century, the expression "Darby and Joan" was commonly used in America. The peddler Ali Hakim gets the term wrong when he tells Ado Annie that Will Parker "will stick to you all your life and be a regular Darby and Jones."

dirt-scratchers: A slang expression for a farmer, because he plows the earth, meant in a very negative way. At the Box Social, the cowman Cord

Elam says, "Whyn't those dirt-scratchers stay in Missouri where they belong?"

Elixir of Egypt: The word *elixir* is an antiquated term for a special potion, either medicinal or magical; some elixirs were guaranteed to induce love, or even keep one from aging. The Elixir of Egypt that Ali Hakim sells to Laurey supposedly helps a person make up her mind, but Aunt Eller recognizes it as "smellin' salts!"

fascinator: Aunt Eller says she is going to wear her "fascinator" to the Box Social. One of the dainties women in rural areas had access to was a fascinator, a headpiece that was frivolous but very feminine. Fascinators usually consisted of feathers, flowers, and/or beads, and were attached to the head with a comb or hair clip.

frog-sticker: In the Midwest and the South, a "frog-sticker" was slang for a knife—one meant to be used more as a weapon than a utility tool. Jud asks the peddler Ali Hakim if he has a frog-sticker to sell. He says he wants to "kill a hog—er, a skunk," meaning Curly.

gas buggies: One of the many slang terms for the early automobile, *gas buggies* were usually small cars with open tops. Will sings of "twenty gas buggies goin' by theirsel's" in the song "Kansas City."

hamper: Any large basket with a lid would be called a hamper. A clothes hamper, for example, would be used to hold laundry. In *Oklahoma!*, the women put their lunches in a "picnic hamper," what we might call a picnic basket today.

horn to hoof: Ado Annie tells Laurey that "when a feller talks purty to me, I git all shaky from horn to hoof." While the horn and the hoof are parts of a horse's foot, Annie likely means she trembles "from head to foot."

hussy: Any female who was brazen, saucy, or mischievous was once said to be a hussy. When Aunt Eller looks into the Little Wonder and sees mostly naked women, she says, "The hussy! Ought to be ashamed of herself."

isinglass curtains: A thin and transparent sheet of mica, an early form of plastic, was termed *isinglass*. Curly sings of the "isinglass curtains y'c'n roll right down" in the song "The Surrey with the Fringe on Top."

magic-lantern show: A primitive form of image projector used for showing photographic slides was termed a *magic lantern*. In the song "Kansas City," Will Parker sings about the sights in the big city and declares, "It's better than a magic-lantern show."

mav'rick: A calf or yearling (a one-year-old cow) that has not been branded is called a maverick, named after Samuel A. Maverick (1803–1870), a Texas rancher who did not brand his cattle. Curly sings of a "little brown mav'rick" in the opening song, "Oh, What a Beautiful Mornin'."

nix: A negative term going back to the eighteenth century, *nix* can mean "no" or "nothing." In the song "I Cain't Say No," Ado Annie sings, "I always say, come on, let's go—Jist when I orta say nix!"

privies: A toilet located in a small shed outside a house or other building used to be called a *privy*, another term for an outhouse. Will sings in "Kansas City" about how you can "walk to privies in the rain an' never wet yer feet."

ragtime: The new kind of music that came from Black musicians in the 1890s was called ragtime because the musical notes were "ragged"—that is, they were uneven and irregular. Will Parker does a dance to the new sound in the "Kansas City" number, telling the others, "That's ragtime. I seen a couple of colored fellers doin' it."

rig . . . gig: A general term for a vehicle with one or more horses harnessed to it is a *rig*. Curly is among those who use the word, as in the song "The Surrey with the Fringe on Top," when he sings "ain't no finer rig, I'm a thinkin'." Similarly, *gig* can also be used to denote a horse-drawn vehicle. Curly sings "the slickest gig you ever see" in the same song.

shivoree: A loud and boisterous serenade for a newlywed couple is a "shivaree." People would gather outside the couple's bedroom window on their wedding night and bang pots and pans, blow horns, and make all the noise they could. Andrew Carnes mispronounces the word when he tells his daughter Ado Annie that the men are planing a "shivoree . . . a good old custom" for Curly and Laurey.

smokehouse: A North American word for a shed or room used for preserving food by exposure to smoke; Jud Fry lives in the smokehouse on Laurey and Aunt Eller's farm.

surrey: A light, four-wheeled carriage with two seats facing forward was called a surrey in the late nineteenth century in Great Britain and America. Originally called a Surrey cart, it was first made in Surrey, England; it later developed into a passenger carriage. The song "The Surrey with the Fringe on Top" has kept the term alive.

take a header: The old expression "take a header" means to collapse or tire out, as well as to diminish or to dip out of sight. Curly sings "the moon is takin' a header" in "The Surrey with the Fringe on Top" when he describes coming back from the Box Social in the surrey as the moon goes down and morning comes.

two-step: A dance in march or polka time in which dancers move in a circle and slide their feet is considered a two-step. Will Parker demonstrates the dance in the song "Kansas City," explaining, "This is the two-step. That's all they're dancin' nowadays."

ON THE TOWN

Libretto by Betty Comden and Adolph Green, based on Jerome Robbins's ballet *Fancy Free*. Lyrics by Betty Comden and Adolph Green. Music by Leonard Bernstein. Original Broadway production: December 28, 1944. Adelphi Theatre. 462 performances. Broadway revivals in 1971, 1998, and 2014.

All of *On the Town* takes place during twenty-four hours in 1944 in New York City. The script and the lyrics by Betty Comden and Adolph Green are filled with New York locations and 1940s slang. The sailor Chip has his father's New York City guidebook from 1934, so he is constantly looking for attractions that have moved or no longer exist. If you are a fan of *On the Town* and wonder if there ever was a real Miss Turnstiles, take heart. That subway promotion actually existed, and Comden and Green made excellent use of it.

Expressions, references, names:

Aquarium: One of the oldest aquariums in the nation, the New York Aquarium opened in 1896 in the Battery's Castle Clinton in Lower

ON THE TOWN   *During the war years of the 1940s, women took on many "male" jobs, such as Hildy (Nancy Walker) the cab driver who picks up the sailor Chip (Cris Alexander) and brings him back to "my place."*
Photofest

Manhattan. In 1941 the Aquarium was temporarily housed in the Bronx Zoo, then later found a home at Coney Island. In the song "Come Up to My Place," Chip tells Hildy to take him to Battery Park to see the Aquarium, but Hildy sings, "The fish have flown away; / They're in the Bronx instead, / They might as well be dead."

Bellbottom: Bell-bottoms are trousers that are wider from the knees downward, forming a bell-like shape. These were worn by sailors, so a slang term for a person in US Navy uniform was a "bell-bottom." Madame Dilly chases Gabey off with "On your way, Bellbottom!"

Betty Hutton: The singer, actress, and comedian Betty Hutton (1921–2007) was a brassy blonde known for her loud mouth and broad gestures. On the subway, Flossie tells her friend, "Betty Hutton herself in person would look like a dead zombie after my day's work in this office."

Bronx . . . Battery: The three sailors sing, "The Bronx is up but the Battery's down" in the song "New York, New York." The Bronx is the only New York City borough that is on the mainland and not a peninsula or island. The Battery was a fort at the southernmost tip of Manhattan, but was later turned into Battery Park.

Carnegie Hall: One of the most prestigious venues in the world for both classical music and popular music, Carnegie Hall in Midtown Manhattan also houses studios, rehearsal rooms, and classrooms. Ivy Smith goes to Carnegie Hall to take voice and ballet lessons from Madame Dilly.

Cat People: *Cat People* is a 1942 American horror film about a fashion illustrator, obsessed with the idea that she is descended from an ancient tribe of Cat People, so she turns into a panther when aroused. The movie was very popular, so audiences knew what Hildy was referring to when she tells Chip, "And when we get through with them, we'll go see the Cat People."

Cleopatra's Needle: An impressive Egyptian obelisk, familiarly known as Cleopatra's Needle, was moved from Egypt to Central Park in 1880, where it still resides. Cleopatra's Needle is on the list of sights Chip wants to see in the song "Come Up to My Place," but Hildy recommends "My place!"

Cloisters: Located in Fort Tryon Park in Upper Manhattan is a Met museum and reconstructed monastery known as the Cloisters, which specializes in European medieval art and architecture. In the song "Come Up to My Place," Chip tells Hildy that he wants to see the Cloisters.

Coney Island: Coney Island is not an island but an entertainment area in the southwestern section of the New York City borough of Brooklyn. In addition to the large beach, there have been amusement parks on the "island" since 1887. In 1944, Coney Island was very popular, but the entertainment was mostly sideshows, rides, and tawdry girlie shows, such as the fictional "Rajah Bimmy's Night in a Harem," where Ivy Smith works.

Congacabana: One of the New York nightclubs the three sailors go to is called the Congacabana Club. It is a fictitious place with a portmanteau name. The conga is a dance in which several people in a single line, one behind the other, move forward after stopping to kick on the downbeat. The Copacabana, familiarly known as The Copa, is a real New York City nightclub that was very popular with celebrities in the 1940s and 1950s.

Congressman Bundy: Pitkin W. Bridgework says to Claire: "Don't worry, darling. I have a date with Congressman Bundy." Mentioning a Congressman Bundy in the script leads one to assume Betty Comden and Adolph Green had someone in mind, and that just mentioning him would get a laugh. But the joke's on us, because there was no one by the name of Bundy in Congress in the 1940s.

cooch dancer: Carnivals and fairs often had shows featuring cooch dancers, women whose dancing included sinuous and often suggestive twisting and shaking of the torso and limbs. Ivy Smith tries to keep it a secret that she earns money as a cooch dancer at Coney Island.

demitasse: In the song "I Can Cook, Too," Hildy sings, "I'm a man's ideal of a perfect meal, / Right down to the demitasse." A small cup of strong black coffee or espresso is a demitasse, which means "half of a cup" in French. The demitasse usually comes at the end of a meal.

Flatiron Building: Completed in 1902 as the Fuller Building, the Flatiron Building is Manhattan's first skyscraper, and a groundbreaking masterwork of architecture. On the list of sights that Chip wants to see is this classic structure.

Herald Square: The area between 34th and 35th Streets and Broadway and Sixth Avenue became known as Herald Square because the *New York Herald* had its main offices there. Herald Square is among the sights Chip wants to see in the song "Come Up to My Place," but Hildy keeps insisting, "My place!"

Hippodrome . . . *Aida*: The Hippodrome Theatre in Midtown Manhattan was once the largest theater in the world. The 5,200-seat venue housed circuses, aquacades, pageants, grand opera, and other extravaganzas. Built in 1905, the Hippodrome rarely showed a profit because of its expensive overhead, so it was demolished in 1939. The Nubian princess Aida is the title character in Giuseppe Verdi's 1868 opera, set in ancient Egypt. Such large-scale operas were sometimes presented at the Hippodrome. In the song "Come Up to My Place," Chip says his father told him to be sure to see the Hippodrome, to which Hildy sings, "It ain't there anymore. / Aida sang an 'A' and blew the place away."

IRT: New York's transportation system, the Interborough Rapid Transit Company (IRT), goes back to 1904. When Chip keeps telling Hildy that he has to go and find Ivy Smith, Hildy tells him, "Here's the phone. We'll call the IRT and find her."

Lindy's . . . Lüchow's: Chip wants to see these two famous eateries in New York in the song "Come Up to My Place," but Hildy recommends dining at "My place!" Leo "Lindy" Lindemann founded the popular deli-restaurant Lindy's in 1921, and it lasted until 1969. Lüchow's was a renowned German restaurant located at 14th Street, in business from 1882 until the 1970s.

MacDougal Alley . . . Green-witch Village: Long a home of artists, writers, and performers, Greenwich Village is a neighborhood on the West Side of Lower Manhattan in New York City. MacDougal Alley is a cul-de-sac off MacDougal Street in Greenwich Village. Chip mispronounces "Greenwich" when he tells his buddies, "There are 20,000 streets in New York City, not counting MacDougal Alley in the heart of Green-witch Village."

Macy's . . . Gimbel's: Two of New York's favorite department stores were located close to Herald Square in the 1940s. R. H. Macy & Co. was founded in 1858 and is still there. Gimbel's Department Store was nearby and served the public from 1887 to 1987. Both stores are on the list of sights Chip wants to see in the song "Come Up to My Place."

marron glacé: A French dessert in which chestnuts are preserved in and coated with sugar is called a marron glacé. In the song "I Can Cook, Too," Hildy sings, "Oh, I'm a pâté, / A marron glacé."

Miss Turnstiles: The Transit Authority of New York, who ran the subways, trains, and buses, had a promotion program called "Miss Subways," which ran from 1941 until 1971. The TA selected a woman each month to represent and promote subway ridership. Posters were printed and plastered throughout the five-borough subway system. As with Miss Turnstiles in the musical, each "Miss Subways" became a neighborhood celebrity for a brief period of time, then had to pass the title on to another girl.

Museum of Modern Art . . . Museum of Natural History: The Museum of Modern Art, located in Midtown Manhattan just a few blocks south of Central Park, opened in 1929 and is the foremost home of modern and postmodern art. The American Museum of Natural History has one of the largest collections of artifacts from nature. The subway poster said Ivy Smith regularly patronized the Museum of Modern Art, so Ozzie goes looking for her, for his pal Gabey, but he mistakenly ends up at the Museum of Natural History, where he meets Claire de Loone.

Nedick's: When the three sailors split up to try to find Ivy Smith, Chip says, "We'll meet . . . at Times Square. At Nedick's at eleven." Nedick's was an American chain of fast-food restaurants that originated in New York City in 1913. In 1944, one was located at Times Square.

Peoria: The city of Peoria is the oldest European settlement in Illinois and has often been used as an example of Middle America. In show business, a familiar question has always been, "Will it play in Peoria?" The sailor Chip is from Peoria, and in the song "Ya Got Me," he sings, "You got my whole family in Peoria, for you to see!"

pizzicato: Plucking the strings of a violin or other stringed instrument with one's finger is called pizzicato. In the song "I Get Carried Away," Claire sings about how she gets overexcited at a symphony: "They're playing pizzicato / And everything goes blotto!"

Quasimodo: The name of the hunchbacked bell ringer in Victor Hugo's novel *The Hunchback of Notre Dame* (1831) is Quasimodo. When Ozzie bumps into the dinosaur skeleton in the Museum of Natural History, he says, "Owww! Out of my way, Quasimodo!"

Reuben's: Reuben's Restaurant and Delicatessen was a landmark in New York City, founded by the German immigrant Arnold Reuben in 1908. In 1944, the restaurant was located on Madison Avenue. Reuben's is on the list of sights Chip wants to see in the song "Come Up to My Place," but Hildy recommends that she cook dinner at "My place!"

Roxy . . . Radio City: Chip wants to see New York's two largest movie palaces in the song "Come Up to My Place." The Roxy Theatre was a 5,920-seat movie theater located just off Times Square. It opened in 1927 and was demolished in 1960. With more than six thousand seats, Radio City Music Hall was the largest movie theater in the world when it opened in 1932. It is still an impressive venue in Rockefeller Center.

Scranton: Scranton is a city in northeastern Pennsylvania's Wyoming Valley, set among coal mines and railroad yards. Ozzie is from Scranton and wants to meet "one of those New York City glamour girls," because "back home in Scranton, everybody's covered with coal dust!"

Tilyou: George C. Tilyou (1862–1914) was an American entrepreneur and showman who built Steeplechase Park, an early amusement park at Coney Island. Madame Dilly tells Gabey that he can find Ivy Smith "at the corner of Tilyou and the Boardwalk—Coney Island."

Tobacco Road . . . Angel Street: In the song "Come Up to My Place," Chip asks Hildy to take him to the Forrest Theatre so he can "get some tickets for *Tobacco Road*," but Hildy sings, "That show has closed up shop. /The actors washed their feet / And called it *Angel Street*." One of the longest-running plays of its era was *Tobacco Road*, about a family of backwater (and dirty) Georgia farmers. It opened in 1931 and ran until 1941. *Angel Street* was the American title for the British thriller *Gaslight*, about a husband who is trying to drive his wife insane. It opened on Broadway in 1941 and ran for three years.

Wanamaker's store: John Wanamaker Department Store was one of the first department stores in the nation, beginning in Philadelphia and later having stores in major cities. Chip wants to see the New York store at Broadway and Ninth Street in the song "Come Up to My Place."

Westchester: Westchester, New York, is an affluent suburb of New York City, located north of the Bronx. At the Museum of Natural History, the archaeologist Waldo Figment tells the onlookers, "This unique skeleton— I have reconstructed without any clue whatsoever, except for one tiny bone, found during a picnic in Westchester, in the bushes."

Woolworth Tower: The Woolworth Building, an early American sky-scraper in the Tribeca neighborhood of Manhattan, was the tallest build-ing in the world from 1913 to 1930, when the Empire State Building was completed. Using his outdated guidebook, Chip asks Hildy to drive him to the "city's highest spot, / Atop the famous Woolworth Tower" in the song "Come Up to My Place." Hildy replies, "That ain't the highest spot. / You're just a little late, / We've got the Empire State!"

Yonkers . . . Bay: In the song "New York, New York," Chip sings "Gotta see the whole town / Right from Yonkers on down to the Bay." His geography is correct, but only as far as the borough of Manhattan goes. New York City begins in the Bronx, just south of the city of Yonkers, New York, and ends at the southern tip of Manhattan, where the body of water is called the Upper New York Bay. What Chip doesn't consider is Staten Island, Brooklyn, and Queens.

THE PAJAMA GAME

Libretto by George Abbott and Richard Bissell, based on Bissell's novel *7½ Cents*. Music and lyrics by Richard Adler and Jerry Ross. Original Broadway production: May 13, 1954. St. James Theatre. 1,063 perfor-mances. Broadway revivals in 1973 and 2006.

For a musical about labor relations, *The Pajama Game* is a very escapist show with little emphasis on the economic and political issues. That makes it a typical 1950s musical comedy rather than the kind of questioning shows of the 1960s and 1970s. *The Pajama Game* is mostly set in the fic-tional Sleeptite Pajama Factory in Cedar Rapids, Iowa, in the mid-1950s. Some of the expressions denote the Midwest, but many were used across the nation in the 1950s. Only a few of them are still used today.

Expressions, references, names:

Captain Bligh: When Sid jokingly tells Babe, "Personally, I think a little physical punishment is good for people once in a while," Babe responds, "Oh, do you, Captain Bligh?" The British naval officer William Bligh (1754–1817) was captain of the HMS *Bounty*, and his cruelty toward his crew led to the famous mutiny.

Dictaphone: A tape recorder that records and reproduces dictation is called a Dictaphone. They were once found in offices across the nation. In the song "Hey, There," Sid sings into the Dictaphone, then replays the recording, allowing him to sing a duet with himself.

doll: A slang term for a woman who is much less than a lady; Babe says about herself to Sid, "Miss Williams is a very cold, hard-boiled doll."

eins . . . zwei . . . drei: The German words for "one . . . two . . . three" are *eins . . . zwei . . . drei*. During his knife-throwing act, Hines says, "Here we go. *Eins . . . zwei . . . drei!*" before he throws his knife.

go roll a hoop: Hoop rolling, also called hoop trundling, was once a popular child's game in which a large hoop is rolled along the ground, generally pushed forward by means of a stick. Prez tells Gladys, "You tell Hineszie to go roll a hoop down Main Street."

hot box . . siding: When Pop returns from his job on the railroad and Babe asks, "How was your trip?," he replies, "Dirty—got another hot box. On the siding for twenty-five minutes." An axle or journal box on a railway car that has become overheated by excessive friction is referred to as a hot box. A railroad siding is a small stretch of railroad track that is used to store rolling stock or enable trains to pass through on the same line.

J. P. Morgan: One of the most powerful banking moguls of his era, John Pierpont Morgan (1837–1913) financed railroads and helped organize US Steel, General Electric, and other major corporations. Factory owner Hasler tells his employees, "Turn off those damn lights. Do you think J. P. Morgan got rich leaving lights burning all over Wall Street?"

limey . . . pub: The American slang nickname for a British person is *limey*. The term came from the practice English sailors had of eating limes to avoid scurvy. In the reprise of "There Once Was a Man," Sid sings, "I love you . . . more than a limey loves his pub." A pub, short for public house, is a British bar or tavern.

lunch bucket: Better known as a lunch pail, a lunch bucket was a container made out of metal. The item came to symbolize the working-class man, and the term *lunch-bucket issues* meant union activities. Prez, the president of the local union, says, "Hey, I lost my lunch bucket. Anybody seen my lunch bucket?"

Marx and Klein: A popular-priced department store chain based in New York City; Mabel says, "Here's a letter from Marx and Klein over to Fort Wayne, Indiana," to which Hasler says, "Marx and Klein? Damn chain outfit. Damn Communists!"

Massillon, Chillicothe, Van Wert, Napoleon: A salesman for the pajama business says, "I knocked them for a loop in Massillon, Chillicothe, Van Wert, Napoleon," all the names of small cities in Ohio.

rhubarb: A slang term that refers to a fight or argument, the term is especially associated with baseball, as when chaos breaks out on the field when an unpopular call is made by the referee. Charlie tells Sid, "The Grievance Committee can start quite a rhubarb," to which Sid replies, "This whole town's a rhubarb."

Rita Hayworth: When Pop says to Babe, "I stopped in at the corner tavern for a beer just now and guess who I run into," Babe sarcastically replies, "Old man Hasler and Rita Hayworth." A glamorous film star of the 1940s and 1950, Rita Hayworth (1918–1987) exuded sex appeal and a sparkling persona.

snow job: Any effort to deceive, persuade, or overwhelm with insincere talk is called a snow job. The slangy expression originated during World War II, probably coming from the idea of being "snowed under" with work and unable to see the truth. The union members at the Sleeptite Pajama Factory complain about the "snow job" they are getting from management.

"tempus fugit": Latin for "time flies," the phrase *tempus fugit* is used to remind one of the quick passage of time. Hines says, "All right, girls. Cut out the laughing. Tempest fugit. Tempest fugit." Later in the song "Think of the Time I Save," he sings, "Tick tock, tick tock, Tempest fugit."

"that ain't hay": An old expression meaning something is more valuable than it appears to be, the term usually refers to money. An employee at the pajama factory says, "You know what they're paying at the packing plant? Ninety-three up. That ain't hay neither."

Walter Winchell: The syndicated American newspaper and radio gossip columnist Walter Winchell (1897–1972) was very powerful, sometimes capable of swaying public opinion. Hasler says, "It's just as Walter Winchell said last night. Do you listen to Walter Winchell, Sorokin?," to which Sid replies, "Well, I'm rather flexible in the matter." Later, Mabel asks, "Say, Sid, who is this Walter Winchell he's always talking about?," and Sid wryly replies, "He plays third base for the New York Yankees."

PAL JOEY

Libretto by John O'Hara and George Abbott, based on O'Hara's *Pal Joey* short stories. Lyrics by Lorenz Hart. Music by Richard Rodgers. Original Broadway production: December 25, 1940. Ethel Barrymore Theatre. 374 performances. Broadway revivals in 1952, 1963, 1976, and 2008.

In John O'Hara's *Pal Joey* stories, Joey Evans moves from city to city in order to escape creditors, hoods, dames, and the law. The musical all takes place in Chicago in the late 1930s, but Joey's itinerant personality is intact. *Pal Joey* is famous for introducing such a disreputable, incorrigible character to American musical theatre. The other characters are not far behind, and most of them, rich or on the outs, use backstage slang and street vernacular. This is an adult musical, maybe the first adult musical, and it still bothers and fascinates audiences with its tough attitude.

Expressions, references, names:

Beatrice Lillie, Clifton Webb, Noel Coward, Gertie Lawrence: Whether he is being interviewed by Melba, acting as emcee at Mike's club, or trying to impress women, Joey lies a lot. One night at the club he tells the patrons, "At two o'clock we have Beatrice Lillie, Clifton Webb, Noel Coward, Gertie Lawrence, and a whole mob coming down from some other big party." Lillie was the beloved British comedian; Webb, the American stage actor who found renown in the movies; Coward, the celebrated actor-playwright-songwriter of theatre and film; and Lawrence, a favorite musical theatre star on both sides of the Atlantic. None of them would be found in a place like Mike's.

Betty Grable: The favorite pinup girl during World War II, Betty Grable (1916–1973) was a blond dancer, model, and singer who was featured in many "campus" musicals in the 1930s. As Joey is lying about the colleges he went to, Melba says, "You make it sound like one of those colleges where Betty Grable's always going."

Bob Hope: The British-American comedian Bob Hope (1903–2003) was only at the beginning of his eighty-year career in 1940, and at the time was mostly known for his radio broadcasts. Joey tells the patrons at Mike's nightclub, "First I come out and tell a few stories. Of course if you want to sit home and listen to Bob Hope [on the radio], you'll hear the same stories."

Brooks Brothers: In operation in New York City since 1818, Brooks Brothers is the oldest apparel brand in continuous operation in America, known particularly for men's wear. Picking out a wardrobe, Vera says to Joey, "The important thing is the evening clothes. Not too Brooks Brothers."

Cab Calloway: Long associated with the Cotton Club in Harlem, Cab Calloway (1907–1994) was an American jazz singer, songwriter, dancer, and bandleader during the swing era, though his career went on for sixty-five years. In the song "Do It the Hard Way," Vera sings, "Working hard did not retard / The young Cab Calloway."

COD: When the receiver of a package must pay for the item, it is considered "cash on delivery" (COD). Linda tells Gladys, "I have a COD for Mr. Evans, but I'm supposed to collect the money from Mr. Mike."

Confucius . . . Lucius: Confucius (551–479 BCE) was China's most famous teacher, philosopher, and political theorist, whose ideas have profoundly influenced much of the Eastern world. Lucius Accius (170–86 BCE) was one of the greatest of the Roman tragic poets. In the song "Zip," the stripper's thoughts are, "I adore the great Confucius, / And the lines of luscious Lucius."

Connie Van Rensselaer: The Van Rensselaers of Old Dutch New York were prominent leaders in business, politics, and society for three hundred years. When interviewed by Melba, Joey tries to impress her with a phony past: "There was this society singer from New York—I grew up with her. Her name was Consuelo Van Rensselaer—Connie."

crib: A slang name for any place, from a home to a saloon; the word fell out of fashion until it started showing up in rap and hip-hop songs in the 1990s. Because of the popularity of the MTV show *Cribs*, the word now usually means a private residence. When Vera and her party leave the nightclub, an angry Mike tells Joey, "She picks my lousy crib by some accident, and what do you do? You give her the business!"

Crosby: Arguably the first multimedia star, Bing Crosby (1903–1977) was a top-selling singer and a star in movies for over four decades. Joey admits to club owner Mike, "All right. So I'm not a Crosby. But do these local clients know that?"

Dalí's paintings . . . passé: The Spanish surrealist artist Salvador Dalí (1904–1989) was renowned for the striking and bizarre images in his work. In the song "Zip," burlesque queen Gypsy Rose Lee's thoughts about the artist are expressed with, "Zip! I consider Dalí's paintings passé." The French word *passé* literally means "gone by." Today it refers to anything no longer fashionable or popular.

Dardanella: Published in 1919, the song "Dardanella" by Fred Fisher, Felix Bernard, and Johnny S. Black was very popular for three decades. Joey says to Melba, "We were sitting around singing all the old songs, Dardanella . . . The oldies."

Dartmouth: Dartmouth College is a private Ivy League research college in Hanover, New Hampshire, established in 1769. It is the ninth-oldest institution of higher education in the United States. Joey lies to Melba, saying, "I was up to Dartmouth University—" and she says, "I thought they called it Dartmouth College."

El Morocco . . . Foreign Legion: When Joey tells Gladys he's going "to El Morocco in New York," she responds, "What? El Morocco. You'd have to join the Foreign Legion to get to Morocco." El Morocco was a Manhattan nightclub frequented by the rich and famous from the 1930s until the late 1950s. The French Foreign Legion is an elite military force originally consisting of foreign volunteers in the pay of France. The Legion has often been associated with fighting in exotic locales, including French Morocco.

Follies: The elaborate Broadway revues called the *Ziegfeld Follies* were simply known as the *Follies*. These extravagant shows appeared annually from 1907 to 1931, with renewals in 1934 and 1936. Annoyed with the way rehearsal is going at Mike's saloon, chorus girl Wagner says, "What does he think this is, the *Follies?*"

Fred Astaire: In the song "Do It the Hard Way," Vera sings, "Fred Astaire once worked so hard / He often lost his breath." By 1940, American actor, dancer, singer, and choreographer Fred Astaire (1899–1987) had established himself as Hollywood's premier dancer.

great Cabala . . . Allah: A complex method, discipline, and school of thought in Jewish mysticism can be found in the books of the Cabala (*Kabbalah* in Hebrew). *Allah* is the common Arabic word for God. Such elevated concepts are on the mind of Gypsy Rose Lee while she undresses on stage, according to the song "Zip": "I have read the great Cabala / And I simply worship Allah."

"have a powder": Old-time slang for "Let's have a drink" or "Go have a drink" is "Have a powder." Joey says to Melba, "Let's have a powder. [calls out] Waldo!—You drink, of course."

"I'm a red-hot mama": The American singer, comedian, and radio personality Sophie Tucker (1886–1966) billed herself as "The Last of the Red-Hot Mamas." She was known for her full-voiced delivery of comical and risqué songs. Gladys pays homage to Tucker when she sings, "I'm a red-hot mama" at the end of the song "That Terrific Rainbow."

Lili St. Cyr: The buxom blonde Lili St. Cyr (1918–1999) was a notable striptease artist of the 1940s and 1950s. After a career in burlesque, St. Cyr promoted women's outer clothes and ran a mail-order lingerie company. A rival of Gypsy Rose Lee, St. Cyr is included in the song "Zip!" with "Who the hell is Lili St. Cyr?"

The Man Who Came to Dinner: One of the biggest comedy hits of its day, George S. Kaufman and Moss Hart's *The Man Who Came to Dinner* opened on Broadway in 1939. On the phone, Vera says to Joey, "You'll have to identify yourself . . . What was the name of the play we saw in New York last summer?" Joey thinks fast and responds, "Why, I think we saw *The Man Who Came to Dinner*."

Margie Hart: Billed as "The Poor Man's Garbo," burlesque star Margie Hart (1913–2000) didn't sing, dance, or even talk in her act, but just stripped, quickly and thoroughly. Hart was one of the headliners at Minsky's burlesque theater in Manhattan. In the song "Zip," Melba sings, "Zip! Who the hell is Margie Hart?"

Marshall Field's . . . floorwalker: Since the end of the nineteenth century, Marshall Field & Company has been the premier high-end, upscale department store in Chicago. A floorwalker is a senior employee of a large store who assists customers and supervises salespeople. Chorus girl Dottie tells the other girls about an ex-dancer at the club: "She's working at Marshall Field's . . . [as] a floorwalker."

Metropolitan: The Metropolitan Opera in New York City was founded in 1883 and was located at 39th Street and Broadway until 1966, when Lincoln Center was built. The Met, as it is often called, has always been an expensive enterprise that depends on donated money to exist. During the song "Zip," Gypsy Rose Lee wonders while she is stripping, "Zip! Can they make the Metropolitan pay?"

Mickey . . . Mouse or Rooney: Both Mickeys have had long and amazing careers. Mickey Mouse was created in 1928 by Ub Iwerks and Walt Disney, who originally voiced the character. The anthropomorphic mouse has been the company's mascot and symbol ever since. Mickey Rooney (1920–2014) had an acting career spanning nine decades, appearing in more than three hundred films. In 1940, he was most known for his teenage role in the Andy Hardy series and in musicals with Judy Garland. In the song "Zip," the stripper Gypsy Rose Lee has negative thoughts about both Mickeys, singing, "I don't care for either Mickey— / Mouse and Rooney make me sicky."

Minsky's . . . Miss Lee: In the song "Zip," Melba tells Mike, "But my greatest achievement is the interview I had / With the star who worked for Minsky . . . I said, 'Miss Lee, you are such an artist.'" The four Minsky brothers managed a burlesque theater empire in the 1920s and 1930s, and their flagship venue was Minsky's in New York City, considered the premier burlesque house in the nation. The biggest star at Minsky's was Gypsy Rose Lee (1911–1970), a stripper whose career later went far beyond burlesque. Her 1957 memoir was adapted into the 1959 stage musical *Gypsy*.

mouse: An old slang word for a female, *mouse* was not a very complimentary expression, and was usually used among men in a dismissive manner. Lowell asks Joey, "[I] deduce that you have a friend. Is this friend a man? Maybe. Or is it a mouse?"

nose candy: Cocaine in powdered form, typically ingested by snorting through the nose, is known as "nose candy" in the drug vernacular. When Joey tells Mike that he doesn't drink, Mike says, "Umm—so you don't drink. How about nose candy?"

Pablo Picasso . . . Countess di Frasso: In the song "Zip," Melba tells Mike: "I've interviewed Pablo Picasso / And a countess named di Frasso." The Spanish painter and sculptor Pablo Picasso (1881–1973) is regarded as one of the most influential artists of the twentieth century. The Countess di Frasso (1900–1985) was the title of the American heiress and model Dorothy Taylor after she married Count Carlo di Frasso in 1923. She was one of the richest women of her era.

Pollyanna: Linda tells the street-smart Gladys, "Oh, I'm not just a dumb Pollyanna, either." Although it's not often used today, in the past, calling someone a Pollyanna meant they were an excessively cheerful or optimistic person. The name came from a 1913 novel by Eleanor H. Porter, considered a classic of children's literature, and the source of many plays, movies, and TV dramas.

Pops Whiteman: The leader of one of the most popular dance bands in the nation during the 1920s and early 1930s was Paul Whiteman (1890–1967). He conducted all kinds of music, helped make jazz respectable, and nurtured the young George Gershwin. Melba asks Joey about his past, in particular about his supposed friendship with a countess: "Then did she say—you ought to be singing professionally, and introduce you to Pops Whiteman, and he gave you your first break? "

Princeton College: Founded in 1746 as the College of New Jersey, Princeton University is the fourth-oldest institution of higher education in America. Among the lies Joey tells Linda when he first meets her: "That was when I resigned from Princeton College." Most likely Joey did not know the difference between a college and a university.

Ravel's *Boléro*: Arguably the most famous orchestral piece by the French composer Maurice Ravel (1875–1937), *Boléro* was written for a ballet and first heard in 1928. In the song "In Our Little Den (of Iniquity)," Vera sings, "But now when it's dark and it's late / Ravel's *Boléro* works just great."

***Rip Van Winkle* . . . Tyrone Power:** In the song "Zip," stripper Gypsy Rose Lee thinks: "Zip! *Rip Van Winkle* on the screen would be smart; Zip! Tyrone Power will be cast in the part." The short story "Rip Van Winkle" by Washington Irving, first published in 1819, has been the inspiration for many plays, films, and television movies. The character of Rip is a lazy Dutch-American villager in colonial America who sleeps through twenty years. Tyrone Power (1914–1958) was an American film actor often cast in swashbuckler roles or romantic leads; casting him as Rip Van Winkle would be odd at best.

Roebuck . . . Sears: One of the most famous of all department stores was founded in 1892 by Richard Warren Sears and Alvah Curtis Roebuck. The Sears and Roebuck catalog opened new markets across the United States. In the song "Bewitched, Bothered and Bewildered," Vera sings, "You might say we are closer / Than Roebuck is to Sears."

Sally Rand: Most famous for her ostrich feather fan dance and balloon bubble dance, stripper Sally Rand (1904–1979) rivaled Gypsy Rose Lee on the burlesque stage. In the song "Zip," Gypsy Rose Lee asks, "Zip! Who the hell is Sally Rand?"

Saroyan: The unique American writer William Saroyan (1908–1981) wrote both fiction and plays. During the time of *Pal Joey*, Saroyan had yet to have any hit plays. So in the song "Zip," Gypsy Rose Lee wonders, "Zip! Will Saroyan ever write a great play?"

Schopenhauer: The German philosopher Arthur Schopenhauer (1788–1860) wrote about the frustration-filled and fundamentally painful human condition. In the song "Zip," Gypsy Rose Lee sings, "Zip! I was reading Schopenhauer last night. / Zip! And I think that Schopenhauer was right."

Sir Harry Lauder: In the song "The Flower Garden in My Heart," the tenor Louis sings, "Heather—Sir Harry Lauder sang of its beauties." The internationally known Scottish singer and comic Harry Lauder (1870–1950) came from music hall and vaudeville theatre. His singing could be very silly, but also very sentimental.

Stravinsky: Russian composer Igor Stravinsky (1882–1971) is generally considered one of the most innovative and influential composers of the twentieth century and the father of modernist music. In the song "Zip," Melba claims, "I've interviewed the great Stravinsky."

Teddy Winston: The salesman Ernest shows Joey a coat and says, "Mr. Teddy Winston, the polo player—Well, he has a jacket quite a little like it." Later in the scene, Vera tells Ernest, "And don't show us any more of Teddy Winston's stuff." Winston is probably a fictitious sportsman created by John O'Hara and George Abbott for *Pal Joey*, for there is no record of a noted polo player named Teddy Winston during that time of the century.

Tony De Marco . . . Veloz and Yolanda: Arguing about his tuxedo, Joey says to Mike: "You know who wears tails? Dancers. Tony De Marco. Veloz, you know. Veloz and Yolanda. They wear tails." The dancer Tony De Marco (1898–1965) was featured in several Broadway musicals of the era. Frank Veloz (1906–1981) and his wife, Yolanda Casazza (1908–1995), were an American ballroom dance team who became highly paid stars in the 1930s and 1940s.

Toscanini . . . Jergen's Lotion: One of the great virtuoso conductors of the first half of the twentieth century, Arturo Toscanini (1867–1957) was a household name because of his many radio broadcasts. Introduced in 1901, Jergen's skin-care products continue to be household names. In the song "Zip," stripper Gypsy Rose Lee sings, "Zip! Toscanini leads the greatest of bands; / Zip! Jergen's Lotion does the trick for his hands."

Waldorf Astoria: One of the most desirable luxury hotels in New York City since it opened in 1931, the Waldorf Astoria on Park Avenue is an Art Deco landmark with restaurants and lounges. Trying to impress Mike,

Joey tells him, "Why, last month when I was at the Waldorf Astoria—" but Mike stops him short with, "Don't give me that."

Walter Lippmann: For sixty years, Walter Lippmann (1889–1974) was an outspoken newspaper and radio columnist commenting on world affairs. In the song "Zip," Gypsy Rose Lee has her own comment: "Zip! Walter Lippmann wasn't brilliant today."

Whistler's Mother . . . Charley's Aunt . . . Shubert's brother: Gypsy Rose Lee dismisses three very different relatives in the song "Zip," in which she sings, "I don't care for Whistler's Mother, / Charley's Aunt or Shubert's brother." Although everyone calls it "Whistler's Mother," James McNeill Whistler's 1871 painting of his mother is titled *Arrangement in Grey and Black No. 1*. The 1893 British farce *Charley's Aunt* by Brandon Thomas is about an Oxford student disguising himself as a fellow student's rich aunt. The Shubert brothers were theatrical managers and producers of the largest theater empire of the twentieth century: Lee (1873?–1953), Samuel S. (1875?–1905), and Jacob J. (1879?–1963) were sometimes ruthless moguls who left behind a chain of theaters across the country.

Yankee Clipper: A swanky nightclub-restaurant in Manhattan in the 1930s and 1940s; in the song "Zip," Melba tells Mike about her interview with the burlesque star Gypsy Rose Lee: "I met her at the Yankee Clipper / And she didn't unzip one zipper."

Zorina . . . Cobina: The Norwegian-born ballet dancer Vera Zorina (1917–2003) was also a favorite on Broadway and in films. The American opera singer Cobina Wright (1887–1970) also had a career in other venues outside the opera house. In the song "Zip," stripper Gypsy Rose Lee dismisses such highbrows with, "I don't want to see Zorina . . . I don't want to meet Cobina."

PIPPIN

Libretto by Roger O. Hirson. Music and lyrics by Stephen Schwartz. Original Broadway production: October 23, 1972. Winter Garden Theatre. 1,944 performances. Broadway revival in 2013.

One of the very few musicals set in medieval times, *Pippin* makes no attempt to be accurate in its dialogue or in its handling of history. Yet there

PIPPIN   *The people and events of the Dark Ages are often more legend than accurate history, which gives this anachronistic musical a lot of room for invention.*
Photofest

are a still a few period references in the book and songs. It is difficult to put an exact date on the events in the musical, but it is not really necessary in such an anachronistic show. If a date were assigned, it would be AD 792, the year during the Dark Ages in which Pepin, or Pippin, tried to overthrow his father, Charlemagne.

Expressions, references, names:

anecdotic revue: In the opening number, "Magic to Do," the Leading Player describes the show to be presented as an "anecdotic revue." An anecdote is a short tale, usually comic, or at least amusing. A revue is a performance composed mostly of songs and dance. So *Pippin* is a combination of the two: an episodic tale told with musical numbers.

Arles: A city in southeastern France, it was the capital of the medieval kingdom of Arles. In the musical, Charlemagne goes to Arles to pray, and it is there that Pippin slays him—but only temporarily.

Berthe: Pippin's grandmother in the musical is called Berthe, but she was actually named Bertrada of Laon. She gave birth to Charlemagne before she was married to Pepin the Short, Pippin's grandfather, whom he was named after. So, technically, Charlemagne was illegitimate.

brine: When water is strongly mixed with salt and is used to preserve food, it is called "the water of the sea," or brine. The Leading Player sings about "the taste of salty summer brine" in the song "Glory."

charlatan: A fraudulent person, one who falsely claims to have a special knowledge or skill, has been called a charlatan since the seventeenth century. In the song "War Is a Science," the king sings, "I'll endeavor to explain what separates a charlatan from a Charlemagne."

Charlemagne: A translation of the French "Charles the Great," Charlemagne (AD 742–814) was the mightiest conqueror and ruler of his time. He was king of the Franks and the first Holy Roman Emperor. He had several wives and many children, both legitimate and not.

defilade . . . enfilade: *Defilade* is a military term for the protection of an army's position by keeping from being observed by the enemy. In a medieval battle, a volley of gunfire directed along a line from end to end is called an *enfilade*. Charlemagne sings of "Bearing principles of enfilade and defilade in mind," in the song "War Is a Science."

Fastrada: Charlemagne's third wife was Fastrada, and they were married for ten years before she died. Fastrada gave Charlemagne two children, but neither was named Lewis, as in the musical.

Frisians . . . Visigoths: The inhabitants of the West German land of Frisia (or Friesland) were known as Frisians. They are the invading barbarians whom Charlemagne in the musical says he defeated "last year." The Visigoths were a Germanic tribe and a member of the branch of the Goths. The Visigoths often invaded the Roman Empire between the third and fifth centuries AD. They were overthrown by the Moors in 711. Charlemagne and his army battle the Visigoths in the "War" section of the musical. Lewis boasts, "Did you know this arm slew twenty Frisians last year? And it's going to slay even more Visigoths."

Holy Roman Empire: During the early Middle Ages, a monarchy that covered most of Europe was known as the Holy Roman Empire. Pope Leo III crowned Charlemagne the first Holy Roman Emperor in AD 800. For the brief time in the musical when Pippin thought he had killed his father, Pippin was Holy Roman Emperor.

infidels: Anyone whose religious beliefs differ greatly from one's own are sometimes called infidels. Charlemagne refers to all the tribes threatening the Church as infidels.

King Aleric: The first king of the Visigoths was Aleric I (AD c. 370–410). Charlemagne goes to war against Aleric and the Visigoths in the "War" section of the musical.

lea: Any open area of grassy or arable land is called a lea. They sing of a battle "on the lea" in the song "War Is a Science."

Lewis: The pompous son Lewis of Charlemagne in the musical is based on Louis the Pious, one of the king's two sons. After Charlemagne's death, Louis became King of the Aquitaine.

pastorally: When the subject of a story or piece of art is about the land or a farm, it is called "pastoral." In the opening number, the Leading Player sings that the musical will have "sex presented pastorally."

Pippin: Spelled "Pepin" in the Middle Ages, the name refers to two different people. Charlemagne's father was Pepin the Short, and Charlemagne named his eldest son after him. Because of a malformation, the son became known as Pepin the Hunchback (AD c. 769–811). He led a rebellion to try to overthrow Charlemagne in 792, but failed, and was banished to Prüm Abbey.

Pompey . . . Darius: Gnaeus Pompeius Magnus (106–48 BCE), also known as Pompey the Great, was a Roman general of renown. Darius the Great (c. 550–486 BCE) was a Persian king and a great warrior, but when he invaded Greece, he was defeated at the Battle of Marathon. In the song "War Is a Science," Charlemagne sings, "A rule confessed by generals illustrious and various / Though as pompous as a Pompey or as daring as a Darius."

Valhalla: In Scandinavian mythology, the hall in which heroes killed in battle were believed to feast with Odin for eternity was called Valhalla. Pippin asks the severed Head of a Visigoth soldier if he will go to Valhalla because he died in battle. The Head tells him that King Aleric "assured us personally."

Vistula: An Eastern European river, the Vistula is remembered by Charlemagne as the place where "I drowned two legions."

Volga: The longest river in Europe, the Volga flows through Russia to the Caspian Sea. Charlemagne recalls a battle he fought on the banks of the Volga in the "War" section of the musical.

RAGTIME

Libretto by Terrence McNally, based on the novel by E. L. Doctorow. Lyrics by Lynn Ahrens. Music by Stephen Flaherty. Original Broadway production: January 18, 2000. Ford Center for the Performing Arts. 834 performances. Broadway revival in 2009.

Few musicals have the wide scope of *Ragtime*. With its many characters, locales, and themes, it can truly be called a musical epic. Terrence McNally did an admirable job adapting E. L. Doctorow's massive novel into an expert libretto. Like the book, the three central stories involve both fictional and historical characters, yet they are all so well drawn that it is sometimes difficult to tell history from fiction. The action is confined to a few years in the first decade of the twentieth century. The settings include various New York City locales, New Rochelle (New York), Lawrence (Massachusetts), and Atlantic City (New Jersey), so there are several references to names and places that need exploring.

Expressions, references, names:

Admiral Peary: Credited with being the first person to reach the North Pole, Admiral Robert E. Peary (1856–1920) was an American navy officer and explorer who made several expeditions to the Arctic. Father says to

Peary, "It is an honor to go on expedition with you, Admiral Peary. It's men like you who've made this country great."

Atlantic City: The coastal metropolis Atlantic City in New Jersey is known today for its casinos, boardwalk, and beaches. In the early part of the twentieth century, Atlantic City went through a significant building boom, and the modest boardinghouses along the boardwalk were replaced with large hotels, including two of the city's most famous: the Marlborough-Blenheim Hotel and the Traymore Hotel. Hoping to escape from all the unwanted publicity, Father tells Mother, "Atlantic City is only a temporary answer, Mother, but I can't think of a better one."

Booker T. Washington: The leading Black intellectual at the turn of the twentieth century, Booker T. Washington (1856–1915) was born into slavery and rose to found the Tuskegee Normal and Industrial Institute. Washington was an educator, author, orator, and advisor to several presidents of the United States. In *Ragtime*, he introduces himself to the audience with, "Booker T. Washington was the most famous Negro in the country. He counseled friendship between the races and spoke of the promise of the future."

Braves . . . Giants . . . Hub Perdue . . . Jack Murray: At a baseball game in the musical, the fans sing, "It's Braves and Giants / Two to two . . . The pitcher's name is / Hub Perdue . . . Jack Murray's now / Up at bat." Boston's professional baseball team became the Doves in 1907 and the Rustlers in 1911 before settling on the Boston Braves in 1912. The New York Giants was founded in 1883 as the New York Gothams, then changed to the Giants in 1885. Herbert "Hub" Perdue (1882–1968) was a Braves pitcher known as the Gallatin Squash. Jack "Red" Murray (1884–1958) was an American outfielder in Major League Baseball who was traded to the New York Giants and helped win three consecutive pennants. Murray tied with Honus Wagner for the most home runs in the majors, from 1907 through 1909.

Children's Crusade: Younger Brother tells the audience, "The strike in Lawrence became famous. The press called it the Children's Crusade. Public indignation grew. The mill owners were not slow in calling in the militia to protect their property." In 1912, ten thousand workers at the American Woolen Company in Lawrence, Massachusetts, went on strike, and violence followed. Around two hundred children of immigrants were sent away on trains to foster homes. The so-called Children's Crusade brought awareness and sympathy to the Lawrence strikers. The authorities then sent the militia to intervene with the next attempt to send children away. Mothers and children were clubbed and arrested. The brutality of this event gained national coverage and led to an investigation by Congress. After three months, the mill owners gave in to the strikers' original demands for higher pay.

coon songs: When Coalhouse sits at the family's piano and starts to play, Grandfather asks him, "Do you know any coon songs?" Coon songs were a genre of music that presented a stereotype of Blacks in the South. These songs were popular in minstrel shows as far back as 1848, and were still being written (usually by white songwriters) and performed (usually by white actors in blackface) into the 1920s.

Emma Goldman: The anarchist Emma Goldman (1869–1940) was a political activist and writer who fought for the workers in America during the first decades of the twentieth century. Goldman introduces herself to the audience with, "The radical anarchist Emma Goldman fought against the ravages of American capitalism as she watched her fellow immigrants' hopes turn to despair on the Lower East Side."

Evelyn Nesbit: The model and Broadway chorus girl Evelyn Nesbit (c. 1884–1967) was the lover of celebrated architect Stanford White and the wife of railroad scion Harry K. Thaw. When Thaw killed White in a jealous rage, the resulting trial made Nesbit famous. She later found a career in vaudeville. In *Ragtime*, Evelyn introduces herself, saying, "Evelyn Nesbit was the most beautiful woman in America. If she wore her hair in curls, every woman wore her hair in curls."

excrescence: A noticeable outgrowth on a human or animal body, especially one that is the result of disease or abnormality, is called an excrescence. The chorus sings about Coalhouse: "He calls [Fire Chief] Conklin the white excrescence."

"a gang, a crazy gang": In the epilogue of the musical, Tateh tells the audience about his idea for a movie: "A bunch of children, white . . . black, Christian . . . Jew, rich . . . poor—all kinds—a gang, a crazy gang getting into trouble, getting out of trouble, but together despite their differences." He is referring to the *Our Gang* film shorts that were made by producer Hal Roach from 1922 to 1944. These silent—then later, talking—movies featured a diverse group of poor neighborhood children and their misadventures. Most know of the "gang" from the later title, *The Little Rascals.*

Harlem: In the opening number of *Ragtime*, Coalhouse tells the audience, "In Harlem, men and women of color forgot their troubles and danced and reveled to the music." The neighborhood of Harlem in Upper Manhattan had been home to Jewish and Italian immigrants, but by 1900 the Great Migration of Black people from the South to Northern industrial cities turned Harlem into a bustling Black community. There would eventually be a Harlem Renaissance in which Black artists thrived.

Harry Houdini: Perhaps the most famous magician in American history, the Hungarian American Harry Houdini (1874–1926) was best known as an escape artist during his lifetime. In *Ragtime*, Houdini introduces himself to the audience with, "Harry Houdini was one immigrant who made an art of escape. He was a headliner in the top vaudeville circuits."

Harry K. Thaw: The son of coal and railroad baron William Thaw Sr. of Pittsburgh, Harry Kendall Thaw (1871–1947) was heir to a multimillion-dollar fortune. He married the model and chorus girl Evelyn Nesbit, and his jealousy over her past lovers drove him to distraction. Thaw shot and killed the renowned architect Stanford White in 1906 on the rooftop of New York City's Madison Square Garden in front of hundreds of onlookers. In the opening musical number, Thaw tells the audience that "the eccentric millionaire, Harry K. Thaw, was a violent man."

Henry Ford: The Industrial Revolution came to America through the ideas of Henry Ford (1863–1947), a business magnate and founder of the Ford Motor Company. Ford developed the assembly-line technique of mass production and was able to make the first cars that middle-class Americans could afford. Ford sings to the workers, "Well, here's my theory / Of what this country / Is moving toward. / Every worker / A cog in motion. / Well, that's the notion of / Henry Ford!"

Jim Europe Clef Club Orchestra: Coalhouse tells Mother, "I am a professional, ma'am. I'm now with the Jim Europe Clef Club Orchestra. They're quite well known." James Reese Europe (1881–1919) was a Black ragtime and early jazz bandleader, arranger, and composer. In 1910,

Europe organized the Clef Club, a society for Black musicians, and two years later the Club made history when it played a concert at Carnegie Hall for the benefit of the Colored Music Settlement School. Europe was only thirty-eight years old when he was murdered by a drummer in his band.

J. P. Morgan: In the title song, Morgan sings to the immigrants, "I'm J. P. Morgan, my friends, / The wealthiest man on this earth! / . . . You immigrants, look up to me / And you'll see what money is worth." In the two decades before World War I, John Pierpont Morgan (1837–1913) was one of the world's foremost financial figures. His reorganization of several major railroads and financing of industrial consolidations led to the formation of the US Steel, International Harvester, and General Electric corporations.

Latvia: Located in the Baltic region of northern Europe, Latvia is a country that was for centuries under German, Swedish, Polish, Lithuanian, and Russian rule. Latvia was among the many Eastern European nations with a large Jewish population who were persecuted by foreign governments. Today's Republic of Latvia was not established until 1918. Tateh tells the audience, "In Latvia, a man dreamed of a new life for his little girl."

Mary Pickford: Frustrated with trying to film Evelyn Nesbit, movie director Tateh says, "Where is Mary Pickford when I need her?" One of the greatest stars of early Hollywood, Mary Pickford (1892–1979) was known as "America's Sweetheart" because of her portrayal of sweet, innocent heroines. Pickford was one of the founders of United Artists and the Academy of Motion Picture Arts and Sciences.

Matthew Henson: The Black explorer Matthew Henson (1866–1955) accompanied Robert Peary on seven voyages to the Arctic over a period of nearly twenty-three years. Henson was with Peary when they first reached the North Pole in 1909. Admiral Peary introduces Henson to Father, saying, "This is my First Officer, Mr. Matthew Henson." Father is surprised to find a Black man in such an important position.

movie books: The Kineograph (or flicker book or flip book) goes back to 1868. It is a small book consisting of a series of images in different positions that create the illusion of flowing movement when the thumb is placed so the pages flip quickly. Tateh sells the train Conductor one of his flip books and says, "They move. I call them . . . movie . . . books!"

New Rochelle: The musical opens with the Little Boy telling the audience, "In 1902, Father built a house at the crest of the Broadview Avenue hill in New Rochelle, New York." Located in Westchester County and not far north of New York City, New Rochelle was the first major suburb in America. By 1900, there were some fourteen thousand residents living there in a planned community of residential neighborhoods.

President McKinley: President during the Spanish-American War of 1898, William McKinley (1843–1901) was assassinated by a troubled immigrant in 1901, allowing Vice President Theodore Roosevelt to become president. Younger Brother tells the audience, "The Secret Service was at the ready. The recent assassination of President McKinley had been a lesson well learned."

Scott Joplin: The people of Harlem sing, "His name was Coalhouse Walker . . . Was a native of St. Louis some years before . . . When he heard the music of Scott Joplin . . . Bought himself some piano lessons." Known as the "King of Ragtime," Scott Joplin (c. 1868–1917) was an American composer and pianist who achieved fame for his ragtime compositions, music that was born out of the Black community.

Shakespeare folios . . . Gutenberg Bible on vellum: J. P. Morgan possessed two of the world's most valuable books. The First Folio was published in 1623 and contained thirty-six of William Shakespeare's works. The Gutenberg Bible is the earliest major book printed in Europe using mass-produced movable metal type. Morgan's copy was printed on vellum, a fine parchment made originally from the skin of a calf. With his library in danger, J. P. Morgan shouts, "Four Shakespeare folios! A Gutenberg Bible on vellum! The treasures of civilization are at stake. You've got to do something!"

shtetl: A small Jewish town or village found in Eastern Europe and Russia at the turn of the twentieth century was called a shtetl. As they sail into New York Harbor, Tateh tells his daughter, "America is our home now. America is our shtetl."

Stanford White: A partner in the prestigious architectural firm of McKim, Mead & White, Stanford White (1853–1906) was famous for the mansions, civic buildings, and religious structures he designed. White was also notorious for his seduction of teenage girls. His affair with Evelyn

Nesbit led to Harry K. Thaw, Nesbit's husband, shooting and killing White in public. In *Ragtime*, White introduces himself to the audience as "the eminent architect . . . designer of the Pennsylvania Station on 33rd Street."

Tom Thumb: Charles Sherwood Stratton (1838–1883) was an American dwarf who achieved great fame as General Tom Thumb under the management of shrewd impresario P. T. Barnum. Evelyn tells the audience that she "became the biggest attraction in vaudeville since Tom Thumb."

Tuskegee Institute: Booker T. Washington was one of the founders of the Tuskegee Institute in Alabama, an early and still-operating place of learning for Black people. Among the institution's famous residents were botanist George Washington Carver and the Tuskegee Airmen of World War II. In the epilogue, Washington says, "Booker T. Washington's Tuskegee Institute became, in time, the capital of Black America."

Union Square: In the song "The Night That Goldman Spoke at Union Square," Younger Brother sings, "The police were standing by / But the crowd was on its feet / The night that Goldman spoke at Union Square." Named for the union of two major thoroughfares in Lower Manhattan, Union Square is bordered by Broadway and Fourth Avenue. By the first decade of the twentieth century, the intersection was a major transportation hub, with several elevated and surface railroad lines running nearby once the 14th Street–Union Square subway station opened in 1904. By this time, many of the old homes on Union Square had been converted into tenements for immigrants and industrial workers. The real Emma Goldman spoke to crowds in Union Square on several occasions.

vaudeville: Riding on her swing, Evelyn sings, "Harry's in trouble / And Stanny's in heaven / And Evelyn is in vaudeville!" The most popular form of entertainment in the early twentieth century was vaudeville, or variety. The vaudeville theaters offered a mixture of specialty acts ranging from singers to magicians. Because the admission was much less than that for traditional theatre and other events, vaudeville performances were attended by all classes of people, until the genre waned and died out during the Depression.

"Warn the Duke!": Six times in the musical, the Little Boy tells Houdini, "Warn the Duke!" He is referring to Archduke Franz Ferdinand

(1863–1914) of Austria, who was assassinated in Sarajevo in 1914, precipitating World War I. In actuality, Houdini and the Archduke never met, but the Little Boy is supposedly clairvoyant, and he tells the magician to warn the Duke. After touring Europe in 1914, Houdini left for America a few days before the assassination.

Zapata: A prominent figure in the Mexican Revolution of 1910–1920, Emiliano Zapata (1879–1919) was the main leader of the people's revolution in the Mexican state of Morelos. In the epilogue, the Little Boy says, "Younger Brother drove south to Mexico, where he joined the great peasant revolutionary Emiliano Zapata."

RENT

Libretto, lyrics, and music by Jonathan Larson, loosely based on the opera *La Bohème* by Giacomo Puccini, and Henri Murger's novel *Scenes de la vie de Bohème*. Original Broadway production: April 29, 1996. Nederlander Theatre. 898 performances.

Although the setting for *Rent*—the East Village in the 1990s—is more contemporary than just about every other musical in this book, it is still removed from many audience members by its details. Greenwich Village in New York City has its own language, with local references, such as Alphabet City and CBGB's. The 1980s saw the first major assault of the AIDS epidemic, and it was felt very strongly in this community of young artists. Also, Jonathan Larson's lyrics are riddled with names and words from pop culture, some of which are not widely recognized by everyone.

Expressions, references, names:

Absolut: Manufactured in Sweden since 1879, Absolut vodka is one of the largest brands of spirits in the world. In the song "La Vie Bohème," Mark sings "To no absolutes—to Absolut!"

Alphabet City: Avenues A, B, C, and D, the only thoroughfares in Manhattan to have single-letter names, are located within the East Village and, because of these letters, the neighborhood is known as Alphabet City. Much of the action in *Rent* takes place in Alphabet City, and the term is used by various characters throughout the musical.

Antonioni . . . Bertolucci . . . Kurosawa . . . *Carmina Burana*: In the song "La Vie Bohème," the young Bohemians sing, "Antonioni, Bertolucci, Kurosawa / *Carmina Burana*." Michelangelo Antonioni (1912–2007) was an Italian film director, screenwriter, editor, and painter best known for his movies about discontented modern individuals. Bernardo Bertolucci (1941–2018) was a film director and screenwriter, considered one of the great filmmakers of the Italian cinema. Akira Kurosawa (1910–1998) was a Japanese filmmaker and painter who is regarded as one of the most important and influential of all filmmakers. Carl Orff's 1937 cantata *Carmina Burana* is one of the most widely known and beloved pieces of modern classical music, based on saucy poems written by medieval university students.

avant-garde: French for "advance guard" or "vanguard," *avant-garde* is used to describe a person or work that is experimental, radical, or unorthodox with respect to art, culture, or society. The artists in *Rent* consider themselves avant-garde, and Collins introduces Angel to the others with, "A new member of the Alphabet City avant-garde / Angel Dumott Schunard!"

AZT: The first approved HIV/AIDS drug was Zidovudine (or Azidothymidine), but often was called AZT. Mark tells Roger to be sure to "take your AZT," and later some of the HIV-positive characters "take an AZT break."

Burberry: Burberry is a British luxury fashion house that designs and distributes ready-to-wear clothing, in particular trench coats. A street vendor in *Rent* tries to sell a "Burberry" coat with "zip-out lining."

Captain Crunch: Cap'n Crunch is a corn and oat breakfast cereal manufactured by Quaker Oats Company since 1963, a childhood favorite in America. Mark and Roger have no food in the house and sing, "A box of Captain Crunch will taste so good."

CBGB's . . . The Pyramid Club: At the beginning of *Rent*, Mark describes the loft apartment on Avenue B shared by Roger and himself: "Old rock-and-roll posters hang on the walls. They have Roger's picture advertising gigs at CBGB's and The Pyramid Club." A Manhattan music venue with a varied clientele over the years, CBGB opened in the East Village in 1973. The letters "CBGB" stood for country, bluegrass, and blues.

Over its short history, it was a dive bar, a biker hangout, a famed venue for punk rock, a place for New Wave bands, and eventually the home of hard-core punk. The Pyramid Club was a nightclub on Avenue A in the East Village. It opened in 1979 and soon was a popular hangout for the drag, gay, punk, and art scenes of the 1980s.

C'est la vie: French for "That's life," and also meaning "That's how things happen," the phrase "C'est la vie" is used by Mark's mother about his breakup with Maureen.

Circle Line: The Circle Line cruise is a popular tourist attraction, with vessels that circle the island of Manhattan and point out the sights. Mark recalls how Angel once guided a group of lost tourists "out of Alphabet City" and helped them "find the Circle Line."

curry vindaloo: Vindaloo (or vindalho) is a spicy Indian curry dish popular in curry houses and Indian restaurants around the world. Mimi and Angel salute the fiery dish in the song "La Vie Bohème."

D . . . C . . . X . . . smack . . . horse . . . jugie boogie . . . blow: On Christmas Eve, Mimi and the junkies sing, "Got any D, man? Got any C, man? . . . Got any X? Any smack? Any horse, any jugie boogie, boy? Any blow?" "D" is street slang for the drug LSD. Short slang for cocaine is "C." A slang term for the drug MDMA, also known as ecstasy, is simply "X." "Smack" and "horse" are names for heroin. Two other common words for cocaine are "jugie boogie" and "blow."

DATs: A "direct antiglobulin test" is a laboratory test for the presence of complement, or an antibody that is bound to a patient's red blood cells (RBCs). The test is used in testing patients with AIDS. A street vendor in *Rent* tries to sell "DATs" along with "hats and bats."

Doc Martens: Also called Dr. Marten, Docs, or DMs, the trendy shoe and clothing company is most known for the comfortable shoes with air-cushioned soles. Joanne's father tells her to wear a dress to her mother's confirmation hearing, and "no Doc Martens this time." Later Maureen sings to Joanne: "I'll kiss your Doc Martens, Let me kiss your Doc Martens."

Elsie: Elsie the Cow is a cartoon character developed as a mascot for the Borden Dairy Company in 1936 to symbolize the "perfect dairy product." Being one of the most recognizable icons in American advertising, Elsie has only to be mentioned in Maureen's performance piece, "Over the Moon," and the audience knows to whom she is referring.

Fender guitar: The Fender Musical Instruments Corporation (FMIC, or simply Fender) is an American manufacturer of stringed instruments and amplifiers that was founded in 1946. It is best known for its high-quality, solid-body electric guitars and bass guitars. Roger owns and plays a Fender guitar, which he later sells to get money to go to Santa Fe.

Geoffrey Beene: Geoffrey Beene (1924–2004) was one of New York's most famous fashion designers, recognized for his comfortable and dressy women's wear. A coat vendor in *Rent* tries to sell "Geoffrey Beene" on the street.

Ginsberg . . . Dylan . . . Cunningham . . . Cage . . . Lenny Bruce . . . Langston Hughes: Tom Collins and Roger in "La Vie Bohème" sing, "Ginsberg, Dylan, Cunningham and Cage / Lenny Bruce, Langston Hughes." The iconic American poet and writer Allen Ginsberg (1926–1997) was an instrumental force in the Beat Generation. Bob Dylan (born 1941) is a singer-songwriter, author, and visual artist, generally regarded as one of the greatest of American songwriters. Merce Cunningham (1919–2009) was an American dancer and choreographer who was at the forefront of American modern dance for much of the twentieth century. John Cage (1912–1992) was an American composer and music theorist who was a pioneer in avant-garde music, including the non-standard use of musical instruments. Lenny Bruce (1925–1966) was an influential American stand-up comedian, social critic, and satirist renowned for his open, freestyle, and critical form of comedy. A major force behind the Harlem Renaissance, Langston Hughes (1901–1967) was a Black poet, social activist, novelist, and playwright.

"golden": A slang expression, meaning one is not in the wrong, "golden" can also mean that all is fine, or everything is settled. This is how Mark uses the word when Bennie asks him for the rent, replying, "You said we were golden."

Gracie Mews: A thirty-five-story residential tower named Gracie Mews on the Upper East Side of Manhattan is the very affluent address of Bennie and his wife, Alison. Angel is paid to get rid of Alison's dog, Evita, so he throws the Akita off the balcony and into the courtyard below.

Heidegger: Martin Heidegger (1889–1976) was a German philosopher who is among the most important and influential philosophers of the twentieth century. Tom Collins sings about opening a restaurant in "Santa Fe," where the guests "come chatting not about Heidegger, but wine."

Hicksville: Hicksville is a hamlet on Long Island, a well-known suburb of New York City. Maureen is from there, and Mark teases her: "You can take the girl out of Hicksville but you can't take Hicksville out of the girl."

Huevos rancheros . . . Maya Angelou: A dish consisting of fried or poached eggs served on a tortilla and topped with a sauce, usually tomato-based, is known as huevos rancheros. The Black poet, memoirist, and civil rights activist Maya Angelou (1928–2014) published seven autobiographies, three books of essays, and several books of poetry. Mimi and Angel toast the Black writer and the Mexican dish in the song, "La Vie Bohème."

la vie Bohème: The French expression for the "Bohemian life" is "la vie Bohème." It is also the title of the song that ends the first act of *Rent*. A "Bohemian" originally referred to a person from Bohemia, a region in today's Czech Republic. Later the word *bohémien* was the French expression for a gypsy. By the late 1880s, a bohemian was any unconventional person, usually one involved in the arts.

L.L.Bean: L.L.Bean is an American retail company headquartered in Freeport, Maine, that specializes in clothing and outdoor recreation equipment. A street vendor in *Rent* tries to sell "L.L.Bean" on Christmas Eve.

MBA: A master of business administration (MBA) is a graduate degree that trains one for a career in business or investment management. A street vendor tries to sell a fur "in perfect shape owned by an MBA from Uptown."

MIT: The Massachusetts Institute of Technology (MIT) is a private research university in Cambridge, Massachusetts. Established in 1861, it ranks among the top academic institutions in the world in the development of modern technology and science. Tom Collins taught at MIT, but "they expelled me for my theory of actual reality."

Moneypenny: Miss Moneypenny is a fictional character in the James Bond novels and films. She is secretary to M, who is Bond's superior officer and head of the British Secret Intelligence Service. On New Year's Eve, Tom Collins pretends he is James Bond, and says to Mimi: "Aha! Moneypenny—my martini!"

"Musetta's Waltz": A soprano aria in Puccini's 1896 opera *La Bohème,* "Musetta's Waltz" is a very familiar piece of classical music. Mark teases Roger during "La Vie Bohème" when he announces, "Roger will attempt to write a bittersweet, evocative song . . . that doesn't remind us of Musetta's Waltz."

Pablo Neruda: The Chilean poet-diplomat and politician Pablo Neruda (1904–1973) won the Nobel Prize for Literature in 1971. The Bohemians salute Neruda in the song "La Vie Bohème" by singing, "To Buddha / Pablo Neruda, too!"

Pee-wee Herman . . . Gertrude Stein: The Bohemians sing, "Pee-wee Herman / German wine, turpentine, Gertrude Stein" in the song "La Vie Bohème." Best known for his films and television series during the 1980s, Pee-wee Herman is a comic fictional character created and portrayed by American comedian Paul Reubens (born 1952). Gertrude Stein (1874–1946) was an influential patron of the arts and a noted author and poet.

Prozac: The antidepressant Prozac is thought to work by increasing the levels of serotonin in the brain. Angel says about Benny, "That boy could use some Prozac."

Pussy Galore: On New Year's Eve, Angel dresses in drag with a blond wig and says, "Pussy Galore—in person!" Pussy Galore is a sexy fictional character in Ian Fleming's 1959 James Bond novel, *Goldfinger,* and the 1964 film of the same name.

Scarsdale: Scarsdale is a moneyed town in Westchester County, New York. Mark comes from Scarsdale, and he tells Joanne that he learned to tango "at the Scarsdale Jewish Community Center."

Sontag . . . Sondheim: Collins salutes Sontag and Angel toasts Sondheim in "La Vie Bohème." Susan Sontag (1933–2004) was an American writer, filmmaker, teacher, and political activist who mostly wrote essays, but also published novels. The highly innovative and influential Broadway composer and lyricist Stephen Sondheim (1930–2021) was one of the most important figures in twentieth-century musical theatre.

Spike Lee: Shelton Jackson "Spike" Lee (born 1957) is a Black film director, producer, screenwriter, and actor who often makes movies on the streets of New York City. When Mimi says there's a moon out, Roger sings, "Maybe it's not the moon at all, I hear Spike Lee's shooting down the street."

Steuben glass: The junkies and street vendors sing about there being "no Steuben glass" this Christmas. A brand of handmade, heavy-lead crystal made by Steuben Glass Works in Corning, New York, Steuben glass is a high-quality luxury item.

Stoli: A well-known Russian brand of vodka made of wheat and rye grain is Stolichnaya, commonly called Stoli. Tom Collins sings, "This boy could use some Stoli" when he sees Roger for the first time in months.

T-cells: T-cells are one of the important white blood cells of the immune system and are destroyed in those suffering from AIDS. In the support group, Gordon, who is HIV-positive, announces that his "T-cells are low."

Ted Koppel: When a cop tries to beat a homeless woman, Mark films the scene and says, "Smile for Ted Koppel, Officer Martin!" Edward "Ted" Koppel (born 1940) is a British-born American broadcast journalist, best known as the anchor for the television show *Nightline*.

Thelma and Louise: When Angel sings about how he tossed Alison's dog off the twenty-third floor of Gracie Mews, he describes it as being "Like Thelma and Louise when they got the blues." The 1991 film is about two female friends who embark on a road trip that ends up with the pair driving off a cliff together.

Tuckahoe: The homeless people and the street vendors sing, "Once you donate you can go and celebrate in Tuckahoe." Approximately sixteen miles north of Midtown Manhattan in Southern Westchester County is the affluent village of Tuckahoe.

Václav Havel . . . Sex Pistols . . . 8BC: In the song "La Vie Bohème," the young Bohemians sing, "To apathy, to entropy, to empathy, Ecstasy / Václav Havel—the Sex Pistols, 8BC, / To no shame— / Never playing the fame game." Václav Havel (1936–2011) was a Czech statesman, playwright, and former dissident who was the last president of Czechoslovakia and the first president of the Czech Republic. One of the most groundbreaking acts in the history of popular music, the Sex Pistols were an English rock band responsible for initiating the punk movement. 8BC was a seminal performance space, art gallery, and nightclub in New York's East Village in the early 1980s.

Village Voice: A weekly newspaper known especially for its articles on entertainment and the arts, the *Village Voice* was published in Greenwich Village and focused on an "alternative" culture. It gradually became more traditional, then ceased publication in 2017. In the song "La Vie Bohème," Mark sings, "To the *Village Voice*—To any passing fad."

Westport: Westport is a very affluent community in Fairfield County, Connecticut. Benny's in-laws live there, and he tells Roger and Mark that "I'd honestly rather be with you tonight than in Westport."

THE SECRET GARDEN

Libretto by Marsha Norman, based on the novel by Frances Hodgson Burnett. Lyrics by Marsha Norman. Music by Lucy Simon. Original Broadway production: April 25, 1991. St. James Theatre. 709 performances.

This musical adaptation of Frances Hodgson Burnett's British novel sounds so authentic that it is somewhat surprising to learn that it was written by an American. Marsha Norman is not afraid to use Yorkshire words and phrases in the dialogue and the lyrics. Sometimes they are explained to Mary by Dickon or Martha, the two thoroughly Yorkshire characters in the musical; other words are left unexplained but add greatly to the rustic atmosphere. The story begins in Colonial India in 1906 and flashes back to the Raj Empire throughout *The Secret Garden*. The majority of the tale is set in that same year—winter to summer—on the grounds of the fictional Misselthwaite Manor in North Yorkshire, England.

Expressions, references, names:

ayah: In India during the era of the Raj, a native nurse or maid is called an ayah. Mary tells Martha, "In India, my ayah dressed me."

canna: In the Scottish dialect, the word *can't* becomes *canna*. Over the centuries, the word was picked up and used throughout northern England. Martha asks Mary, "Canna tha' dress thyself, then?"

columbine: A flower of the buttercup family, the columbine has white petals and white to blue sepals that form long, backward spurs. When Dickon gives Mary a handful of seeds, he says, "There's columbine and poppies by the handful."

fakir: In the Muslim and Hindu worlds, a fakir is an itinerant religious wonder-worker, thought to have exceptional gifts. Near the beginning of *The Secret Garden*, the fakir in Colonial India chants in Hindu.

THE SECRET GARDEN   *The Yorkshire lad Dickon (John Cameron Mitchell) teaches Mary (Daisy Egan) the meaning of "wick" in the local vernacular.*
Photofest

lassie . . . lass: As in Scotland, the words *lass* and *lassie* refer to a girl or a young woman not yet wed in Yorkshire. Martha says to Mary, "But I didn't know what to expect from you, lassie." And later in the musical, Dickon sings to the robin about Mary, "She's a lass and tha' art right / As need a spot where she can rest in."

lorry: In Great Britain, a lorry is a truck or any large, heavy motor vehicle for transporting goods or troops. An angry Mary says to the schoolmistress, Mrs. Winthrop, "I hope you get hit by a lorry on the way home and your ugly head rolls off in a ditch and gets eaten by maggots!"

Misselthwaite Manor: The fictional home of Archibald Craven has a made-up name but a Yorkshire one all the same. A "thwaite" is a piece of land used as a meadow, field, or pasture. It can also refer to land that is cleared with the intention of building structures on it. Also, there is a small village in the Yorkshire Dales named Thwaite. The "missel" part of Misselthwaite perhaps refers to the prayer book with hymns in it, called a missal.

"Mistress Mary, quite contrary": This simple nursery rhyme goes back to the 1600s, and a version was published for the first time in 1744. Among the variations is one that begins with, "Mary, Mary, Quite Contrary." There are different theories about who Mary is. It is believed by many that the nursery rhyme refers to Mary Tudor, the first daughter of Henry VIII, who was called Bloody Mary because of her persecution of the Protestants. Near the beginning of the musical, children's voices are heard singing different variations of "Mistress Mary" as the British subjects in India dance and gradually die off from cholera.

moor . . . heather . . . gorse . . . broom: Early in *The Secret Garden*, Mrs. Medlock explains to Mary, "It's the moor. Miles and miles of wild land that nothing grows on but heather and gorse and broom." A moor is a tract of open land that is uncultivated. Such a place can also be called a heath. Heather is a wild shrub with small purple flowers that grows abundantly on moorland and heathland. Another wild shrub is gorse, this one with yellow flowers that sheep graze on. Broom is a third shrub with long thin stems and bright flowers that are cut and used for decorative purposes or for making brooms.

nowt . . . soart: In Yorkshire, "now" is written and pronounced "nowt," and "sort" becomes "soart." Together they can mean "nothing of the sort." Dickon sings to the robin, "She's took thee on / For like to vex thee. / Nowt o' the soart."

oatcakes: A common food found in Scotland and Yorkshire is the oatcake, a hard, unleavened cake made by putting wet oats under pressure. In the song "A Girl in the Valley," Archibald sings about Lily and recalls, "'Share my tea,' she bade me so gently / Oatcakes and cream, sweet plums in a jar." Later in the musical, when asked what food he has eaten in his mother's garden, Colin replies, "Oatcakes and roasted eggs and fresh milk."

rajah: An Indian king or prince is called a rajah. The title was also given to dignitaries and nobles in India during the British Raj. When Colin starts to throw a temper tantrum, Mary says to him, "You little rajah!"

scullery: In most nineteenth-century homes, there was a small kitchen or room at the back of the house used for washing dishes and other dirty household work. A "scullery maid" was perhaps the lowest position in a household staff. Martha tells Mary, "I'm like to be sent back to the scullery, and I don't like the scullery."

wick: Probably coming from the word "quick," something that is lively or very active is said in Yorkshire to be wick. When Mary thinks that Lily's garden is dead, Dickon sings the song "Wick," explaining, "If a thing is wick, it has a life about it."

Yorkshire: The setting for most of *The Secret Garden*, Yorkshire is a county in northern England, traditionally divided into East, West, and North Ridings. In the novel, Misselthwaite Manor is located in northern Yorkshire.

1776

Libretto by Peter Stone. Music and lyrics by Sherman Edwards. Original Broadway production: March 16, 1969. 46th Street Theatre. 1,217 performances. Broadway revivals in 1997 and 2022.

Just about every character in *1776* comes from history. That said, librettist Peter Stone and lyricist Sherman Edwards have taken a few liberties with people and places. Yet what is so remarkable about this musical is how much of it is true. The authors did not have to invent high drama; it was already there. The action takes place in Philadelphia during May, June, and July of 1776. Most of the drama (and music) can be found in the chamber in which the Second Continental Congress meets, located in a building that is today called Independence Hall. When one visits the place today, one is not only walking into history, but right into the setting of a famous Broadway musical.

Expressions, references, names:

Abigail Adams: The wife of one president (John Adams) and the mother of another (John Quincy Adams), Abigail Adams (1744–1818) was active in American politics even though women did not have the vote, nor could they serve as government officials. She is most remembered today for the hundreds of letters that she wrote to her husband, making her one of the most documented of all First Ladies. In one of the letters quoted in the musical, Abigail writes to her husband, "After all, I am Mrs. John Adams—that's quite a lot for one lifetime."

apoplexy: A cerebral hemorrhage that causes one to become unconscious or incapacitated used to be called apoplexy. Today the word *stroke* is used. During a heated discussion in Congress, Ben Franklin warns Adams, "John, you'll have an attack of apoplexy if you're not careful."

Benjamin Franklin: An American Renaissance man who was active as a writer, scientist, inventor, statesman, diplomat, printer, publisher, and political philosopher, Benjamin Franklin (1706–1790) was seventy years old at the time of the events in the musical. As the senior member of the Second Continental Congress, Franklin inspired respect but was also controversial in some of his ideas. He was also known for his quick wit and humorous writings. In the musical, Franklin tells Dickinson, "You should know that rebellion is *always* legal in the first person—such as 'our rebellion.' It is only in the third person—'their' rebellion—that it is illegal."

Botticelli . . . Venus: The most famous painting by the Italian Renaissance painter Sandro Botticelli is *The Birth of Venus*. When Franklin asks Adams what he thinks of the portrait of him, Adams says about the artist, "He's no Botticelli," and Franklin adds, "And the subject's no Venus." In Roman mythology, Venus is the goddess of love.

Congress: In his opening speech in *1776*, Adams tells the audience, "By God, I have had this Congress!" Any formal meeting, or series of meetings, for discussion between delegates representing political parties or organizations is considered a congress, though the word is not always used. The Second Continental Congress of 1776 was held in Philadelphia, and delegates from the thirteen colonies were represented. The word *congress* was retained when the new government was created after the Revolutionary War.

crossed the Rubicon: In the song "Is Anybody There?," Adams sings, "I have crossed the Rubicon, / Let the bridge be burn'd behind me!" In 49 BCE, Julius Caesar and his troops crossed the Rubicon River in Gaul, a move that meant he planned to defy the Roman Republic and make himself dictator. Ever since then, the phrase "crossing the Rubicon" has meant a major or momentous decision. The decision Adams is referring to is the final vote on the Declaration of Independence.

gout: A disease in which defective metabolism of uric acid causes arthritis, especially in the smaller bones of the feet, is known as gout. Although today there is medication that helps, gout can still cause acute pain. Franklin says about his limping, "Yes, I have the honor [of being Franklin]—unfortunately the gout accompanies the honor."

grenadiers: Adams calls the members of Congress "these indecisive grenadiers of Philadelphia!" Soldiers armed with grenades or a grenade launcher are known as grenadiers. Before the invention of the modern hand grenade, grenadiers were members of a special formation, usually selected for strength and height, and were trained to throw handheld projectiles.

Hastings and Magna Carta . . . Strongbow and Lionhearted . . . Drake and Marlborough . . . Tudors, Stuarts, and Plantagenets: More interested in being an Englishman than an American, John Dickinson asks Adams: "Would you have us forsake Hastings and Magna Carta, Strongbow and Lionhearted, Drake and Marlborough, Tudors, Stuarts, and Plantagenets?" In the Battle of Hastings in 1066, William the Conquered defeated Harold II and established the Normans as the rulers of England. The Magna Carta, or the Great Charter, in 1215 forced King John to acknowledge the rights of the nobles and, indirectly, the common man as well. The King of Leinster, also known as Strongbow, led the Norman invasion of Ireland in 1170. King Richard I, known as the

Lionhearted, was a great military leader and warrior of the twelfth century. Sir Francis Drake was the famed English explorer of the sixteenth century. The first Duke of Marlborough was a noted military leader in the eighteenth century. The Tudors, Stuarts, and Plantagenets were all dynasties of British rule.

inventor of the stove: In 1742, Benjamin Franklin invented a cast-iron stove having the general form of a fireplace with enclosed top, bottom, sides, and back, the front being completely open or able to be closed by doors. It has since been called the Franklin stove. When Adams introduces Franklin to Martha Jefferson, he says, "Inventor of the stove."

John Adams: Perhaps the strongest advocate for American independence among the Founding Fathers, John Adams (1735–1826) was a shrewd statesman and a dedicated lawyer. He was forty-one years old when he signed the Declaration of Independence, and he went on to serve two terms as vice president (under George Washington) and one term as president. Throughout the musical, Adams is called "obnoxious and disliked" by everyone, including his friends. John Dickinson, who opposes all of Adams's ideas, describes him as an "incendiary little man . . . this Boston radical, this *a-gi-ta-tor*, this demagogue—this madman!"

King George: Near the beginning of *1776*, Adams addresses the audience with: "For ten years King George and his Parliament gulled, cullied, and diddled these colonies with their illegal taxes." During the events of *1776*, King George III (c. 1738–1820) was on the British throne. He was a member of the Hanover dynasty and was monarch for fifty-nine years. Losing the American colonies was his greatest defeat, and, it is believed, it drove him to insanity near the end of his long life.

look sharp: Dating from the early 1700s, the idiom "to look sharp" means to keep a strict watch or to be vigilant. In the song "Momma, Look Sharp," the Courier sings of a mother of a soldier who went out looking for the body of her slain son. The Courier sings the dead boy's thoughts: "Hey, hey—Momma, look sharp!"

Martha Jefferson: As depicted in the musical, Martha Jefferson (1748–1782) was only twenty-eight years old in 1776 and had only been married to Thomas Jefferson for four years. Because she died young (thirty-three years old) and Jefferson rarely wrote or spoke of her, Martha Jefferson is perhaps the most enigmatic of the First Ladies. In the musical, she sings about her husband in the song "He Plays the Violin": "Oh, he never speaks his passions, He never speaks his views, / Whereas other men speak volumes, / The man I love is mute."

mercenaries: A professional soldier who is hired to serve in a foreign army is called a mercenary. Great Britain hired trained German soldiers called Hessian mercenaries to fight in the New World. In one of Washington's communiqués, he writes, "General Howe has landed 25,000 British regulars and Hessian mercenaries on Staten Island."

minuet . . . gavotte: A very popular dance in the eighteenth century was the minuet. It is a slow, stately ballroom dance for two, in triple time. Also frequently danced in the eighteenth century was the gavotte, a medium-paced French dance that was less formal. When Dickinson asks Hancock, "Mr. Hancock, you are a man of property—one of us. Why don't you join us in our minuet?" Hancock answers, "I'd rather trot / To Mr. Adams's new gavotte."

Mr. Paine's *Common Sense*: Arguably the most important piece of writing of the American Revolution was Thomas Paine's 1776 pamphlet *Common Sense*, encouraging independence from Great Britain. Franklin tells Adams, "The people have read Mr. Paine's *Common Sense*; I doubt the Congress has."

Plato: The Greek philosopher Plato (c. 428–348 BCE) wrote *The Republic*, one of the first works about political theory. Franklin says, "Democracy! What Plato called a 'charming form of government, full of variety and disorder.' I never knew Plato had been to Philadelphia."

quartermaster: The military officer responsible for providing quarters, rations, clothing, and other supplies is called a quartermaster. The term, in use in the British military since 1600, developed from the German *quartiermeister*, the master of the soldiers' living quarters. George Washington writes in one of his communiqués, "My quartermaster has no food, no arms, no ammunition, and my troops are in a state of near mutiny!"

saltpetre: In a letter to his wife, Abigail, Adams says, "I asked you to organize the ladies and make saltpetre (in Britain) or saltpeter (in America) for gunpowder." A common name for potassium nitrate is saltpetre. When salt crystals are treated with potassium nitrate, the result is a mixture that can be used in gunpowder and other combustible materials.

second Flood: A Flood spelled with a capital *F* usually refers to Noah's Flood in the Bible. A "second Flood" suggests a natural catastrophe on the level of the biblical Flood. Adams says he could understand "a second Flood, a simple famine, / Plagues of locusts everywhere," but he cannot understand this Congress.

Thomas Jefferson: During his long and distinguished lifetime, Thomas Jefferson (1743–1826) served as president, vice president, secretary of state, and governor of Virginia. He was also an architect and a diplomat. Jefferson was thirty-three years old during the events in *1776*. As the author of the Declaration of Independence and other writings, Jefferson is considered one of the most important political philosophers of his era. In the musical, Adams says to Jefferson, "You write ten times better than any man in the Congress—including me!"

triangle trade: In the song "Molasses to Rum," Rutledge asks the New England delegates, "Whose fortunes are made / In the triangle trade?" In the eighteenth century, a pattern of colonial commerce connecting three regions in the Atlantic Ocean was known as the "triangle trade." Ships transporting slaves from West Africa to the New World and goods from the Americas going to Europe created a triangle in which each trip was profitable. The Southern colonies bought the slaves, but it was the New England colonies who owned the ships and made big profits.

Washington: Because George Washington (1732–1799) was made commander of the Continental Army, he did not attend any of the meetings held by the Second Continental Congress. However, he did send a series of dispatches, or "communiqués," to the Congress to report on the war and request more supplies. In the musical (and in reality), these communiqués always end with "Y'r Ob'd't—G. Washington," a short form of "your obedient servant."

William and Mary: The College of William and Mary in Williamsburg, Virginia, was founded in 1693 and named after King William III and his queen, Mary. After Harvard University, it is the oldest institution of higher learning in the United States. When Jefferson and Adams argue over the word *inalienable*, Adams says, "I happen to be a Harvard graduate," to which Jefferson replies, "And I attended William and Mary."

SHOW BOAT

Libretto by Oscar Hammerstein, based on the novel by Edna Ferber. Lyrics by Oscar Hammerstein. Music by Jerome Kern. Original Broadway production: December 20, 1927. Ziegfeld Theatre. 572 performances. Broadway revivals in 1932, 1946, 1948, 1954, 1983, and 1994.

The American musical moves from the three-act comedy (boy meets girl, boy loses girl, boy gets girl) to epic storytelling with *Show Boat*. Both the setting (various places along the Mississippi River and Chicago) and the time frame (1887 to 1927) are expansive, not to mention the themes in the musical. Oscar Hammerstein was not only able to adapt and condense Edna Ferber's complex novel, but he was able to present the first fully developed, three-dimensional characters in the history of the Broadway musical. Different versions of *Show Boat* exist, and productions vary significantly. References from all of these versions are discussed here.

Expressions, references, names:

Chicago World's Fair: The World's Columbian Exposition (commonly known as the Chicago World's Fair) was an international event held in Chicago in 1893 to celebrate the four hundredth anniversary of Christopher Columbus's arrival in the New World in 1492. The exposition covered 690 acres, and nearly two hundred new (but deliberately temporary) buildings were built, most in the neoclassical style. More than twenty-seven million people attended the exposition during its six-month run. In *Show Boat*, Ravenal and Magnolia are in the money and are enjoying the fair, but hard times are foreshadowed when Parthy says that Ravenal is "spending money like a fool," and Magnolia naively replies, "Oh, Gay can always make more."

coon songs: Popular in the United States from 1880 to 1920, "coon songs" were a genre of music that presented a racist and stereotyped image of Black Americans. Some songs were sentimental about the South, while others were ribald and offensive by modern standards. When Magnolia is trying to get a job at the Trocadero, she says, "I . . . do Negro songs," to which the manager Max says, "Oh—coon songs, eh?"

SHOW BOAT *There were still a few show boats in operation when this legendary musical opened in 1927, and they usually presented melodramas like the ones Captain Andy (Charles Winninger, center stage) offered.*
Photofest

demi-mondy role: French for "half-world," *demimonde* referred to a class of women on the fringes of respectable society who were supported by wealthy lovers. The term was popularized by the 1855 Alexandre Dumas play *Le Demi-Monde*. In the song "Life upon the Wicked Stage," Ellie sings, "I would like to play a demi-mondy role—with soul."

dis . . . dat . . . de . . . : Hammerstein uses a Southern Black vernacular for the Black characters in *Show Boat*. *Dis* means "this," as when Queenie says to Peter, "You mean dis scrumptious piece of jewelry?" *Dat* is "that," as when Julie sings, "Can't Help Lovin' Dat Man of Mine." *De* is the same as "the," as with the stevedores singing, "Gittin' no rest till de Judgment Day." The "d" sound is also heard in other words in which no "d" is found. For example, "with" becomes *wid*, as when the dockhands sing, "Loadin' up boats wid de bales of cotton." Other times the "d" sound disappears completely, as with "Ol' (instead of Old) Man River."

flotsam and jetsam: As part of the melodrama performed on the *Cotton Blossom*, Ellie compares women to blossoms that "are cast aside to float along on the tide of eternity like flotsam and jetsam on the sea." Thanks to Disney's *The Little Mermaid*, the words *flotsam* and *jetsam* are very familiar to audiences, though what they actually mean is not so well known. Flotsam is debris in the water that was not deliberately thrown overboard, usually the result of a shipwreck or other sea accident. Jetsam is debris that was deliberately thrown overboard by a crew of a ship in distress, most likely to lighten the ship's load. The word *flotsam* comes from the French word *floter*, to float; *jetsam* comes from the word *jettison*.

gas buggies: An antiquated term for motor cars that run on petrol or diesel. Frank tells Magnolia, "I was thinkin' of buyin' one of those gas buggies—either a Mercedes or a Packard. I ain't decided."

hoochie coochie: In the second half of the nineteenth century, there was a sensual dance, something like a belly dance, that was done by the scantily dressed woman at a carnival. The dance is also commonly spelled as *hootchy kootchy*. At the Chicago World's Fair, Parthy asks why all the men are coming out of one pavilion, and Magnolia answers, "That's the hoochie coochie dance."

keel boatin': The river pilot Windy says to Sheriff Vallon, "I was keel boatin' time you was runnin' around a barefoot on the landing." A keel boat was a shallow, flat-bottom boat that was usually rowed, poled, or towed, and was used for moving freight up or down a river. The name comes from the sail, or keel, that allowed the boat to sail into the wind.

"lift dat bale": The Black stevedores sing "lift dat bale" in the song "Ol' Man River." Today, a standard bale of cotton is large (seventeen cubic feet) and heavy (five hundred pounds), but cotton bales were not standardized in the nineteenth century, and sizes and weights varied. Most of the time, bales were "rolled" rather than lifted because of the weight. When such bales were lifted, it was usually by a winch and pulley rather than being picked up by an individual worker. So to "lift dat bale" probably meant the stevedores pulled on ropes to lift the cotton high enough to be loaded or unloaded.

miscegenation: In the most powerful scene in *Show Boat*, Sheriff Vallon tells Andy, "I understand there's a miscegenation case on board." An old term, used mostly in old laws, *miscegenation* is the interbreeding of people who are considered to be members of different races. The word, now usually considered pejorative, is derived from a combination of the Latin *miscere* ("to mix") and the Greek *genus* ("race"). In the American South, in particular, there were laws on the books forbidding such mixed marriages or relationships.

"old favorite": During the New Year's Eve show at the Trocadero, the announcer says, "We are fortunate in obtaining the services of Miss Magnolia Ravenal, who will sing you an old favorite." That old favorite is "After the Ball," a popular song from 1892, and the only song in the *Show Boat* score not by Jerome Kern. It was written by Charles K. Harris and was introduced in Milwaukee when it was interpolated into the score for the touring musical comedy *A Trip to Chinatown*. "After the Ball" went on to sell five million copies of sheet music and was the first theatre song to earn over $10 million.

Punchinello: The Italian puppet character Punchinello was a fat, short, and often hunchbacked clown or buffoon. In Britain the character was known as Punch, and he often fought with Judy. In the song "You Are Love," Gaylord sings, "Life was just a joke to tell, / Like a lonely Punchinello."

roué: A man who recklessly indulges in sensual pleasures was once called by the French name *roué*. The word often was applied to elderly, debauched men who thought themselves irresistible to young women. In the song "Life upon the Wicked Stage," Ellie sings, "Though you're warned against a roué ruining your reputation."

Sappho: The Greek poetess Sappho lived in the seventh century BCE and resided on the island of Lesbos. Because she wrote many poems of love for women, Sappho is often associated with female homosexuality. Ellie has no idea of who Sappho is when she incorrectly says to Frank, "If it wasn't for you, I'd be on Broadway this minute doing Sappho in Shakespeare's *Merchant of Venice*."

sports of gay Chicago: In the song "At the Fair," the chorus girls sing, "When the sports of gay Chicago / Pay a visit to the fair / You can tell / Ev'ry swell / By his dashing air!" While the words *sport* or *sports* usually refer to athletic games, there is an older use of the word. A person, usually a male, who behaves in a carefree manner and is unconcerned about a difficult situation was called a sport.

stage door Johnnies: Little used today, the term *stage-door Johnny* was used to describe a man who often goes to a theater or waits at a stage door to court an actress. Sometimes a nuisance, stage door Johnnies could also be wealthy men out to wine and dine female performers. In the song "Life upon the Wicked Stage," Ellie sings, "Stage door Johnnies aren't raging over you with gems and roses."

Sweeney Todd: Captain Andy tells the show boat audience, "I always put on strong moral plays . . . There ain't never been no Sweeney Todds in my shows." In the 1846 British melodrama *The String of Pearls*, the character of Sweeney Todd was introduced, and he has become a legend since, appearing in plays, movies, and musicals. Todd is a vengeful barber who slits the throats of his enemies and gives the bodies to his cohort, Mrs. Lovett, to make into meat pies. Although not as famous in the States, Sweeney and his grotesque legend were not unknown.

"tote dat barge": This phrase in the song "Ol' Man River" has been much discussed over the decades. The word *tote* usually means to carry, as in a tote bag. Since it is not possible for the Black stevedores in the musical to "carry a barge," some have found Oscar Hammerstein's lyric at fault. Yet others have pointed out that "to tote a barge" means to pull a small barge by a rope as one walked along the towpath of a river or canal. Others have pointed out that the Black vernacular could easily have turned "tow" into "tote."

Trocadero Music Hall: The original London Trocadero entertainment venue was in the theatre district known as the West End, and opened in 1865. It was so popular that the name was used for theaters and nightclubs in cities around the English-speaking world. The Trocadero Music Hall in Chicago was one of them, flourishing in the last decades of the nineteenth century, and for a time in the next century. The New Year's Eve party at the Trocadero in *Show Boat* celebrates the arrival of 1905.

SHREK THE MUSICAL

Libretto by David Lindsay-Abaire, based on the book by William Steig. Lyrics by David Lindsay-Abaire. Music by Jeanine Tesori. Original Broadway production: December 14, 2010. Broadway Theatre. 441 performances.

This satirical musical is a spoof of famous fairy tales and nursery rhymes. Consequently, the cast of characters is filled with familiar faces, and many of the references are to other fairy tales. Happily, even children will get these references. When a character sings, "Story of my life. / Always doomed to fail. / Cheated by a fox. / Swallowed by a whale," everyone knows that is the story of Pinocchio. But there are some not-so-obvious references worth exploring. In many ways, the fairy-tale world of *Shrek the Musical* is very modern, full of sass and mirth.

Expressions, references, names:

Angela's Ashes: In the song "Donkey Pot Pie," the Dragon tells Donkey to read her book on fire breathing, and Donkey replies, "I'm actually already in a book club. We're reading *Angela's Ashes*." The Irish-American author Frank McCourt's 1996 memoir about his very early childhood in Brooklyn and his life in Ireland is titled *Angela's Ashes*.

bipolar: A psychiatric illness characterized by both manic and depressive episodes is commonly called bipolar. The Adult Fiona sings, "But I know he'll appear, though I seem a bit bipolar" in the song "I Know It's Today."

cardio: Short for cardiovascular exercise, cardio is an aerobic exercise that stimulates and strengthens the heart and lungs. In "Travel Song," Donkey sings to Shrek, "This is good cardio."

colossus of moxie: The citizens of Duloc introduce Lord Farquaad with, "Here's the man who made it happen! That towering colossus of moxie!" A colossus is a statue of huge proportions. Today it can refer to any person of great size or power. *Moxie* can mean a person's energy or pep, but also courage and determination. The diminutive Lord Farquaad has moxie but is hardly a colossus.

conga line: In the song "Big Bright Beautiful World," Shrek sings, "Doin' what I can with a one-man conga line." A kind of Cuban carnival dance, a conga line is a long, processing line of dancers holding on to each other's waists and following the circular pattern of the leader. As Shrek suggests, a conga line with only one person is very limiting.

cookie cutter: Something that is mass-produced, repeating the same look many times over, is described as "cookie cutter." The phrase comes from the metal frames used to shape cookie dough. Wanting all his citizens looking and behaving alike, Lord Farquaad sings, "Embrace the cookie cutter in Duloc" in the song "What's Up, Duloc?"

Cupid and Psyche . . . Pop Rocks and Mikey: In the song "Don't Let Me Go," Donkey sings to Shrek about two pairs: "Like Cupid and Psyche—like Pop Rocks and Mikey." The tale of Cupid and Psyche is a Roman myth about the love relationship between a mortal and a god. It is a rarity in classical literature in that it has a happy ending. Pop Rocks is a candy that differs from typical hard candy in that pressurized carbon dioxide gas bubbles are embedded inside the candy, creating a small popping reaction when it dissolves. One of the most frequently aired television advertisements in the 1970s and 1980s was one for Life cereal. Mikey is a very cute youngster with a round face and freckles who is a picky eater. His older brother and a friend feed Mikey some Life cereal, and when the tot likes it, they decide it must be good. Years after the commercial aired, an urban legend developed that said the actor who played Mikey died by eating Pop Rocks and carbonated soda, the candy exploding inside his stomach. The rumor persisted until "Mikey" publicly declared he was alive and well.

Dutch elm disease: In the song "Story of My Life," Pinocchio says, "This is worse than that case of Dutch elm disease I caught in Tijuana!," referring to a fungi that destroys elm trees. Spread by elm bark beetles, when it worked its way over from Europe, the disease killed millions of elm trees in the United States.

flamenco: A kind of music, dancing, and guitar style, flamenco originated with gypsy musicians and dancers in southern Spain. The dance involves intricate and rapid foot stomping. In the song "What's Up, Duloc?," the citizens sing about Lord Farquaad: "He's trained in ballet, flamenco, and jazz!"

Hey nonny-nonny: A very popular nonsense refrain going back to Elizabethan England, the expression can be translated as "Whatever," "What the heck?," or "That's life." Lord Farquaad sings, "Hey nonny-nonny-nonny-no!" several times in the song "What's Up, Duloc?"

"horses who pull wagons": Donkey boasts to Shrek, "I could be one of those horses who pull those wagons full of beer." He is referring to the famous Budweiser Clydesdales, huge draft horses originating in Scotland that are featured in parades and commercials pulling elaborate wagons for the Anheuser-Busch brewing company.

Paxil: When one of the Three Pigs is discovered to have panic attacks, the Sugar Plum Fairy says, "This little piggie needs Paxil." Used for people with depression, anxiety, or other disorders, Paxil is an antidepressant containing Paroxetine, which affects chemicals in the brain that may be unbalanced.

pheromones: Pheromones are chemicals released by an animal that trigger a social response in members of the same species. In humans, pheromones are usually associated with sexual response or attraction. In the song "Make a Move," Donkey sings, "With a giggle and a flip of her hair / I smell pheromones in the air."

"prenup will be binding": A prenuptial agreement, commonly known as a prenup, is a contract entered into by two people who are about to get married. The agreement outlines the financial obligations of each party, and includes a plan for dividing assets and debt obligations if the marriage should come to an end. In the song "I Know It's Today," teenage Fiona sings, "He'll propose on one knee and our prenup will be binding."

vamping: Adult Fiona sings, "Cut the villains, cut the vamping" in the song "I Know It's Today." In music terminology, *vamping* is essentially repeating a musical sequence as needed to cover a spoken introduction to a song or as background behind dialogue in a musical play.

velvet glove: The proverb "to handle someone with a velvet glove" means to treat a person very carefully, usually to get what one wants from them. In the song "Donkey Pot Pie," the Dragon tells Donkey, "I'll velvet-glove you."

yin and yang . . . Sturm und Drang . . . Eng and Chang: In the song "Don't Let Me Go," Donkey sings to Shrek, "You and me, we belong together . . . Like yin and yang—Sturm und Drang—like Eng and Chang, attached at the hip." Yin and yang is a Chinese philosophical concept that describes how obviously opposite or contrary forces may actually be complementary and interconnected. The German expression *Sturm und Drang* (translated as "storm and stress") was a late-eighteenth-century literary movement in Germany characterized by very serious works with somber philosophy, high emotion, and the individual's struggle against society. The world's most famous "Siamese twins," Chang and Eng Bunker (1811–1874), were conjoined twin brothers whose fame propelled the expression "Siamese twins" to become synonymous for all conjoined siblings. During their lifetime, Eng and Chang were widely exhibited as curiosities and studied by the medical profession.

THE SOUND OF MUSIC

Libretto by Howard Lindsay and Russel Crouse, based on Maria von Trapp's memoir *The Trapp Family Singers*. Lyrics by Oscar Hammerstein. Music by Richard Rodgers. Original Broadway production: November 16, 1959. Lunt-Fontanne Theatre. 1,443 performances. Broadway revival in 1998.

Set in Austria in early 1938, the musical is based on an autobiography, so many of the places and terms are actual and accurate. The real Maria was a novice at Nonnberg Abbey, and Captain von Trapp did indeed live in a villa outside of Salzburg. Among the changes Howard Lindsay and Russel

Crouse made in their libretto was to create the Kaltzberg Music Festival, paying homage to the famous one in Salzburg.

Expressions, references, names:

abbess: The woman who is the head of all the nuns in an abbey is known as the abbess. The nuns in the musical address the Abbess as Reverend Mother, which is accurate, and typical of most religious orders of women.

abbey: A building or, more often, a complex of buildings that house a community of monks or nuns is called an abbey. Going back to the early Middle Ages, a European abbey usually included farmland and vineyards in addition to the stone structures where the inhabitants lived, worked, and prayed. The abbey in the musical is Nonnberg Abbey, an actual community in Salzburg.

Anschluss: In 1938, Hitler forced the resignation of the Austrian chancellor, replaced him with a new pro-Nazi leader, then annexed Austria without a struggle. This turn of events was called the *Anschluss*, the German word for "connection." In the second act, Zeller says, "It's been four days since the Anschluss."

auf Wiedersehen: The familiar way of saying good-bye in German, *auf Wiedersehen* translates literally to "Until we see each other again." In the song "So Long, Farewell," the children sing, "So long, farewell, / auf Wiedersehen, good night."

basso profundo: A singer with a deep bass voice is known as a basso. A bass singer with an exceptionally low range is called a "basso profundo." Preparing the annual music festival, Max complains, "All I've got up to now is a basso who isn't even profundo."

bosun: The ship's officer in charge of equipment and the crew is called a bosun. The butler Franz, an ex-navy man, tells Frau Schmidt, "In the Imperial Navy, the bosun always whistled for us."

Camille: In the song "How Can Love Survive?," Elsa von Schraeder sings to the Captain, "I cannot die like Camille for you." The character of the high-class courtesan Camille was introduced in the 1848 novel *La Dame aux Camélias* by Alexandre Dumas (fils). Camille has since appeared in plays, operas, and movies. In most versions, Camille dies a romanticized death from consumption (tuberculosis).

edelweiss: The national flower of Austria is the edelweiss, a small alpine perennial with a white blossom surrounded by downy gray-green leaves. The simple folk song "Edelweiss" (the last Rodgers and Hammerstein song ever written) has a strong political meaning when the Captain sings it at the musical festival.

flibbertigibbet: Any frivolous or excessively talkative person is called a flibbertigibbet. It is an onomatopoeic word, created to make the sounds of meaningless chatter. In the song "Maria," Sister Berthe sings about Maria being a "flibbertigibbet!"

frau . . . fraulein: A married woman in German is addressed as *Frau*. In the musical, the married housekeeper is called Frau Schmidt. An unmarried woman in German is a *fraulein*. The Captain addresses Maria as Fraulein Maria.

gauleiter: Under Nazi rule, the political official governing over a district is called the gauleiter. In the musical, the gauleiter for Austria is Zeller. Frau Schmidt says, "The gauleiter is here. He wants to know why we aren't flying the new flag."

goatherd: A person who tends goats is a goatherd. Maria sings about one in "The Lonely Goatherd," whose yodel is returned by "a girl in a pale pink coat."

herr: The German equivalent to mister, *Herr* is used to address any adult male. Max Detweiler is addressed formally as Herr Detweiler in the musical.

Kaltzberg Festival: The fictional annual music festival that Max is producing is called the Kaltzberg Festival, paying homage to the Salzburg Festival, which was established in 1920 and today is world-famous. It is held each summer for five weeks, starting in late July, in various venues within the Austrian city of Salzburg. The Captain tells Elsa that Max is "desperate about getting singers for the Kaltzberg Festival."

ken: One's range of knowledge, or experience, or sight, can be called one's ken. Something that is outside of one's ken is foreign or strange. In the song "You Are Sixteen," Liesl sings to Rolf, "Timid and scared and shy am I / Of things beyond my ken."

ländler: Before the waltz, there was an Austrian folk dance in 3/4 time called the ländler. At the party given to honor Elsa von Schraeder, Maria tells Kurt, "I haven't danced the ländler since I was a little girl."

Maria Theresa . . . Emperor: The Habsburg ruler Maria Theresa (1717–1780) was the archduchess of Austria and queen of Hungary and Bohemia in the eighteenth century. The Military Order of Maria Theresa was one of the highest honors in the Austro-Hungarian Empire. Mother Abbess says about Captain von Trapp, "He was given the Maria Theresa medal by the emperor." That emperor was probably Emperor Francis Joseph I (1830–1916).

Nonnberg Abbey: The oldest continuously existing nunnery in the German-speaking world is Nonnberg Abbey, a Benedictine monastery in Salzburg, Austria. In *The Sound of Music*, it is the abbey where Maria prepares to become a nun before she meets and marries Captain von Trapp.

postulant . . . novitiate: A person who is admitted to a religious order as a probationary candidate for membership is called a postulant. In the musical, Maria is a postulant. After a period of time, a postulant can be allowed to join the novitiate, a religious house where the novices live. Mother Abbess says to the other nuns in charge of the abbey, "Out of twenty-eight postulants, sixteen or seventeen [are] ready to enter the novitiate."

roués . . . cads: In the song "You Are Sixteen," Rolf sings to Liesl, "Eager young lads / And roués and cads / Will offer you food and wine." The French expression for a dissolute or licentious man is a *roué*. A cad is a man who deliberately acts with disregard for another's feelings or rights.

saengerbünde: A social and cultural club made up of singers is referred to as a *saengerbünde* (or *sängerbünde*) in German. Max says he will be auditioning "saengerbündes, choirs, quartets" for his music festival.

table d'hôte: *Table d'hôte* is French for "the host's table." The term is used to denote a table set aside for residents of a guesthouse who get to sit at the same table as their host. Over the years, *table d'hôte* has come to mean any meal featuring a set menu at a fixed price. In the song "The Lonely Goatherd," Maria sings, "men in the midst of a table d'hôte heard [the yodeling of the goatherd]."

whirling dervish: In the song "Maria," Sister Berthe sings, "She could throw a whirling dervish out of whirl." The dervishes are members of an order of Sufi Muslims in Turkey who are known for their ceremonies in which they perform a whirling dance as an act of devotion. Later a "whirling dervish" came to mean any person displaying boundless amounts of energy.

will-o'-the-wisp: In folklore, a will-o'-the-wisp is a ghostly light seen at night over swamps or marshes. In some legends, the will-o'-the-wisp is a sprite or elf who uses a special glow to lure travelers to their deaths in a bog. In the song "Maria," Sister Sophia sings about Maria being "a will-o'-the-wisp."

wimple: A cloth headdress that covers the head, neck, and the sides of the face is a wimple. In the Middle Ages, wimples were often worn by women. In modern times, only nuns wear wimples, though most religious orders have abandoned them. In the song "Maria," Sister Berthe sings "Underneath her wimple / She has curlers in her hair."

SOUTH PACIFIC

Libretto by Oscar Hammerstein and Joshua Logan, based on *The Tales of the South Pacific* by James Michener. Lyrics by Oscar Hammerstein. Music by Richard Rodgers. Original Broadway production: April 7, 1949. Majestic Theatre. 1,925 performances. Broadway revivals in 1955 and 2008.

The authors of *South Pacific* put the location of the musical at "Two islands in the South Pacific" and the time as "World War II." One of the islands—the beautiful volcanic isle of Bali Ha'i—is now famous because of the song from the musical; unfortunately, it doesn't exist. But much of *South Pacific* is very true to the time and the place. To put a more specific date on the action, it is most likely the fall of 1943, when the Allied Forces in the South Pacific are starting to move from a defensive position to an offensive one. The Operation Alligator discussed in the musical is fictitious, but the preparations being made are for real.

Expressions, references, names:

betel nuts: In the song "Bloody Mary," the GIs sing, "Bloody Mary's chewing betel nuts." Native to Southeast Asia, the betel nut grows on an evergreen, dioecious perennial, with glossy heart-shaped leaves. Sometimes used to make medicine, the betel nut is usually chewed alone or in the form of quids—a mixture of tobacco and powdered or sliced betel nut. Quite often, chewing betel nuts makes one's mouth and lips turn red.

Bettys: Over the radio, Lieutenant Cable tells Brackett, "Twenty-two bombers—Bettys—went by at 0600, headed southwest." The Japanese attack bomber nicknamed the "Betty" by GIs during World War II was a deadly, cigar-shaped aircraft. More "Bettys" were built by the Japanese than any other aircraft during the war.

"bowl of Jell-O": In the song "A Cockeyed Optimist," Nellie sings, "I could say life is just a bowl of Jell-O." It is a nod to the 1931 popular song "Life Is Just a Bowl of Cherries" by Ray Henderson and Lew Brown. While gelatin products go back centuries, the fruit-flavored Jell-O we know today was first manufactured in America in 1897.

bromidic: A trite and unoriginal idea or remark used to be called a bromide. The corny expression was meant to soothe or placate, usually by being overly optimistic. Oscar Hammerstein turned the word into an adjective in the song "A Wonderful Guy" when Nellie sings, "I'm bromidic and bright / As a moon-happy night."

Bronze Star: After hearing about Billis's stunt in the rubber raft, Bracket asks Adams, "What the hell do you want me to do? Give this guy a Bronze Star?" One of the most heralded military medals is the Bronze Star, a US Armed Forces decoration awarded for either heroic achievement, heroic service, meritorious achievement, or meritorious service in a combat zone.

demitasse: French for "half cup," a demitasse is a small coffee cup that holds only two or three fluid ounces. Such containers are usually used for espresso. Nellie asks for three lumps of sugar, then says to Emile, "I know it's a big load for a demitasse to carry."

DiMaggio's glove: In the song "Bloody Mary," the male chorus sings mockingly about Mary's leather-like skin: "Her skin is tender as

DiMaggio's glove!" The American baseball center fielder Joe DiMaggio (1914–1999) had several nicknames, including "Joltin' Joe," "The Yankee Clipper," and "Joe D." His entire thirteen-year career in Major League Baseball was with the New York Yankees.

Dinah Shore: A favorite singer during the Big Band era, Dinah Shore (1916–1994) was the top-charting female vocalist of the 1940s. Nellie says to Cable, "For instance, if the man likes symphony music and the girl likes Dinah Shore . . . Well, what do you think?"

"Dites-Moi": The musical opens with the Eurasian children Ngana and Jerome singing a French children's song, whose title means "Tell Me." Its simple lyrics can be translated as: "Tell me why / Life is beautiful? / Tell me why / Life is gay? / Tell me why / Dear miss? / Is it because / You love me?"

Dragon Lady: When Billis tries to bargain with the Tokinese native Bloody Mary, he says, "Now look here, Dragon Lady." A stereotypic name for certain Asian women is Dragon Lady. The title implies a female who is strong, deceitful, domineering, mysterious, and sometimes sexually alluring. Bloody Mary is all of these except the last.

Florence Nightingale: The symbol of the heroic nurse is Florence Nightingale (1820–1910), an English social reformer and the founder of modern nursing training and theory. She significantly reduced death rates during the Crimean War by improving hygiene and living standards. Nellie shows Emile a newspaper clipping from her hometown of Little Rock, and he reads it aloud: "Ensign Nellie Forbush, Arkansas's own Florence Nightingale."

frangipani: Prominent in the islands of the Pacific Ocean, the frangipani is a fragrant flowering tree, also known as plumeria. The oil of the colorful flower has been used in perfumery since the sixteenth century. Emile is heard offstage telling Nellie, "That is frangipani . . . You will find many more flowers out here."

LCTs: The landing craft tank (or tank landing craft) was an amphibious assault craft used for landing GIs or tanks on beachheads. They were initially developed by the British Royal Navy, and later, by the US Navy, used during World War II and as late as the Vietnam War. Billis asks a marine, "Are you booked on one of those LCTs? . . . They'll shake the belly off you, you know."

Little Rock: Little Rock is the capital and most populous city in the state of Arkansas. The city is located on the south bank of the Arkansas River, close to the state's geographic center. Nellie says to Emile, "I wanted to see what the world was like—outside of Little Rock, I mean."

Marcel Proust . . . Anatole France: The educated Emile tells the "hick" Nellie, "I have many books here . . . Marcel Proust? Anatole France?" Nellie has never heard of them. Marcel Proust (1871–1922) was a French novelist and essayist who wrote the monumental *À la recherche du temps perdu* (*Remembrance of Things Past*), completed in 1927. Proust is considered to be one of the most influential authors of the twentieth century. Anatole France (1844–1924) was a French poet, journalist, and novelist, considered in his day to be the ideal French man of letters.

mimeograph: Before photocopying, one used a mimeograph machine to duplicate something without printing it. The mimeograph produced copies from a stencil; the more copies made, the more the image faded. At the Thanksgiving show, Nellie says to the audience, "It has been called to our attention that owing to some trouble with the mimeograph, the last part of the program is kind of blurry."

P-40s: The Curtiss P-40 was an American single-engine, single-seat, all-metal fighter and ground attack aircraft. It was used by twenty-eight nations during World War II. Airman Buzz Adams tells Brackett, "Some New Zealanders in P-40s spotted [Billis] though and kept circling around him while I flew across the island."

PBY: The Consolidated PBY Catalina is a flying boat and amphibious aircraft that was produced in the 1930s and 1940s. It was one of the most widely used seaplanes of World War II. When Billis asks Cable if he's new on the island, he answers, "Just came in on that PBY." Later in the musical, Brackett asks Billis, "And how the hell can you fall out of a PBY anyway?"

Pepsodent: In the song "Bloody Mary," the male chorus sings about her teeth and notes: "And she don't use Pepsodent." A toothpaste that contains pepsin, a digestive agent designed to break down and digest food deposits on the teeth, is known as Pepsodent. It was introduced in the United States in 1915 by the Pepsodent Company of Chicago.

Rutgers . . . Princeton: When Cable says he went to college in New Jersey, Billis asks, "Rutgers?" but Cable answers, "No, Princeton." By the 1940s, Princeton University had established itself as an Ivy League school with a worldwide reputation. Rutgers at the time was still a land-grant college concentrating on agriculture, engineering, and chemistry. Today Rutgers is a university with four campuses in New Jersey.

Sadsack . . . Droopy-drawers: When Bloody Mary gets mad at a GI, she calls him a bunch of names: "Come back! Chipskate! Crummy GI! Sadsack! Droopy-drawers!" *Sad Sack* was an American comic strip and comic book character created by Sergeant George Baker during World War II. Sad Sack was a lowly US Army private caught up in the absurdities and humiliations of military life. The title was a euphemistic shortening of the military slang "sad sack of shit." The phrase has come to mean an inept person or soldier. A droopy-drawers is a person whose pants are falling down, typical of a sloppy, incompetent individual.

Seabees: The men in naval combat demolition units and underwater demolition teams during World War II were called Seabees. When Brackett hears that GIs are making grass skirts for Billis, he angrily asks, "Do you mean to tell me the Seabees of the United States Navy are now a lot of—!"

Tokyo Rose: In the song "There Is Nothin' Like a Dame," the GIs sing, "We get . . . advice from Tokyo Rose." The most famous broadcaster of Japanese propaganda during World War II was an Asian American woman who went by the name Tokyo Rose. Her English-language programs were broadcast from Tokyo to the South Pacific and North America, to demoralize Allied forces abroad and their families at home.

Tonkinese: The language and the people of Tonkin are termed *Tonkinese.* Tonkin is a region that is now northern Vietnam, the origin of the popular Tonkinese cat breed. The Gulf of Tonkin, located off the coasts of Tonkin and South China, played an important part in the Vietnam War. When Cable asks Billis who Bloody Mary is, he answers, "She's Tonkinese—used to work for a French planter."

SWEENEY TODD: THE DEMON BARBER OF FLEET STREET

Libretto by Hugh Wheeler, based on a play by Christopher Bond. Music and lyrics by Stephen Sondheim. Original Broadway production: March 1, 1979. Uris Theatre. 557 performances. Broadway revivals in 1989 and 2005.

Long familiar to Britons, the tale of Sweeney Todd was new to most Americans when the musical version opened on Broadway in 1979. Also new were several of the British words and expressions. The setting is London during the Industrial Revolution, which vaguely covers much of the nineteenth century. Most of the action takes place in the area around Fleet Street, a neighborhood in the old city of London that included a cross-section of Londoners, from court judges to the homeless. That means both high-class language and lower-class slang is heard throughout the musical.

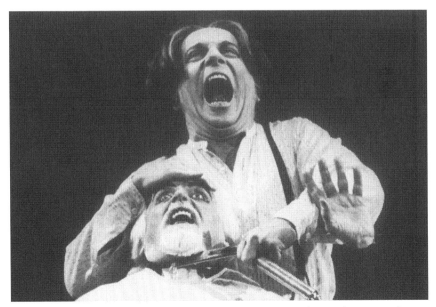

SWEENEY TODD: THE DEMON BARBER OF FLEET STREET *Barbers in the nineteenth century were prized not for cutting hair but for smooth, painless shaves. The vengeful Sweeney (Len Cariou) will give the Judge (Edmund Lyndeck) a close but painful shave.* Photofest

Expressions, references, names:

alms: Money or food given to the poor used to be known as alms. It was mostly used by beggars who called out, "Alms for the poor!" In the musical, the Beggar Woman frequently approaches Sweeney and others singing, "Alms! . . . Alms!"

Australia: In 1824, the first penal colony in Australia was founded in Morton Bay (today Brisbane), and over the next seventy-five years Great Britain regularly sent its most dangerous convicts (men and women) to the continent. Most had life sentences and never returned to Europe. Some managed to escape, as in the case of Sweeney Todd. Mrs. Lovett, noticing the physical and mental change in Todd, says to him, "Good God, what did they do to you down there in bloody Australia or wherever?"

bank holiday: In the United Kingdom, Ireland, and a handful of other countries, a national public holiday is referred to as a "bank holiday." The name comes from the fact that banking institutions typically close for business on such holidays. Mrs. Lovett recalls when she was young and "my rich Aunt Nettie used to take me to the seaside August Bank Holiday."

barber: Before razors for shaving were made safer and easier to use, most men were shaved by a barber using a straight blade. Barbers also cut hair, but that was secondary in their craft. Some barbers also pulled teeth, the only cure for a painful toothache. In the prologue, the chorus sings of Sweeney Todd, who "shaved the faces of gentlemen." Later, Todd and Pirelli have a contest to see who can pull a tooth faster and least painfully.

Beadle: When Mrs. Lovett tells Todd about what happened to his wife, she sings, "There were these two, you see, / Wanted her like mad, / One of 'em a judge, / T'other one his beadle." Today a beadle is an official who takes part in some church or university ceremonies. But in the nineteenth century, a beadle referred to an officer of the law who dealt with small offenses in the neighborhood.

Bedlam: Todd explains to Anthony where the wig makers get their hair: "Bedlam. They get their hair from the lunatics at Bedlam." The Hospital of Saint Mary of Bethlehem was an institution in London for the mentally ill. The word *Bethlehem* morphed into *Bethlem*, then *Bedlam*, and soon that hospital, and all other psychiatric institutions, were called Bedlam. Today the word means any scene of uproar and confusion.

Botany Bay: The inlet of the Tasman Sea just south of Sydney, Australia, is known as Botany Bay. It was where Captain James Cook landed in 1770. By the nineteenth century, it was a British penal settlement. Pirelli tells Todd that he knows he is "Benjamin Barker, later transported to Botany Bay for life."

coo: The British informal exclamation for surprise is *coo*. When Mrs. Lovett tells Tobias that she's knitting a muffler for him, he says, "Coo, ma'am—for me?"

cor: An oft-used exclamation for alarm, delight, or any other emotion is the informal British word *cor*, most commonly heard by Cockneys who say, "Cor blimey!" When business is bustling at her pie shop, Mrs. Lovett sings, "Cor, me bones is weary . . . Cor, me eyes is bleary."

curate: A clergyman who serves as an assistant to a vicar, rector, or parish priest is called a curate. In the song "A Little Priest," Todd pretends to taste a meat pie made from a priest and says to Mrs. Lovett, "Not as hearty as bishop, perhaps, but not as bland as curate, either."

Dardanelles: Near the beginning of the musical, Anthony sings, "I have sailed the world, beheld its wonders / From the Dardanelles / To the mountains of Peru." The narrow thirty-eight-mile strait between Europe and Asiatic Turkey is called the Dardanelles. Known as the Hellespont in classical times, the Dardanelles link the Sea of Marmara with the Aegean Sea.

dropsy: A condition in which an excess of watery fluid collects in the cavities or tissues of the body is called edema, the more antiquated term being *dropsy*. Mrs. Lovett tells Todd about her deceased husband, Albert, whose "leg give out from the dropsy."

elixir: An old and exotic name for a magical or medicinal potion. In the song "Pirelli's Miracle Elixir, Toby sings, "'Twas Pirelli's / Miracle Elixir, / That's wot did the trick, sir."

epiphany: Any sudden manifestation or moment of sudden revelation or insight can be called an epiphany. In the song "Epiphany," the crazed Todd sings, "Welcome to the grave! / I will have vengeance, / I will have salvation!"

Fleet Street: One of the oldest streets in the City of London is Fleet Street. The name comes from the Fleet River, which used to run through the old city. It has been an important through-route since Roman times. Fleet Street became known for printing and publishing at the start of the sixteenth century; by the twentieth century, most British national newspapers operated from this area. They have since moved elsewhere, but the expression "Fleet Street" still means the British national press. In the musical, Mrs. Lovett's pie shop and Todd's barbershop are located on Fleet Street.

fop: An antiquated term for a dandified person, usually a male who is obsessed with clothes and manners; in the song "A Little Priest," Mrs. Lovett offers an imaginary pie to Todd, and sings, "It's fop. / Finest in the shop."

gillyflowers: Not an authentic botanical name, *gillyflower* can refer to any number of fragrant flowers. Mrs. Lovett hopes to brighten up Todd's shop with flowers. In the song "Wait," she sings, "Gillyflowers, I'd say. Nothing like a nice bowl of gillies."

harmonium: A popular drawing-room instrument in Victorian times was the harmonium, a keyboard instrument in which the notes are produced by air driven through metal reeds by foot-operated bellows. They were also found in small churches that could not afford a proper pipe organ. Mrs. Lovett sits counting her money and says, "That makes seven pounds, nine shillings, and four pence for this week. Not bad—and that don't include wot I had to pay out for my cheery wallpaper or the harmonium . . . And a real bargain it was, dear, it being only partially singed when the chapel burnt down."

Kearney's Lane: A quiet street in London, which in Victorian days was occupied by the upper classes, it's where Judge Turpin lives with his ward, Johanna. Anthony sees Johanna and sings, "For all its wonders, / When in Kearney's Lane / Lies the greatest wonder yet."

kippers: Fish that has been split open and salted and dried in the open air, or in smoke, is known as a kippered fish, or kippers. Herring was the most common fish that was kippered. In the song "By the Sea," Mrs. Lovett sings, "By the sea, in our nest, / We could share our kippers / With the odd paying guest."

lavabo: A small wooden structure that holds a washbasin and a towel is known as a lavabo. In the prologue, the chorus sings of how Todd's "room was bare: / A lavabo and a fancy chair."

linnet bird . . . ringdove . . . robinet: In the song "Green Finch and Linnet Bird," Johanna sings about the variety of sounds different birds make: "Green finch and linnet bird, / Nightingale, blackbird . . . ringdove and robinet . . . teach me how to sing." A linnet is a brown or gray finch with a reddish breast and forehead. Not a proper ornithological term, *ringdove* (or *ringbird*) can refer to any bird that has contrasting feathers that appear as a ring around the neck. *Robinet* is the diminutive form of *robin*, a bird whose name comes from the name Robert.

meat pies: In many cultures around the world, pies are more than a dessert item. Such pies, filled with meat and vegetables, are considered savories. In the song "Worst Pies in London," Mrs. Lovett admits she makes "The worst pies in London. / Only lard and nothing more."

Old Bailey: The outer wall of a castle is called the bailey. The central criminal court in London is on Bailey Street, where the walls of such a castle once stood, and is familiarly referred to as the Old Bailey. The courts have been on this site since the sixteenth century, and Judge Turpin presides over one. Anthony tells Todd, "Now I must hurry, for surely the Judge is off to the Old Bailey."

pomade and pumice stone: When the Judge is about to get a shave, he tells Todd, "So fetch the pomade and pumice stone." A pomade is a scented ointment or oil that is applied to the hair. Pumice stone is a very light and porous volcanic rock that was used to remove hard or callused skin. Later in the musical, Beadle asks Todd, "Tell me, Mr. Todd, do you pomade the hair? I dearly love a pomaded head."

quid: The informal British term for one pound sterling is *quid*. Mrs. Lovett shows Todd his shaving tools and tells him, "Times as bad as they are, I could have got five, maybe ten quid for 'em, any day."

reticule: An antiquated word for a woman's small handbag; in Victorian times, a reticule typically had a drawstring and was decorated with embroidery or beading. In the song "Kiss Me," Anthony says they will steal away, and Johanna sings, "I'll take my reticule. / I need my reticule. / You mustn't think / Me a fool / But my reticule / Never leaves my side."

savory/sweet pies: A savory pie is salty or spicy rather than sweet and contains meat and vegetables. A sweet pie has fruit or some other confection with mincemeat to make it a dessert dish. In the song "God That's Good!," Tobias sings to the customers, "There you'll sample / Mrs. Lovett's meat pies, / Savory and sweet pies."

squiff: The word *squiff* is a fusion of *skew* and *whiff*, and refers to intoxication or drunkenness. It can also refer to a woman who wears slutty clothes and is promiscuous. First coming into use in the mid-nineteenth century, the word was usually used as an adjective, as in a "squiffed" person. The Beggar Woman uses the word to suggest sexual favors when she sings to Anthony, "'Ow would you like a little squiff, dear?"

tinker: An old-fashioned term for a person who travels from place to place mending metal utensils as a way of making a living; in the song "A Little Priest," Mrs. Lovett offers an imaginary pie to Todd and sings, "We've got tinker."

vespers bell: A church service of evening prayer is known as vespers. Calling parishioners to such a service was the vespers bell. In the song "City on Fire," the Beggar Woman sings, "Smell it, sir! An evil smell! / Every night at the vespers bell / Smoke that comes from the mouth of hell!"

SWEET CHARITY

Libretto by Neil Simon, based on the film *Nights of Cabiria*. Lyrics by Dorothy Fields. Music by Cy Coleman. Original Broadway production: January 29, 1966. Palace Theatre. 608 performances. Broadway revivals in 1986 and 2005.

Federico Fellini's 1957 film *Nights of Cabiria*, about a goodhearted, indomitable Italian streetwalker, was reset in the mid-1960s in New York City, with the heroine now a dance hall hostess. Fighting off lecherous men who paid to dance with you was an effective substitute for prostitution, and no one knew how to write about New York and New Yorkers with sass like Neil Simon. But for all its atmospheric qualities, *Sweet Charity* was a star vehicle. (Ironically, Gwen Verdon, who starred as Charity, had played an ex-prostitute in the musical *New Girl in Town* nine years earlier.) The slang in the musical is very 1960s, some of which we still use today. But there are also many names and products that have fallen by the wayside.

Expressions, references, names:

"B" picture: Back in the days when films were shorter and were usually shown as part of a double feature, the "B" movie was often a low-budget commercial motion picture. An angry Ursula calls Italian movie star Vittorio Vidal a "two-bit, 'B' picture, fading Romeo."

Bronx . . . Washington Square: In the song "Where Am I Going?," Charity sings, "Why do I care? / Run to the Bronx / Or Washington Square." The New York City borough named the Bronx is separated from Manhattan by the Harlem River and is the only district in New York located on the mainland. Once a modest ethnic neighborhood, the Bronx was beginning to get dangerous and undesirable in the 1960s. With its impressive arch and historic homes, Washington Square is a favorite public park in Lower Manhattan.

Chase and Sanborn: Established in 1862 in Boston, Chase and Sanborn claims to be the first coffee company to pack and ship roasted coffee in sealed tins. Charity tells Oscar she doesn't "even have a bank account. I keep my money in an empty can of Chase and Sanborn coffee."

Chateaubriand: Supposedly named after the French aristocrat François-René de Chateaubriand, whose chef developed the recipe, Chateaubriand is made by taking a large, boneless cut of beef, wrapping it in poor-quality steaks, tying it up, and grilling it until charred. At the Pompeii Club, Vidal says to the Waiter, "Bring us two Chateaubriand."

Church of the Month Club: In 1926, the Book of the Month Club was established, to great success. It is a subscription-based service that offers its members a selection of five to seven new hardcover books each month. Later, clubs for other products followed, such as the Fruit of the Month Club and the Wine of the Month Club. When Charity asks Oscar how he found the Rhythm of Life Church, he says, "I'm on a mailing list. It's the Church of the Month Club." There has never been any such club; it is a comic creation by Neil Simon.

Count Basie: The American jazz pianist, bandleader, and composer Count Basie (1904–1984) formed the Count Basie Orchestra in 1935, and for the next forty years he was one of the major Black artists on the music scene. In the song "I'm a Brass Band," Charity sings, "I'm a . . . Big Count Basie blast."

dance hall hostess . . . taxi dancer: The practice of men paying dance hall women to dance with them goes back to the 1920s, and the dime-a-dance concept gained popularity in the 1930s. The women were called "hostesses" or "taxi dancers," and for a fee would dance with a customer for the length of one song. Such dance halls were waning by the 1960s, and are long gone now, but taxi dancing is still practiced in some other countries. When the Cop asks Charity what her occupation is, she says, "I'm a Social Consultant . . . [at] the Fandango Ballroom," so the cop writes down, "Dance hall hostess." Later in the musical, Nickie says, "I'm not gonna become the world's first little old taxi dancer. I'm gettin' out."

Dior: In the song "There's Got to Be Somethin' Better Than This," Nickie sings, "When I sit at my desk on the forty-first floor, / In my copy of a copy of a copy of Dior." Fashion designer Christian Dior (1905–1957) was the founder of one of the world's premier fashion houses. His clothes were in great demand, so copies by others flooded the market.

dowry: Charity says to Charlie, "An' I've got the money for the down payment right here. My dowry." The money or valuable objects that a woman brings to her husband in marriage is called a dowry. Rarely practiced today, the idea of a dowry still exists in some cultures.

eccola: The Italian word *eccola* can be translated as "Here she is." Vidal hands Charity the signed photo of himself and says, "Eccola."

Howard's: Charity says about her ex-boyfriend, "That louse wouldn't wear a Howard's suit." With its factory in Brooklyn and over one hundred stores across the nation, Howard's Clothes was a retail giant. The company was founded in 1924, and the men's clothing empire had its flagship store on Broadway and 50th Street.

Irish Sweepstakes: At the dance hall, Carmen announces to the dance hall girls, "Ladies, they have just announced the winners of the 1966 Irish Sweepstakes. And since none of you ladies are among the winners, get your ass out there." In 1930, the Irish government authorized a lottery to benefit Irish hospitals, which flourished until a state lottery replaced it, in 1987.

jet set: Wealthy and fashionable people who flew far and often to pleasure sites around the world were labeled the "jet set" in the 1960s. In the song "Baby, Dream Your Dream," Helene and Nickie sing, "We'll ask the local jet set / To dine on our dinette set."

Modern Jazz Quartet: In the song "I'm a Brass Band," Charity sings, "I'm the Modern Jazz Quartet." Classical, cool jazz, blues, and bebop music were all part of the repertory of the Black foursome known as the Modern Jazz Quartet.

Norman Mailer: At the 92nd Street Y, a girl asks the receptionist, "Excuse me. Could you tell me where Norman Mailer is reading his poetry tonight?" An American novelist, journalist, essayist, playwright, activist, filmmaker, and even actor, Norman Mailer (1923–2007) had a prolific career spanning over six decades. He was an outspoken and controversial author who also wrote poetry.

Old Glory: An informal (yet respectful) name for the flag of the United States is Old Glory. In the song "You Should See Yourself," Charity sings to Charlie, "You're Old Glory, man; yes, you are! / In my flag, you are the fi-fifty-first star."

"O, Promise Me": For nearly one hundred years, "O, Promise Me" (1887), by Reginald De Koven (music) and Clement Scott (lyrics), was the song of choice for weddings. First heard in the operetta *Robin Hood*, the sentimental song went on to sell over a million copies of sheet music. In the song "I Love to Cry at Weddings," Rosie sings, "Ah! What's as sweet and sloppy as: / 'O, Promise Me' . . . and all that jazz?"

Orbach's: Between 1923 and 1987, Orbach's was a go-to place for moderately priced clothing, footwear, bedding, furniture, jewelry, beauty products, and housewares. Charity tells Oscar, "I was once trapped in a dress for twenty minutes. I screamed all over Orbach's."

Parachute Jump: Built for the 1939 New York World's Fair, and then a landmark amusement park ride at Coney Island, the Parachute Jump was the ultimate thrill ride. A steel tower had arms from which riders were lifted to the top in a two-person canvas seat and then dropped. In the scene from *Sweet Charity* at Coney Island, the Policeman says to a crowd gathered, "Can't you see? There's a fellow and a girl stuck up there on the Parachute Jump."

Passaic: Located north of Newark on the Passaic River, Passaic is a community in New Jersey that offers residents a modest commute to New York City. Talking about their future together, Oscar tells Charity, "There's this little place on Route 66 in Passaic."

Pul-it-itzer Prize: Established by the will of Joseph Pulitzer in 1916, Pulitzer Prizes are given annually for outstanding literary or journalistic achievement. In the song "You Should See Yourself," Charity sings to Charlie, "You're a blue ribbon Pul-it-itzer prize!" She not only mispronounces the name, but the Pulitzer does not come with a blue ribbon.

***Sabrina Fair* . . . Julie Andrews:** Trapped in the elevator with Oscar, Charity says, "Play the game. Awright, what actress was in *Sabrina Fair?* . . . Julie Andrews?" Audrey Hepburn was the star of the 1954 romantic comedy *Sabrina*, not Julie Andrews, who did not make her first movie until ten years later.

Scarsdale: One of the most desirable bedroom communities of New York City is the village of Scarsdale in Westchester County, New York. Nicki tells the newcomer Rosie, "This is where you'll meet Prince Charming who'll carry you off on his white horse to Scarsdale. You should live so long."

Sealy Posturepedic: Tempur Sealy International, Inc., is an American manufacturer of mattresses and bedding products. One of their most popular products in the 1960s was the Sealy Posturepedic mattress. Charity pats the film star Vidal's mattress and says, "Sealy Posturepedic."

Southampton: Located partly on the South Fork of Long Island, the town of Southampton is one of the wealthiest communities in the nation. When Charity says she is sick of the ballroom, Nicki sarcastically tells her, "Well, you can always go back to Mummy and Daddy's place in Southampton."

"Sweet Adeline": "(You're the Flower of My Heart,) Sweet Adeline" is a ballad by Richard Husch Gerard and Harry Armstrong that has been a sentimental favorite since it was published in 1903. "Sweet Adeline" has also been a favorite of barbershop quartets. In fact, there are still choral groups who call themselves the "Sweet Adelines." In the song "I Love to Cry at Weddings," the partygoers sing, "I drink champagne and sing 'Sweet Adeline.'"

"upstate government hotel": Nickie tells Charity, "Despite the fact that I may have spent a few years in an upstate government hotel, I am still warm, kindhearted, and basically sincere." She is probably referring to Sing Sing Correctional Facility, located thirty miles up the Hudson River in Ossining, New York.

Vaseline: In several languages, the word *Vaseline* is used as generic for petroleum jelly. Although Vaseline is used as an ointment and lubricant, in the 1950s and 1960s many of the hair creams for men contained large amounts of Vaseline. Helene says that Charity's so-called fiancé has "a pound and a half of Vaseline in his hair."

Williamsburg: In the borough of Brooklyn, Williamsburg is a neighborhood that has always been home to working-class New Yorkers. Charity lies to Oscar and says she works at a bank: "First National City, Williamsburg branch."

"the Y": Founded in 1874 as the Young Men's Hebrew Association, the 92nd Street Y (often simply called "the Y") went from being a social club to a major cultural center in New York City in the twentieth century. Besides offering a variety of classes, many of the world's top literary and political figures have given lectures there. When Charity tells the receptionist at the "Y," "I'm interested in joining a cultural group," the woman replies, "Certainly. Are you a member of the 'Y'?"

WEST SIDE STORY

Libretto by Arthur Laurents, loosely based on Shakespeare's *Romeo and Juliet*. Lyrics by Stephen Sondheim. Music by Leonard Bernstein. Original Broadway production: September 26, 1957. Winter Garden Theatre. 734 performances. Major Broadway revivals in 1960, 1964, 1980, 2009, and 2020.

Perhaps nothing dates faster than street slang, especially the vernacular of the younger generation. The two gangs in *West Side Story* each have their own lingo, but they communicate with each other better than the gang members do with the older generation. Today's audience finds the tough street talk in *West Side Story* both quaint and foreign. One of the marvels of the musical is how Stephen Sondheim's lyrics match Arthur Laurents's libretto. Both have expressions and references that need explaining.

WEST SIDE STORY   *The gang known as the Jets uses a street lingo that is long gone but is still potent when heard in this landmark musical.*
Photofest

Expressions, references, names:

branded . . . tomato: Baby John examines A-rab's bloody ear and says, "Them PRs! They branded you!" and Snowboy adds, "That makes you a Puerto Rican tomato. Cha-cha-cha, Señorita?" In the past, "branding" was used to describe ear piercing, something most Latinx women did. One of the Sharks has "branded" A-rab by cutting his earlobe. An old slang term for a sexy female is *tomato*.

bruja: An old hag, particularly one who is supposed to have powers of dark magic, is called a *bruja* in Spanish. When the owner of the dress shop is gone, Anita says, "She's gone! That old bag of a bruja has gone!"

casual . . . "the road": A common practice in street vernacular is to shorten a word or a phrase and still make it clear what is meant. When Baby John notices blood on A-rab's ear, A-rab says proudly, "I'm a casual, Baby John," by which A-rab means he is a casualty. When Riff wants to get rid of Anybodys, he tells her, "The road, little lady, the road," meaning "hit the road" or "leave."

Daddy-o: The long-gone but still recognized term "Daddy-o" was an informal way to address any male who was considered cool or hip. It is used several times in *West Side Story*, as when Riff says he's going to challenge Bernardo at the dance and A-rab says, "Great, Daddy-o!"

d.t.'s: The street abbreviation for "delirium tremens," meaning a severe reaction to withdrawal from alcohol. The police detective Schrank goads A-rab with, "How's your old man's d.t.'s?"

ennaprise: Any venture in business or entrepreneurial project is called an enterprise. Baby John butchers the word when he says to the Jets, "My old man says them Puerto Ricans is ruinin' free ennaprise."

frabbajabba: A colorful but dated word for "gibberish" or "nonsense"; when an argument breaks out among the Jets, Riff says to them, "Cut the frabbajabba."

gassin' . . . crabbin': Related to the term *gasbag*, *gassing* is to talk nonsense. The slang word *crabbing* also involves idle talk, usually in an effort to procrastinate or cover up for a lie. When Action asks, "What're we doin' about [the Puerto Ricans]," Anybodys sarcastically says, "Gassin', crabbin'—!"

Glory Osky: The exclamation "Glory Osky" was already outdated by the 1950s, it being a gushing way of saying "How wonderful!" in the 1920s and 1930s. Sometimes spelled *gloriosky*, it probably came from the word *glorious*. In the song "Gee, Officer Krupke," Action mockingly uses the old expression when he sings, "Glory Osky, that's why I'm a jerk!"

the gold-teeth: For a time, the term *gold-teeth* was a pejorative name for Puerto Ricans in New York City. Schrank asks the Jets, "Say, where's the rumble gonna be? Ah, look. I know regular Americans don't rub with the gold-teeth otherwise."

hip . . . dig . . . : Two of the most overused slang expressions in the 1950s and early 1960s were *hip* and *dig*. One who was knowledgeable about the latest trends or very fashionable and stylish was said to be "hip." To like a thing, or at least understand something, meant that one could "dig" it. In a tense moment, A-rab says to Doc, "You was never my age, none of you! The sooner you creeps get hip to that, the sooner you'll dig us."

kick it: A slang way of telling someone to leave or get lost was to tell them to "kick it," probably a variation of "Kick up your heels and go." To get rid of Doc, Riff says to him, "Kick it, Doc . . . Kick it!"

Krup you! . . . spit hits the fan: In 1957, when *West Side Story* opened on Broadway, four-letter words were not yet heard on the stage or screen. Lyricist Stephen Sondheim wanted Riff to sing "If the shit hits the fan" in "Jet Song," but had to settle for, "When you're a Jet, / If the spit hits the fan, / You got brothers around." Sondheim also wanted to end "Gee, Officer Krupke" with "Gee, Officer Krupke, fuck you!" The compromise was: "Gee, Officer Krupke, / Krup you!" Both scatological words could have been used onstage at the time, which would have raised eyebrows but not broken any local laws. However, if they had been used in recording the original cast album, the record would have broken laws about pornography if the albums had been shipped across state lines. Thus, the decision was made by the producers to go with the less-abrasive words for both the production and the recording.

"Leapin' lizards!": This expression, popularized by the character of Little Orphan Annie, often appeared in the comic strip and was popular throughout the 1930s. By the 1950s, the term was decidedly old-fashioned but still widely known. In the song "Gee, Officer Krupke," Action sarcastically sings, "Leapin' lizards—that's why I'm so bad!"

Micks . . . Wops . . . Polacks: Derogatory terms for immigrant groups were not limited to Puerto Ricans. The Irish (Micks) and the Italians (Wops) are also mentioned in *West Side Story*. The Jets say to the Sharks: "Who asked you to move here? . . . Back where you came from! . . . Spics!," to which the Sharks reply, "Micks! . . . Wops!" Tony is of Polish extraction and is called a Polack several times by the Sharks. Bernardo tells Anita, "Chino makes half of what the Polack makes."

Old Man Rivers: The tomboy Anybodys in *West Side Story* is smarter and braver than the Jets give her credit for; one of her insults involves her knowing the song "Ol' Man River" from *Show Boat* and the lyric, "He must know sumpin' / But don't say nuthin'." Anybodys says to the Jets, "Wotta bunch of Old Man Rivers: they don't know nuthin' and they don't say nuthin'."

pen: The shortened slang term for a penitentiary, these are prisons where persons convicted of serious crimes are sent. In the song "Gee, Officer Krupke," Baby John sings, "This boy don't need a job, he needs a year in the pen."

por favor: The Spanish for "please" is *por favor*. Maria is trying on her dress for the dance and, holding out the scissors, asks Anita, "*Por favor*, Anita. Make the neck lower."

PRs . . . Spics: Two slang terms for Puerto Ricans are *PRs* and *Spics*, the latter being a very derogatory expression equivalent to the N-word for Blacks. Schrank tells the Jets, "There's been too much raiding between you and the PRs." Later in the musical, Schrank tells the Sharks, "Clear out, spics. Sure, it's a free country and I ain't got the right. But it's a country with laws: and I can find the right. I got the badge, you got the skin."

Puerto Rico: Officially titled the Commonwealth of Puerto Rico, or the Free Associated State of Puerto Rico, the Caribbean island is an unincorporated territory of the United States. The population of Puerto Rico in 1957 was just over 2.2 million people. That same year there were over 600,000 Puerto Ricans in New York City. As Anita, Rosalia, and Consuelo sing in the song "America," "Puerto Rico's in America!"

querida . . . una poca poca: A term of affection in Spanish is *querida*, referring to a loved one. The Spanish for "little" is *poca*. Asking Anita to lower the neckline of her dress, Maria says, "Querida, one little inch; una poca poca."

rumble: A no-holds-barred fight between two rival street gangs or any other organized groups is given the slang term *rumble*. When the Jets decide to confront the Sharks, Riff says, "Okay, buddy boys, we rumble!"

San Juan: The capital of Puerto Rico is the seaport city of San Juan, the most populous community on the island. In the song "America," Rosalia sings, "I like the city of San Juan . . . When I go back to San Juan . . . I'll bring a TV to San Juan."

"Smoke your pipe and put that in": Going back to London in 1822, the idiom "Put that in your pipe and smoke it" has been a slangy way to tell someone to accept or put up with what has been said or done, even if it is unwelcome. In the song "America," Anita twists the familiar expression and sings, "Smoke your pipe and put that in!"

soda jerker . . . schmuck: In the song "Gee, Officer Krupke," Action sings, "They say go earn a buck, / Like be a soda jerker, / Which means like be a schmuck." Usually a young man, a soda jerk was a person who operated the soda fountain in a drugstore and made soda drinks and ice-cream sodas for customers. The slang word for a stupid or foolish person is *schmuck*, coming from the vulgar Yiddish, for "penis."

stool pigeon: A person who informs the authorities (usually the police) about the illegal or immoral doings of another has been given the slang term *stool pigeon*. Shrank tells A-rab, "Didn't nobody tell ya there's a difference between bein' a stool pigeon and co-operatin' with the law?"

tea: In Jack Kerouac's 1957 novel *On the Road*, he used the slang term *tea* for marijuana. Since then, one of the street words for the drug has been *tea*. In the song "Gee, Officer Krupke," Action sings, "My grandma pushes tea."

te adoro: "To love or adore" in Spanish is *adoro*, and *Te adoro* is "I love you." During the fire escape scene, when Tony and Maria must part, they say, "Te adoro, Anton" and "Te adoro, Maria."

turf . . . with skin: Riff says to the Jets, "I say this turf is small, but it's all we got. I wanna hold it like we always held it: with skin!" A place that a group or gang thinks they own is called their turf. To fight someone using your bare hands, rather than some kind of weapon, is to battle "with skin."

zip gun: A crude weapon made from the parts of a gun is called a zip gun. After A-rab pretends to be shot and falls to the floor, Baby John asks him, "Could a zip gun make you do like that?"

WONDERFUL TOWN

Libretto by Joseph Fields and Jerome Chodorov, based on the Fields-Chodorov play *My Sister Eileen* and Ruth McKenney's stories. Lyrics by Betty Comden and Adolph Green. Music by Leonard Bernstein. Original Broadway production: February 25, 1953. Winter Garden Theatre. 559 performances. Broadway revival in 2003.

This is a 1950s musical comedy set mostly in Greenwich Village in the 1930s, and it relies on Depression-era names and terms to set the atmosphere. Because Ruth Sherwood is a writer, the dialogue and lyrics in *Wonderful Town* are filled with literary references as well. Most of the places mentioned in Greenwich Village still exist, but the area has gone from a low-rent, undesirable neighborhood frequented by struggling artists, writers, and actors to a very desirable, expensive part of Manhattan filled with historic and quaint structures.

Expressions, references, names:

Albert Einstein: In the song "Pass the Football," Wreck sings of the time "Albert Einstein came to speak: Relativity!" and, because he was a football star, Wreck was chosen to introduce him. Acknowledged to be one of the greatest and most influential physicists in the history of science,

Albert Einstein (1879–1955) is best known for developing the theory of relativity. He was very much in the news in the 1930s and was known around the world.

André Gide: A giant of French literature, André Paul Guillaume Gide (1869–1951) was a winner of the Nobel Prize in Literature in 1947. Wreck sings, "Never learned to read / Mother Goose or André Gide" in the song "Pass the Football."

Astor Hotel: One of New York's most exclusive and expensive hotels, the Astor was on Times Square in Midtown Manhattan from 1905 until it was demolished in 1967. In one of Ruth's stories that Baker reads aloud, she describes "a plush opening night party at the Astor Hotel," even though she has never been there.

Barbizon Plaza: For many decades, the Barbizon Plaza was a female-only residential hotel for young women who came to New York City for professional opportunities. It was also considered a safe and friendly place for single women. The Barbizon still exists, though it began admitting men as guests in 1981. When Wreck asks at the police station if he can see Eileen Sherwood, the cop replies, "What do you think this is, the Barbizon Plaza?"

Bulova Watch Time: Bulova is an American clock and watch manufacturing company that was founded in 1875 and was known for its advertising campaign on the radio, in which a voice announced, "At the tone, it's eight o'clock, Bulova Watch Time." It was an announcement known to millions of Americans. When Appopolous tells Ruth that she has to be out of the apartment in fifteen minutes, Baker asks, "What was that?," to which Ruth replies, "Bulova Watch Time."

bunny hug . . . turkey trot: In the song "Wrong Note Rag," the chorus sings about the bunny hug and the turkey trot, two popular dances from the era. The bunny hug is an American ballroom dance in ragtime rhythm in which the couple holds each other closely. The turkey trot is also a ragtime dance in which the feet are well apart and one rises on the ball of the foot followed by a drop upon the heel.

Charles G. Dawes . . . Warden Lawes: In the song "Conga," Ruth asks the Brazilian cadets, "What do you think of . . . Charles G. Dawes,

Warden Lawes?" but they just want to dance the conga. An American banker, general, diplomat, and Republican politician who was vice president of the United States under Calvin Coolidge, Charles Gates Dawes (1865–1951) won the Nobel Peace Prize in 1925 for his work on the Dawes Plan for World War I reparations. Lewis Edward Lawes (1883–1947) was the prison warden at the Sing Sing Correctional Facility for twenty-one years, well known for the prison reforms he instituted.

Chekhov . . . Shakespeare . . . Wilde: In the song "What a Waste," Baker sings about an actress whose repertoire included "Chekhov's and Shakespeare's and Wilde's" plays, but she ended up as a waitress at Child's Restaurant. Anton Chekhov (1860–1904) was a renowned Russian playwright and short story author, and Oscar Wilde (1854–1900) was a celebrated Irish wit, poet, and dramatist. Along with Shakespeare, they are considered giants in world drama.

Childs' . . . flapjacks: In the song "What a Waste," Baker sings about an actress who came to New York to act but ended up "flipping flapjacks at Childs'." One of the first national dining chains in the United States and Canada, Childs' Restaurants peaked in the 1920s and 1930s with over one hundred eateries across the nation. One of the many slangy synonyms for pancakes is *flapjacks*.

Christopher Street: Perhaps the thoroughfare that best epitomizes Greenwich Village in New York City is Christopher Street. The opening number of *Wonderful Town* describes the nature of Christopher Street in the 1930s, and gives examples of the artists, actors, con men, prostitutes, and writers in the West Village. Today the street is most known for the Stonewall Inn, where riots in 1969 instituted the gay recognition movement. In *Wonderful Town*, the tour guide ironically sings about everything being "Pleasant and peaceful on Christopher Street," when in fact it is a beehive of activity.

colleen: An Irish girl is called a "colleen" in Ireland and among the Irish in America. In the song "My Darlin' Eileen," the cops sing about her being the "Fairest colleen that ever I've seen."

Collier's: Initially launched as *Collier's Once a Week*, *Collier's* was an American magazine known for its short stories. The magazine ceased publication in 1957, but was widely read during the time period of *Wonderful Town*. Wreck tells Ruth that *Collier's* returned one of her stories in the mail.

conga: A Latin American dance of African origin, the conga was usually performed with several people in a single line, one behind the other, stepping forward with intermittent kicks. Ruth insists the dance is from South America, but one of the Brazilian cadets says, "Conga American dance. You show conga!" and Ruth is forced to demonstrate how it is danced. The production number "Conga" is one of the comic highlights of *Wonderful Town*.

cornball: Slang term for an unsophisticated person who is overly sentimental, or corny; Speedy Valenti says to Appopolous, "I'll see ya, cornball."

Emily Post: For many years the queen of proper behavior, Emily Post (1872–1960) wrote a syndicated newspaper column on etiquette, which was not only read but followed by many Americans. Unable to get rid of the Brazilian sailors, Ruth says to Eileen, "Listen, Emily Post—how do you say 'Get the hell out of here' in Portuguese?"

Eskimo Pies: A vanilla ice-cream bar totally covered in chocolate. A vendor on the street tries to sell Ruth some Eskimo Pies, but she doesn't have any money, so she tries to sell him empty milk bottles.

Felix Frankfurter: The US Supreme Court associate justice Felix Frankfurter (1882–1965) was on the bench during the time period of *Wonderful Town*. He was a widely known judge, having founded the American Civil Liberties Union in 1920. After Appopolous interrogates Ruth about the ownership of her typewriter, she asks, "Who are you, Felix Frankfurter?"

"For Whom the Lion Roars": Ruth's short story "For Whom the Lion Roars" is an obvious spoof of Ernest Hemingway's 1940 novel, *For Whom the Bell Tolls*, about a guerrilla unit during the Spanish Civil War. Baker reads aloud from the story, which is set in the jungles of Africa and is filled with clichés.

good neighbors: In 1933, Franklin Roosevelt established the Good Neighbor Policy to create friendly relations and mutual defense agreements with the nations of Latin America. In the song-and-dance number

"Conga," Ruth sings to the Brazilian sailors, "Good neighbors, good neighbors—remember our policy."

Greenwich Village . . . Waverly Place: In the opening number, the Guide sings, "On your right, / Waverly Place, / Bit of Paree in Greenwich Village." Most of the action of *Wonderful Town* takes place in the neighborhood on the West Side of Lower Manhattan known as Greenwich Village. Because of low rents, the Village was inhabited by artists, actors, and writers who turned the area into a hub for cultural activity. Although the Village is trendy and expensive today, in the 1930s it was considered a run-down, unappealing neighborhood. Waverly Place is a narrow street in the Village named after Sir Walter Scott's 1814 novel, *Waverley*.

Harold Teen . . . Mitzi Green . . . Dizzy Dean: In the song "Conga," Ruth asks the Brazilian sailors, "What's your opinion of Harold Teen, Mitzi Green, Dizzy Dean?" A popular comic strip by Carl Ed in the 1930s was *Harold Teen*, about a farm boy named Harold who moves to the city and becomes a popular figure at his new high school by playing football and directing the school play. Mitzi Green (1920–1969) was an American child actress whose career continued in movies and on Broadway as an adult. She was at the peak of her popularity in the 1930s. Jay Hanna "Dizzy" Dean (1910–1974) was an American professional baseball pitcher with a colorful and popular personality who played for the St. Louis Cardinals, the Chicago Cubs, and the St. Louis Browns.

Helen Hayes: American stage and film actress Helen Hayes (1900–1993) had a celebrated career that spanned seven decades, giving her the label "First Lady of the American Theatre." After Eileen manages to get rid of the Brazilian sailors by getting hysterical over an earthquake (actually, an explosion from building the subway), Ruth says, "What a performance! Helen Hayes couldn't have done it better."

hornswoggled: An old expression meaning to swindle or cheat someone. Telling a story about a customer who ordered a banana split at the soda fountain, Frank Lippencott says, "I'll be hornswoggled if he doesn't leave the whole banana!"

Kiwanis Club: Founded in 1915, the Kiwanis Club is an international service organization that raises money to strengthen communities and serve children. Until 1987, the Kiwanis only accepted male members. In the song "Ohio," Ruth recalls "The Kiwanis Club Dance" with a shudder.

MacDougal Alley, Patchin Place, Minetta Lane, Bank Street and Church Street, John Street and Jane: In the opening number, the tour guide says, "Come along, follow me / Now we will see MacDougal Alley, Patchin Place, Minetta Lane, Bank Street and Church Street, John Street and Jane." One of New York City's shortest streets is the cul-de-sac thoroughfare called MacDougal Alley, in Greenwich Village. Patchin Place is a gated cul-de-sac located off of 10th Street; Minetta Lane is a quaint and quiet street in the Village; Bank Street is a primarily residential street in the West Village; and Church Street meets up with Trinity Place to form a single north–south roadway in Lower Manhattan. Located in downtown New York's historic Financial District is the short thoroughfare named John Street, and Jane Street is in the West Village.

Madhatter: The fictional magazine *Madhatter* is most likely a nod to *The New Yorker* magazine, which still features original fiction and poetry. The title also references the Mad Hatter in *Alice in Wonderland* and suggests the word "Manhattan," as well. Ruth tells Eileen, "I'm taking these stories down to the *Madhatter*," which is where she meets the editor, Robert Baker.

Major Bowes . . . Steinbeck's prose: In the song-and-dance number "Conga," Ruth asks the Brazilian sailors, "What's your opinion of women's clothes, Major Bowes, Steinbeck's prose?" The American radio personality Edward Bowes (1874–1946), known to listeners as Major Bowes, was the host of *Major Bowes' Amateur Hour*, which ran for eighteen years. The distinguished American author John Steinbeck (1902–1968) won the 1962 Nobel Prize in Literature.

Moby Dick: During a lull in the conversation, Ruth says, "I was rereading *Moby Dick* the other day," but no one picks up on the topic; so Ruth bluntly notes, "It's about this whale." Herman Melville's 1851 novel *Moby Dick* is considered a masterpiece but remains largely unread.

monkey glands . . . Stokowski's hands: In the song "Conga," Ruth asks the Brazilian sailors, "What do you think of . . . monkey glands, hot dog stands? . . . Stokowski's hands?" The surgeon Serge Voronoff developed a technique of grafting monkey testicle tissue onto the testicles of men for purportedly therapeutic purposes. The trend for monkey gland therapy faded away in the 1930s, and the topic was later something of a joke. Leopold Stokowski (1882–1977) was one of the leading conductors of the concert stage, best remembered for his long association with the Philadelphia Orchestra and his appearance in the Disney film *Fantasia*, with that orchestra.

Montmartre: The artistic center of Paris is Montmartre, once a low-rent district where artists lived and one could find low-class entertainment. In the song "What a Waste," Baker sings about an artist who "lived in Montmartre" before coming to New York.

Mothersill's seasick pills . . . Helen Wills: In the song "Conga," Ruth asks the Brazilian cadets, "What do you think of . . . Mothersill's seasick pills? How do you feel about Helen Wills?" First registered as a trademark in 1926, Mothersill's Seasick Remedy was billed as "the pill that ruled the waves." At one time very popular with ocean voyage passengers, the pills went out of favor in the 1960s. The renowned American tennis player Helen Wills (1905–1998) dominated women's tennis in the 1920s and 1930s.

NRA . . . TVA: In the song "Conga," Ruth asks the Brazilian sailors, "What do you think of the USA—NRA—TVA?" Franklin Roosevelt's National Recovery Administration (NRA) was part of the New Deal, created to battle the Great Depression by funding certain projects. The Tennessee Valley Authority (TVA) is a federally owned electric utility created by Congress in 1933, also part of Roosevelt's New Deal. The series of dams provides electricity to areas of seven states.

"O, Promise Me": In the song "One Hundred Easy Ways (to Lose a Man)," Ruth sings, "You'll never hear 'O Promise Me'" if you let on to a man that you are smart. The most popular song for wedding ceremonies in America and the United Kingdom for nearly one hundred years was "O, Promise Me" (1887) by Reginald De Koven (music) and Clement Scott (lyrics). It was first heard in the operetta *Robin Hood* and went on to sell over a million copies of sheet music in 1890.

Picasso: The renowned Spanish-born artist Pablo Picasso (1881–1973) was an international celebrity for several decades, including the 1930s.

In the song "What a Waste," Baker sings about an artist who "went to Picasso—Pablo said 'Wow!'"

prexy: *Prexy* is a shortened term for *president*, especially the president of a college. In "Pass the Football," Wreck sings about the time he was in college and "the prexy's mom, age ninety-three, Got up and gave her seat to me."

Rasputin: The infamous Russian monk Grigori Rasputin (1871–1916) exerted a powerful influence over Tsar Nicholas II and his family, helping to lead them to a tragic end. The name was later used for any despotic and controlling villain. Ruth identifies Appopolous as "Our landlord—Rasputin."

Rigoletto: In the song "What a Waste," Baker sings about a singer who came to New York to "sing *Rigoletto*, his wish," but now sells fish. Giuseppe Verdi's Italian opera *Rigoletto* premiered in 1851 and has remained one of the composer's most cherished works.

Sheridan Square: Sheridan Square is a well-known location in Greenwich Village that is a crossroads for many New Yorkers and, consequently, a bustling place. Speedy Valenti tells a man carrying a sign advertising his nightclub, "You take Sheridan Square."

soda jerk: A person who dispenses carbonated drinks and ice cream at a soda fountain is called a soda jerk, or a soda jerker. In *Wonderful Town*, Frank Lippencott is a soda jerk. When Eileen gets Frank confused with Mr. Baker from the *Madhatter*, Ruth asks her, "How can you mix up a soda jerk with an editor?"

Stanislavski: In the song "What a Waste," Baker sings about an actress who "met Stanislavsky . . . He said the world would / Cheer her someday." The Russian actor, director, and producer Konstantin Stanislavski (1863–1938) founded the Moscow Art Theatre and laid the foundation for modern acting techniques.

summa cum laude . . . tripe: "Summa cum laude" is an honorary title used by educational institutions to signify a degree that was earned "with the highest distinction," as opposed to "cum laude" and "magna cum laude." In the song "What a Waste," Baker sings about himself as someone who was "Summa cum laude—all of that tripe" before he came to New York and became an editor, rather than an author. The stomach tissue from an ox or cow is known as *tripe*. The word has come to mean something of poor quality—offensive, even.

Trenton Tech: There is no such college as Trenton Tech. Wreck's alma mater is a spoof of the famed research university, Georgia Institute of Technology, whose fight song is "(I'm a) Ramblin' Wreck from Georgia Tech." Wreck tells the Sherwood sisters, "I'm a ramblin' wreck from Trenton Tech—and a helluva engineer."

truck on down . . . let down your hair . . . barrel-house air: In the song "Swing!," Ruth promotes the Village Vortex by singing, "Truck on down and let down your hair; / Breathe that barrel-house air." To "truck" is 1940s and 1950s slang for moving in a casual, carefree manner toward your destination. To "let down your hair" is also slang, meaning to stop behaving in a conservative or formal manner. An old expression for a bar or saloon is a barrel-house. The name comes from the time when barrels of alcohol used to line the walls of such places.

Van Gogh's herring: The Dutch-born painter Vincent van Gogh (1853–1890) often painted still lifes of food. When Appopolous is painting Wreck's portrait, he tells him, "You will be immortalized like van Gogh's herring."

Walgreens: Charles R. Walgreen founded his first drugstore in 1901 in Chicago, and it eventually became one of the biggest chain stores in America, making the Walgreen family very rich. Ruth cracks a joke about the Walgreens when she says, "The Liggetts speak only to the Walgreens, and the Walgreens speak only to God." The wealthy Liggett family co-founded the Liggett & Myers Tobacco Company, Inc.

Walt Whitman: American poet Walter Whitman (1819–1892) was an innovative writer whose works are in both the transcendental and realistic styles. Ruth says the letter *W* is missing on her typewriter because "it fell off after I wrote my thesis on Walt Whitman."

Washington Square: Washington Square Park is the celebrated public park in Greenwich Village, with an impressive arch marking the start of Fifth Avenue. The square is home to historic residences and has always been a meeting place and center for cultural activity. In the opening number, "Christopher Street," the tour guide sings, "Painters and pigeons in Washington Square."

Williamsburg: Not the colonial town in Virginia, Williamsburg is a neighborhood in the New York City borough of Brooklyn. Always a working-class district, Williamsburg has seen many German and, later, Jewish residents. In one of Ruth's stories that Baker reads aloud, she describes the setting as a "squalid . . . one-room flat in Williamsburg without windows."

WPA: The Works Progress Administration (WPA) was the biggest of the New Deal public works programs, created in 1935 to battle mass unemployment by putting millions of Americans back to work. The WPA also sponsored theatre, music, and art programs. Appopolous tells the Sherwood sisters, "I'm entering my painting in the WPA Art Contest."

SELECTED BIBLIOGRAPHY

Alpert, Hollis. *Broadway: 125 Years of Musical Theatre*. New York: Arcade, 1991.

Atkinson, Brooks. *Broadway* (revised). New York: Macmillan, 1974.

Block, Geoffrey. *Enchanted Evenings: The Broadway Musical from* Show Boat *to Lloyd Webber* (2nd ed.). New York: Oxford University Press, 2009.

Bloom, Ken, and Frank Vlastnik. *Broadway Musicals: The 101 Greatest Shows of All Time*. New York: Black Dog & Leventhal Publishers, 2004.

Bordman, Gerald, and Thomas S. Hischak. *The Oxford Companion to American Theatre* (3rd ed.). New York: Oxford University Press, 2004.

Bordman, Gerald, and Richard Norton. *American Musical Theatre: A Chronicle* (4th ed.). New York: Oxford University Press, 2011.

Everett, William A., and Paul R. Laird (eds.). *The Cambridge Companion to the Musical*. (3rd ed.). Cambridge, UK: Cambridge University Press, 2017.

Ganzl, Kurt. *Ganzl's Encyclopedia of the Musical Theatre*. New York: Schirmer Books, 1993.

Grant, Mark N. *The Rise and Fall of the Broadway Musical*. Boston: Northeastern University Press, 2004.

Green, Stanley. *The World of Musical Comedy*. New York: A. S. Barnes & Co., 1980.

Green, Stanley, and Cary Ginell. *Broadway Musicals Show By Show* (9th ed.). Guilford, CT: Applause Theatre & Cinema Books, 2019.

Grode, Eric. *The Book of Broadway: The 150 Definitive Plays and Musicals*. Minneapolis: Voyageur Press, 2015.

Hischak, Thomas S. *Off-Broadway Musicals since 1919*. Lanham, MD: Scarecrow Press, 2011.

———. *The Oxford Companion to the American Musical: Theatre, Film and Television*. New York: Oxford University Press, 2008.

Jackson, Arthur. *The Best Musicals from* Show Boat *to* A Chorus Line. New York: Crown Publishers, 1977.

Jones, John Bush. *Our Musicals, Ourselves*. Lebanon, NH: University Press of New England, 2003.

Kantor, Michael, and Laurence Maslon. *Broadway: The American Musical*. Guilford, CT: Applause Theatre & Cinema Books, 2020.

Kennedy, Michael Patrick, and John Muir. *Musicals*. Glasgow, UK: HarperCollins, 1997.

Lamb, Andrew. *150 Years of Popular Musical Theatre*. New Haven, CT: Yale University Press, 2000.

McMillan, Scott. *The Musical as Drama: A Study of the Principals and Conventions Behind Musical Shows from Kern to Sondheim*. Princeton, NJ: Princeton University Press, 2006.

Miller, Scott. *Rebels with Applause: Broadway's Groundbreaking Musicals*. Portsmouth, NH: Heinemann Drama, 2001.

Mordden, Ethan. *Beautiful Mornin': The Broadway Musical in the 1940s*. New York: Oxford Press, 1999.

———. *Coming Up Roses: The Broadway Musical in the 1950s*. New York: Oxford Press, 1998.

———. *The Happiest Corpse I've Ever Seen: The Last 25 Years of the Broadway Musical*. New York: Palgrave Macmillan, 2004.

———. *Make Believe: The Broadway Musical in the 1920s*. New York: Oxford Press, 1997.

———. *Sing for Your Supper: The Broadway Musical in the 1930s*. New York: Palgrave Macmillan, 2005.

Musicals: The Definitive Illustrated Story (2nd ed). London: Dorling Kindersley Limited (DK) Publishers, 2021.

Norton, Richard C. *A Chronology of American Musical Theatre*. New York: Oxford University Press, 2002.

Patinkin, Sheldon. *No Legs, No Jokes, No Chance: A History of the American Musical Theatre*. Evanston, IL: Northwestern University Press, 2008.

Portantier, Michael (ed.). *The TheatreMania Guide to Musical Theatre Recordings*. New York: Backstage Books, 2004.

Robinson, Mark A. *The World of Musicals: An Encyclopedia of Stage, Screen, and Song*. Santa Barbara, CA: Greenwood Press, 2014.

Schneider, Robert W., and Shannon Agnew (eds.). *Fifty Key Stage Musicals*. New York: Routledge, 2022.

Sheward, David. *It's a Hit: The Back Stage Book of Longest-Running Broadway Shows, 1884 to the Present*. New York: Watson-Guptill Publications-BPI Communications, Inc., 1994.

Singer, Barry. *Ever After: The Last Years of Musical Theatre and Beyond*. New York: Applause Theatre & Cinema Books, 2004.

Smith, Cecil, and Glenn Litton. *Musical Comedy in America* (2nd ed.). New York: Theatre Arts Books, 1981.

Suskin, Steven. *More Opening Nights on Broadway*. New York: Schirmer Books, 1997.

———. *Opening Night on Broadway: A Critical Quotebook of the Golden Era of the Musical Theatre*. New York: Schirmer Books, 1990.

Swain, Joseph P. *The Broadway Musical: A Critical and Musical Survey*. New York: Oxford University Press, 1990.

Wilmeth, Don B., and Tice Miller (eds.). *Cambridge Guide to American Theatre*. New York: Cambridge University Press, 1993.

INDEX

Page numbers in *italics* indicate a photograph.

ABOUT THE AUTHOR

Thomas S. Hischak is an internationally recognized author and teacher in the performing arts, and one of the foremost authorities on American musical theatre. He is author of over forty nonfiction books about theatre, film, and popular music, notably *The Oxford Companion to the American Musical*; *The 100 Greatest American Plays*; *The Rodgers and Hammerstein Encyclopedia*; *Through the Screen Door: What Happened to the Broadway Musical When It Went to Hollywood*; *Theatre as Human Action*; *The Tin Pan Alley Encyclopedia*; *Off-Broadway Musicals since 1919*; *Word Crazy: Broadway Lyricists*; *American Literature on Stage and Screen*; *1939: Hollywood's Greatest Year*; *The Abbott Touch: Pal Joey, Damn Yankees, and the Theatre of George Abbott*; *Musicals in Film: A Guide to the Genre*; *The Mikado to Matilda: British Musicals on the New York Stage*; *The Thornton Wilder Encyclopedia*; *The Oxford Companion to American Theatre* (with Gerald Bordman); *The Disney Song Encyclopedia*; and *Musical Misfires: Three Decades of Broadway Musical Heartbreak* (the last two with Mark A. Robinson).

Hischak is also author of more than fifty published plays that are performed throughout the United States, Canada, Great Britain, and Australia. Hischak is a Fulbright scholar who has taught and directed in Greece, Lithuania, and Turkey. From 1983 to 2015, he was professor of theatre at the State University of New York (SUNY) at Cortland, where he has received such honors as the 2004 SUNY Chancellor's Award for Excellence in Scholarship and Creative Activity and the 2010 SUNY Outstanding Achievement in Research Award. Four of his books have been cited as Outstanding Nonfiction Books by the American Library Association, and *The Oxford Companion to the American Theatre* was cited as an Outstanding Reference Work by the New York City Public Library in 2008. His playwriting awards include the Stanley Drama Award (New York City) for *Cold War Comedy* and the Julie Harris Playwriting Award (Beverly Hills, California) for *The Cardiff Giant.*

Hischak is currently on the adjunct faculty of Flagler College, where he teaches courses on theatre and film (www.thomashischak.com).